The Writer's Guide
to
the Courtroom:

Let's Quill All the Lawyers

by
Donna Ballman, J.D.

Behler™
PUBLICATIONS

California
USA

Behler Publications
California

The Writer's Guide to the Courtroom: Let's Quill All the Lawyers
A Behler Publications Book

Copyright © 2010 by Donna Ballman, J.D.
Cover design by Cathy Scott—www.mbcdesigns.com

Library of Congress Cataloging-in-Publication Data

Ballman, Donna.
  The writer's guide to the courtroom : let's quill all the lawyers / by Donna Ballman.
     p. cm.
  Includes bibliographical references and index.
  ISBN-13: 978-1-933016-53-5 (pbk.)
  ISBN-10: 1-933016-53-1 (pbk.)
  1. Justice, Administration of--United States. 2. Civil procedure--United States. 3. Authors--Handbooks, manuals, etc. I. Title.
  KF390.A96B35 2009
  347.73--dc22
                            2009023949

FIRST PRINTING

Published by Behler Publications, LLC
Lake Forest, California
www.behlerpublications.com

Manufactured in the United States of America

To every aspiring writer everywhere
especially to those members of Litopia Writer's Colony
the best writer's colony on the planet

Table of Contents

Foreword by Alex Ferrer ("Judge Alex")

Introduction, *v*

Foreword
By Alex Ferrer
Host of the nationally syndicated show, *Judge Alex*

I have lived most of my life deeply involved with the American system of justice. Starting as a police officer when I was 19; continuing through law school and the practice of law as a civil litigator; ten years as a Miami-Dade Circuit Court Judge in the Criminal and Family Divisions and now as the host of the nationally syndicated court show *Judge Alex*, in which I handle disputes between people from all over the country.

Needless to say, I am very comfortable with how our system of justice functions. While everyone does not share my lifelong contact with the legal system, I am still amazed at how little the public really knows about their judicial system.

Make no mistake, the judicial system belongs to us. We pay handsomely for it through our taxes. In some states we elect the judges who make decisions that may seriously impact our lives, often without even knowing for whom we are voting. In other states, we elect people who will select the judges for us. When things go wrong, we ask our courts for protection or remedy in the form of "justice."

A court verdict can make you a pauper or a prince. It can break up your family in ways that are unjust or ease you through the most difficult time of your life. It can set your children back on track after some transgression or change their life for the worse by reinforcing the wrong path. It can reunite families and start them anew. It can lock you up with the most dangerous of our society until your body is carried away in a box. It can give you a sense of closure, a feeling that justice was done. It can end your life by hanging, firing squad, lethal injection, gas chamber, or electrocution. And yet, most people have, at best, a vague, if not mistaken, sense of how our system of justice works.

The problem stems from the fact that most people do not get their legal education from a law library. Other than lawyers, most people have neither the time nor the inclination to put forth that kind of effort. So for better or for worse, television, movies, and novels have become the educators of today. And when it comes to education, nothing fascinates viewers as much as the law. Just peruse the TV listings and see how many popular law-related shows continue to air from season to season, only to be replaced by similar shows when they are eventually cancelled. But despite the quantity of law-related entertainment, the quality is often sadly lacking. With movies and television leading the pack, the public is left with a mistaken impression about how their system of justice really works, along with its strengths and limitations. Most people cannot tell you whether a judge can override a jury verdict, or whether an attorney can put her client on the stand if she knows he is going to lie.

And while some might brush these details off as minutiae, unnecessary in the world of entertainment, the opposite is actually true. Daytime court shows like mine are hugely successful, in large part because the public wants to learn about the law and the legal system. Granted, they also enjoy seeing people pay for their wrongs, but the mail I receive from viewers, as well as blog postings about court shows in general, make it clear that it is the law and the legal system that has them fascinated.

In movies, the more compelling legal thrillers are those that tie in true aspects of the law within the storyline. Just think how you felt when the judge was required to grant defense counsel's objection and exclude the damning evidence of medical malpractice at the end of *The Verdict*. The Scott Turow's and John Grisham's of the world are hugely successfully in large part because of the reality of their writing. Accuracy counts in so many ways.

That brings us to *The Writer's Guide to the Courtroom*. In this invaluable handbook, Donna Ballman covers every fact necessary to accurately write about the law or the legal system; from the roles of the characters in and out of the courtroom to the many and varied causes of action that can be raised as a legal claim. How judges are selected. The duties of bailiffs, juries, prosecutors, defense attorneys, court reporters, clerks and anyone else you can imagine. How law firms of every size function including the roles of everyone involved, from the managing partner to the law clerk. The discovery process, pre-trial motions, jury selection and matters that the jury never gets to hear.

In this one book, Ms. Ballman has given every writer, whether of novels, scripts or screenplays, access to a world of ideas with accurate fact patterns that lend credibility to their work.

Despite my comfort with our legal system, I find myself learning even more about the interrelationship of all of the players. I will definitely keep it handy. Perhaps I will write a book.

~ Alex Ferrer – "Judge Alex"

Introduction

If you're reading this book, you probably have a novel, story, screenplay, or other writing project that has a character involved with the court system. Or you're a journalist writing a story about a court case. Or maybe you're thumbing through this at the bookstore thinking to yourself, "I don't write about law. Why would I need this?"

If you're like me when I write, sometimes you don't know where your mind will take you. Maybe there's a character in your head but you haven't decided what to do with them. Or you have a plot that's stuck. The law is a great device for writers. It can add an obstacle, a sexy twist, or a fun character to your story.

The law can also accidentally drift into your plot, and laypeople who read your books, watch your shows, or read your articles will learn what they know about the justice system from you. Everything your characters touch during their day has something to do with the law. They wake up. Their alarm clock went through customs and is regulated. Their toothpaste has ingredients the law says it can and can't have. Their cereal box has legal requirements about how contents are listed and what claims it can make.

They drive to work in a car that doesn't explode when hit from behind because of civil lawyers. The gas pump they use has a fume guard because of the law. They go to work and, because of employment laws, have to be paid wages and overtime, can't be subjected to discrimination, can't be retaliated against because they objected to illegal activity.

When they make a purchase, the laws say what businesses have to disclose, what trade practices are unfair, what advertisements can say. Doctors have to treat them within acceptable practices or face a suit. Pharmaceutical companies have to test their drugs extensively before your characters can take them. Companies handling hazardous materials must dispose of them in particular ways.

When they get a divorce, your characters have to do it through the civil justice system. If a character dies, their will has to go through probate.

The claims characters can make in the law are almost infinite. Anything that can go wrong for them can end up in court. Whether in an accident, the workplace, a business, or in a relationship, the law can offer a slight plot twist or an entire plot. And if you're a journalist, you probably have legal issues in your stories regularly.

Entire libraries are devoted to the laws that govern us. I cannot possibly cover every type of claim, every potential suit, and every aspect of the law. My purpose is to touch on some of the highlights, to give you a starting point for your research or just trigger an idea for your story. This book is for every writer who doesn't have a law degree, and even for those lawyer/writers who are writing outside their area of practice.[1]

Most lawyers I know can't read or watch stories about law because the factual errors are too frustrating. Gross misunderstanding of how the justice system works can take away from even the best plot. There are over 1.1 million lawyers in the United States, so alienating us with mistakes that are easily corrected can affect your sales and ratings. If I can help even one novelist keep from having their book thrown down in disgust, or one TV writer from having the channel changed, my work is done here.

I asked some lawyers and judges to tell me what really bugged them about how the civil justice system is portrayed in books and screenplays, and to tell me which ones really got it right. I've quoted some of their responses throughout this book to help you see the ways in which "getting it wrong" can alienate readers/viewers, whereas "getting it right" can enhance the story for your audience.

This is a guide for writers whose characters end up encountering the civil legal system. I can't help with the criminal justice system – that's for another book. And I can't help with your writing – that's for your critique group or editor. But I can help you get the characters, claims, and court system right. The rest is up to your imagination.

If there's anything you want to share or ask, whether a research question, a TV show with a giant legal gaffe, or a book that was exactly right on a matter of civil justice, feel free to leave a comment on my blog, http://writereport.blogspot.com and I'll respond as best I can. If you write a book or story after using my book, tell me and I'll probably buy it. Maybe I won't throw it down if you got it right.

---

[1] And I've had some law students tell me it's a great "plain English" reference for their classes, although I make no warranty about its exam-worthiness.

Chapter 1 – The Characters

Any writer with a story involving the legal system has plenty of opportunity to develop interesting characters. Everyone involved in the justice system has specific training and qualifications for their job. Whether writing within or against type, it is important to understand how each character got their job and what they do. This chapter will discuss some of the major players you may want to write about.

Lawyers

Lawyers are, simply put, people who advise and represent people and corporations on legal matter. Lawyers are the most common legal characters in fiction because they are so versatile. A lawyer can be encountered almost anywhere and under an infinite number of plots. Yet lay writers frequently misunderstand what lawyers do, their backgrounds, and what lawyers cannot do. This section will provide some general information about lawyers that may help you add authenticity to your lawyer character.

Legal Training

Almost all lawyers have at least two degrees. They must attain a four year degree, either a B.A. or B.S.[2] from an undergraduate institution. They can major in anything. Law schools like diverse backgrounds in their students. While most law students come from liberal arts backgrounds, many from political science, there are music and art majors, physics and math majors, in law school.

Even if you have a story about a lawyer already in practice, you can give them an interesting background by having an unusual undergraduate major. Or maybe they cheated through law school. Were they on law review or did they just slide by? These background items can give depth to your story.

---

[2] Go ahead, say it now. Get it out of your system. Just know that most of us have B.A.s, despite the appropriateness of the other.

While the major is not important, grades and L.S.A.T. (pre-law school standardized test) scores are paramount. Most law students did well in college, and received high L.S.A.T. scores (meaning that they test well). There are also admission essays, recommendation letters, and extracurricular activities that play roles in the admission process. Your story will lose credibility if your lawyer character was a C student in undergraduate school (unless mommy or daddy pulled strings to get them into law school). If you want to have an intelligence-challenged character, write about a lawyer who graduated at the bottom or middle of their law school class.

Law school is sometimes viciously competitive. Stolen study outlines, cheating schemes, and sabotage can add interest to a law school-based plot.

> I had been to the law school once earlier in the summer when David, a close friend who'd recently graduated, had given me a tour. HLS occupies fifteen buildings on the northern edge of the Harvard campus, and is bounded on one side by Massachusetts Avenue, Cambridge's clogged main thoroughfare. The architecture is eclectic. The student commons and dormitories are square and buff-colored and functional. Old Austin Hall, a classroom building, looks like a sooty fortress with arches. Langdell, the school's largest building, is a long gray expanse of concrete. When I toured the law school in the summer, it had all looked so solid, so enduring, that I'd felt a majestic thrill to think I'd soon be allied with this and the time-ennobled traditions of the law. Now, getting off the bus, I felt mostly my nerves, which were lit all the way down to my knees.

One L, by Scott Turow, was his first book, purely non-fiction, and is still considered a bible for first year law students. It chronicles his experiences at Harvard Law School and is a great reference for any book with an Ivy League law student as a character.

Law school lasts three years on a regular track. Some law schools offer faster tracks, and some offer evening programs that can be completed in four or more years. Lawyers mostly graduate with a J.D. – a doctorate of jurisprudence. Some students attain an L.L.M., a legal master's degree in a specialty area like tax.

While law schools do teach some substance, one of the great delusions people have is that lawyers "know the law." What law schools mostly teach is how to look up the law, and how to spot possible legal issues. If the lawyer is a specialist, maybe, just maybe, they can spout some law from memory. Most lawyers have to look stuff up before they give answers.

Admission

Your characters can't just bounce from court to court and show up for hearings without jumping through lots of hoops first. Lawyers must be admitted to the Bar in each state where they practice. They must graduate from an accredited law school and pass a background check. The qualifications vary from state to state. Most states have a Bar Exam covering the key areas of law and procedure in the state. Did your character flunk the Bar three times before they got in? Do they have to take a Bar Exam in another state after twenty years of practice?

Lawyers must also be admitted to specific courts. Your character can't just show up in, say, a bankruptcy court or a hearing in Iowa. Admission to the state Bar normally allows the lawyer to practice in the state courts. Federal courts each require a separate admission – for each district (the trial courts), appellate (the ones where lawyers claim the trial courts did something wrong) and the Supreme Court (where lawyers argue that trial courts did something wrong that was of national importance), the lawyer must apply, sometimes test, and usually provide references. For instance, just because your character is admitted in the United States District Court for the Southern District of New York doesn't mean they can run up to the Northern District of New York to cover a hearing.

Some states allow lawyers from other states to be admitted without having to take a new Bar Exam. For the most part, those states only admit lawyers from states that offer reciprocity to the lawyers from the admitting state. In other words, let my guys in and I'll let your guys in. Otherwise, sit for the exam like everybody else.

Lawyers also have to pass a background check. Some states allow law students to submit the application for a background check in the first year of law school so the time- consuming process can finish by the time the student passes the Bar Exam. Did your character have a life before law school? Were they in business? Were they ever arrested? The background check involves listing every case in which the applicant has been involved, all criminal charges, every address, and every school. The application must be filled out accurately or the background check can be dragged out for years. The most unintentional omission could require the applicant to attend a hearing to explain the omission.

The State Bar Associations have much discretion in deciding the applicant's fitness for admission. Did your character tick off somebody powerful? They could be delayed indefinitely. A criminal conviction can sometimes be an insurmountable barrier to admission, and even a charge that was dismissed can be a barrier. You could have a character who was arrested for something during law school, say, a traffic stop where they were racing to the airport to pick up a loved one. The character makes the mistake of mentioning that he's in law school, and, voila, he's in jail for resisting arrest. He can have years of Bar hearings over something that stupid. If you have a law student character who is anxious about admission to the Bar, or events that may put up barriers to admission, this can lend depth to the story.

I will cover some of the basic types of lawyers in Chapter 3.

Judges

Judges are the deciders in court. They can mess your characters up in all kinds of interesting ways, or be your main character, a la *Judging Amy*.

They have to be lawyers first, and then generally have to have a number of years of practice, frequently five or ten, before they qualify to be a judge. Judicial selection varies from state to state, and is extremely controversial. Is your character a big contributor? Somebody who contributed to the opposition? Is your judge character so entrenched they have become a demi-god on a power trip? How they got into office can determine something key about their character.

The two general selection methods are election and appointment. Even these vary wildly.

Election

There are three types of judicial elections. Which kind was yours? It may make a difference to your story.

1. **Nonpartisan election** means that the candidate does not identify with a political party on the ballot. Many nonpartisan selection states even prohibit the candidate from identifying their political party in campaign advertising and in campaigning. For heavens' sake, don't have your judge character in Florida or Idaho campaigning on a party ticket, or you'll look like an amateur.

2. **Partisan election** means that the candidate is selected by the political party, either by primary election or other selection process, and then appears on the ballot identified by party. In *Bootlegger's Daughter* by Margaret Maron, her main character, a judge, gets involved in some hilarious political activities that could get a character in another state removed from the bench.

3. **Retention election** is where only the sitting judge's name appears, and the citizens vote to retain or not to retain. In the history of some states' merit retention elections, no judge has ever lost office this way. It's mostly still a lifetime appointment. Imagine how your judge character could get a little full of themselves if they couldn't be removed from office.

States that have partisan judicial elections
Alabama, Illinois, Louisiana, New York, Ohio, Pennsylvania, Texas, West Virginia

States that have nonpartisan judicial elections
Arkansas, California, Florida, Georgia, Idaho, Kentucky, Michigan, Minnesota, Mississippi, Montana, Nevada, North Carolina, North Dakota, Oklahoma, Oregon, South Dakota, Washington, Wisconsin

States that appoint trial judges
Alaska, Arizona, Colorado, Connecticut, Delaware, Hawaii, Indiana, Iowa, Kansas, Maine, Maryland, Massachusetts, Missouri, Nebraska, New Hampshire, New Jersey, New Mexico, Puerto Rico, Rhode Island, South Carolina, Tennessee, Utah, Vermont, Virginia, Wyoming

Elections are generally for a specific term of office, after which judges have to campaign to hold their seats. This process is controversial because campaign contributions are mostly from lawyers and law firms, and there is a concern that judges will look at contribution reports before ruling on the law. Does your judge character peruse the contribution list right before the hearing? Or do they refuse to be swayed by such trivial things as contributions? Did your lawyer character forget to contribute right before the hearing? Are they up against a firm that can round up $50,000 in contributions in a week?

The positive aspects of the elective method are that it opens the process up to any interested party, is easier to remove bad judges, forces judges to meet ordinary people once in awhile so instills humility, and creates a more diverse bench. Does your judge character have to make the rounds of political events? Do they have to look solemn at every Memorial Day service? Is your all-powerful judge facing a tough opponent? Take a look at *The Appeal* by John Grisham if you have any doubts that a judicial election can make an interesting part of your story.

Appointment

If your judge character was appointed, you'd better make sure they are well-connected. Appointments are frequently by a nomination commission, the governor, or a hybrid. Some legislatures get to approve the appointment. Some states appoint through a legislative election, but I'm counting those as appointments since real people[3] don't get to vote.

Some states have term limits, some do not. Federal judges are presidential-appointees who are then confirmed in the Senate. Federal judges sit for life. If your judge character sits for life, they may be more arrogant than, say, a judge who faces election every four years. Or you could play them against type. Your federal judge could be a prince among men who sends lawyers get-well cards. Or maybe she requires the lawyer to attend a trial, even though the attorney's doctor ordered her to undergo emergency cardiac testing, in order to favor her political crony and try to force a settlement. Could that really happen? You bet.

People who despise judicial appointments will say it's because they generally are perceived as only going to lawyers from influential firms or wealthy backgrounds, they can keep judges in ivory towers insulated from ever having to meet the common man, and they let judges forget they were ever ordinary mortals.

---

[3] Real people defined as voters, not elected officials. No offense to my cousin or friends who are elected officials. Well, maybe a little jab.

Those who like appointments say they keep campaign contributions out of the picture, are supposed to mean that lawyers have less influence, and keep the judges from having to campaign.

Does your judge character appear to be humble around voters then act like a jerk to lawyers? Do they ask lawyers for contributions the day before trial? You can definitely have fun writing about how your judge character gets into and stays in office.

Types of Judges
Federal Judges

"[W]hat is really frustrating and infuriating – that the media almost always gets wrong – is the portrayal of federal judges as being liberal activists. They portray the federal courts as actually being more liberal than the general public. This is the exact opposite of what any competent federal court practitioner knows to be true."
- **Dan Williams**, Florida Labor and Employment Attorney.

These are the high and mighty. They are appointed for life, have had enough political influence to be appointed by the President of the United States, and be confirmed by the Senate, and never have to associate with you or me again. They handle federal criminal trials and civil matters involving either disputes of federal law (such as discrimination, overtime, trademark, patent, copyright, or international matters) or matters involving citizens of different states.

Supposedly, federal judges are less subject to local concerns and influences, and therefore will give out-of-towners a fair shake. Which is why there's something called "diversity jurisdiction" that lets federal judges hear cases involving citizens of different states. Is your main character from South Dakota suing somebody who lives in Maine? They may well end up in federal court.

Federal court used to be the place to go for civil rights and discrimination issues. But with the changing winds of political appointments, many plaintiffs' lawyers now utilize their state courts for those issues.

Appellate Judges

Appellate courts decide whether or not the trial judges did something wrong.

> This is an important job—probably more important than any job you'll ever have. For over two hundred years, the Supreme Court has steered our country through its greatest controversies. Congress may pass the laws, and the President may sign the laws, but it's the Supreme Court that decides the law. And starting today, that power is yours. Alongside the Justices, you will draft decisions that change lives. Your input will constantly be sought, and your ideas will certainly be implemented. In many instances, the Justices will rely entirely on your analysis. They'll base their opinions on your research. That means you affect what they see and what they know. There are nine Justices on this Court. But your influence, the power that you hold, makes you the tenth Justice.

In his novel, *The Tenth Justice*, Brad Meltzer uses dead-on accurate descriptions of the heady world of the Supreme Court to enhance his legal thriller. By getting the tone of the court and the workings of the system of that level right, he increases the readability of the story and decreases our need to suspend our disbelief.

Both state and federal courts have appellate courts that can throw your characters' cases into turmoil. In the state system, there are interim courts, called circuit courts, courts of appeal, or district courts, and then top-level courts called supreme courts (except in New York, where they perversely call the trial courts the supreme courts). Make sure your characters call the courts by the right names!

The federal appellate courts are the Circuit Courts of Appeal, organized by region and numbered. Your lawyer characters will refer to these courts by number ("the 11th Circuit," "the 5th Circuit," etc., or just "the 9th"). For instance, "Did you see that case that just came down out of the 9th Circuit? But the 11th disagrees." The top-level court is called the Supreme Court of the United States (not the U.S. Supreme Court).

Appellate judges were frequently appellate lawyers, but many more were trial judges who moved up. Could your appellate judge be a little confused on how things work because they are new? Are they geeky loners who never saw the inside of a trial court? Appellate courts don't hear witnesses or admit evidence. They hear oral arguments based solely on what was presented in the court below, and issue opinions based upon whether or not there was error. There are exceptions where cases can go straight or almost straight to appellate court, which we'll discuss more in the section on appeals.

Appeals courts rarely rule with one judge. They sit in panels of judges, and reach decisions after they discuss them as a panel and they have processes internally to determine which judge or judges will write the majority opinion. Does your appellate panel get along, or do they argue? Do they have petty internal politics? Is there a newbie judge who doesn't quite fit in? There are also concurring opinions, where the judges disagree with the basis for the ruling but agree with the outcome, and dissenting opinions where the judges disagree with the outcome. Does your judge character usually rule on the losing side and have to write dissents? Are they so arrogant they hate to see other judges write opinions?

Appellate judges are frequently called justices rather than judges. Getting this wrong in court can be a rookie mistake. Your characters will need to know what their judges are called. "Your Honor" is almost never wrong. If they are justices, then they are referred to as "Mister Justice" or "Madam Justice." Your nervous lawyer could call them by the wrong names or titles and suffer some humiliation, not that we writers would ever humiliate our characters, would we?

Trial Judges

These are the judges who hear the evidence and testimony in lawsuits. They are frequently organized into divisions, such as criminal, family, and civil. Is the judge in your character's case new to family court? Could they be hopelessly confused about anything but criminal law?

In jury trials, they decide which evidence is heard, keep the attorneys in line, and are supposed to make sure that the process is fairly run. In bench trials, they make the decision about the whole case. Is your character in a jury trial or a bench trial? There's quite a difference between the two. Maybe the lawyers have to discuss which kind of trial to pick and why.

Trial judges have lots of power. As characters, they can make your other characters' lives miserable or happy, can be fair or unfair, biased or unbiased, smart or stupid, and pay attention or not.

Judges are subject to the same human foibles as other mere mortals. Most know it, and some forget. Like it or not, they are some of the most powerful and influential members of our society. They can throw out a case, influence a jury, toss the lawyers in jail, or make the case wildly expensive. These characters can be villains or heroes, can cause major plot twists, and can impose good fortune or great hardship on your characters.

In this book, you'll see some of the things judges can do to affect the cases in your story.

Small Claims Judges

Small claims judges hear and decide the tiny cases – generally from zero to $2500 or $5000. These judges are *The People's Court*. Indeed, that show and the host of other legal reality shows, generally involve real-life small claims cases. My friend from law school Alex Ferrer, of the *Judge Alex* show, swears to me that these are real cases that real people filed in small claims. Watch these shows and you can get a feel for just how crazy and entertaining small claims cases can be. Small claims court is a great place for characters to get quick resolution to a small dispute. It has fewer rules because most people are unrepresented.

Small claims judges need to have an abundance of patience, and a real passion for justice. They have to deal with the frustrating process of hearing claims of ordinary people who have no clue about the law.

Bailiffs

Bailiffs keep order in the court. If your character's cell phone goes off, if there is talking, or if someone gets violent, the bailiff is the one who will remove the offending party. They generally have law enforcement backgrounds or training and can have college degrees or college education in police science or criminal justice. They wear badges and uniforms, and some have guns.

Bailiffs see and hear everything that goes on in court, so it's their job is to observe. As characters, they can be witnesses, blackmailers, or heroes. They are the ones who protect the judges if there is any violence, and they protect the jurors, witnesses, and lawyers as well. They frequently have to lend a hand checking lawyers in for hearings, handling evidence, calling witnesses in, and other administrative tasks. They escort the jury to and from the jury room, and stay outside the door to make sure they stay safe, sequestered, and get what they need.

Judicial Assistants

The judicial assistant, or JA, handles scheduling of hearings, trials, and other court proceedings. They usually handle and mark the evidence when it is admitted. In other words, they are the judge's right arm. The demeanor of a judicial assistant is usually a good reflection of the demeanor of the judge.

If a JA is rude to lawyers, it usually means that the judge hates lawyers. A polite JA will usually work for a polite judge. The JA can make or break the judge's calendar. A judge whose calendars always run late, who takes months to set a hearing, usually has a JA who can't maintain control.

Dealing with a great JA is one of the great pleasures of legal secretaries, paralegals and lawyers. A nasty or incompetent JA can make legal life miserable. Your characters can show up to hearings that aren't on the calendar, sit in the courtroom for hours as proceedings run late, have courtesy copies of motions and cases that were sent to the judge well in advance suddenly lost, and other JA-caused tribulations.

Paralegals

Paralegals assist lawyers in all aspects of law. All states allow paralegals to do investigation and research, prepare documents, organize and review client files, draft court documents, interview clients and witnesses, and assist at trials. These are the most likely functions any paralegal character in your story will have. These must be done under the strict supervision of an attorney.

The fact that the paralegal works so closely with the attorney puts them in a unique position for your story. They may know about some bit of malpractice that has been committed, or they may know a witness is lying. Maybe they were instructed to destroy some crucial piece of evidence by a slimy boss. A good example is the paralegal character in *The Riches*, who finds out Doug Rich may not be who or what he says he is.

In some states, they can even perform minor legal duties and have their own practices where they serve clients. Those states are listed in the chart on this page. If you have a paralegal character in these states you can give them more responsibility. But if your character is setting up corporations in, say, Delaware, you'd better have them aware that they may end up in jail.

Most states will not allow paralegals to work except under an attorney's direct supervision. They aren't allowed to file court documents for clients, submit forms such as immigration forms on behalf of clients, or to have most direct dealings with clients and opposing counsel. Does your paralegal character think they're smarter than the lawyers? Do they overstep their bounds? Or are they smart enough to go to law school but too scared?

No states allow paralegals to take depositions (lawyer talk for sworn testimony) or sign court documents. Paralegals may not appear before state courts or in other hearings in any state unless the rules of that entity authorize their appearance.

The following federal entities permit "non-lawyer" practice: Social Security Administration; IRS; Consumer Product Safety Commission; Department of Labor, EPA. You could have a paralegal character who helps clients with tax issues getting into trouble because they get cocky and decide to appear in court. Or you could have a paralegal instead of a lawyer handling a labor issue and getting in over their heads because they're not a lawyer.

States That Allow Paralegals to Perform Duties
Traditionally Performed by Lawyers

CA	
	1. draft partnership agreements and related filings with state and county agencies;
	2. draft statements of partnership and certificates of limited partnerships;
	3. draft agreements for dissolution of partnership and non-competition agreements for selling partners;
	4. draft articles of incorporation, by-laws, etc.;
	5. prepare and file documents with Secretary of State, Department of Corporations, IRS, and/or Franchise Tax Board;

	6. prepare appropriate forms for securities; 7. prepare stock certificates, loan documents and other documents required by financial institutions; 8. draft buy-sell agreements, employment agreements, assignments, promissory notes, leases; 9. draft petitions for probate and supporting documents; 10. draft inventory and appraisal list; 11. maintain financial records of estate; 12. prepare and file probate documents in administration of estate; 13. draft state and federal tax returns, including final returns for decedent; 14. draft wills, codicils, trusts, powers of attorney
CO	Has duties outlined for 18 specialty areas. Responsibilities for corporate law paralegals and estate planning paralegals are similar to California. Has a specialty area known as "Special District Law," in which the paralegal is given responsibilities which include organizing special districts and their public hearings.
CT	1. attend will executions and act as a witness, but may not provide legal advice at will executions; 2. attend real estate closings, even though no lawyer from the law firm employing the legal assistant is also present. The legal assistant may not express any independent opinion or judgment about execution of the documents, changes in adjustments or prices, or other matters involving documents or funds. 3. prepare client income, estate, gift and other tax returns but the returns must be reviewed by the lawyer.
FL	A law firm may permit a non-lawyer employee to conduct a real estate closing if the following conditions are met: 1. lawyer supervises and reviews all work done up to the closing; 2. supervising lawyer determines that handling or attending the closing will be no more than a ministerial act. Handling the closing will constitute a ministerial act only if the supervising lawyer determines that the client understands the closing documents in advance of the closing; 3. clients consent to the closing being handled by a non-lawyer employee of the firm. This requires that written disclosure be made to the clients that the person who will handle or attend the closing is a non-lawyer and will not be able to give legal advice at the closing; 4. supervising lawyer is readily available, in person or by telephone, to provide legal advice or answer legal questions

		should the need arise;
	5.	non-lawyer employee will not give legal advice at the closing or make impromptu decisions that should be made by the supervising lawyer.
RI	1.	Draft contracts, deeds, leases, mortgages, wills, trusts, probate forms, pension plans and tax returns;
	2.	Assist at closings;
	3.	Witness execution of documents;
	4.	Maintain estate/guardianship trust accounts;
	5.	Transfer securities and other assets;
	6.	Assist in daily administration of trusts and estates

Legal Secretaries

Legal secretaries handle scheduling, prepare some court notices, draft some minor court documents, prepare letters, type (although this is becoming less of the job now that most attorneys prepare their initial drafts on their own computers), transcribe (again, more and more rare), file, deal with client and opposing counsel calls, and keep the lawyer's office running smoothly.

A legal secretary is sometimes shared and sometimes is exclusive to one attorney. Do you have lawyers in your story who get into a fistfight over whose work gets done first? Don't laugh. I've seen it happen. Many now have at least an associate degree and some have paralegal degrees. They can perform paralegal duties, or have more traditionally secretarial type duties. You could have a legal secretary who feels underappreciated and underpaid, who thinks she or he should be making the big bucks. The legal secretary knows everything about the attorney, so they make great witnesses, or blackmailers.

Office Managers

Office managers handle the business and human resources end of the law practice. If your paralegal or legal secretary character starts mouthing off to the boss, the office manager may be the one to step in. Whether making sure office supplies are in stock, dealing with vendors and repair people, or handling staff issues, these managers can take some of the non-legal tasks off the hands of the lawyers so they can focus on practicing law. Office managers can also be used in your story to do the dirty work: getting rid of staff, hiding documents, moving people from department to department to keep any one person from knowing too much. Does this get them killed? Do they quit under stress? Embezzle the trust money? They will probably have passwords and access to the firm's accounts. Frequently seen in larger firms, this role is now being handled in midsize and smaller firms by someone trained in either accounting or administration. Could they be quietly figuring out how to retire? Could they be undercover trying to bring in a crooked attorney? Or did they end up in witness protection?

Runners/Messengers

Runners and messengers make deliveries, do copies and run errands for the attorneys. This puts them in a place where they can move around and observe activities of all your characters. Courier services will usually handle most same-day deliveries, but many larger firms have in-house people dealing with deliveries. Did the runner in your story deliver flowers to a judge with whom the partner is having an affair? Did they have the package of incriminating tapes they were supposed to mail but took home and listened to instead? In-house runners or messengers will also assist with copying and other more menial tasks. These make great characters because they know everything that is going on in the office. And maybe what was shredded.

Process Servers

Process servers hand official documents to people who don't want them. Lawsuits, orders to testify in court or bring documents, and orders to stop doing something are items your characters won't be happy about. Many people try to evade process servers, who have to get clever to serve those individuals. Fake pizza deliveries, exterminators, pulling fire alarms, could be used to humorous advantage in a story. Or get your process server killed. Most people realize that the process server is just doing their job. The likely reaction of your character served with a suit is to thank the process server. Boring, but accurate. But maybe they see the character with a mistress. Many process servers are also private investigators, and some have law enforcement backgrounds. Having a character who moves around lots, who is observant, and who knows something about the law could come in handy in all kinds of creative ways, couldn't it?

Court Reporters

A court reporter's job is to write down every word said in court, listen to every word of every legal proceeding they cover, and be able to write it down accurately. They train for two or more years, and from what I can tell, they have supernatural powers: the ability to transcribe at about 300 words per minute without missing a word. A missed word can be catastrophic to a trial. Imagine the deposition transcript in your story with an omitted "not" or "no." Or with the wrong speaker listed.

The attorneys are usually the ones who order a court reporter for, say, a deposition, and the attorney who orders them pays their fee. Each attorney ordering the transcript of the proceeding pays a per-page fee for the transcript. Usually the trial courts will have a court reporter who attends, but sometimes it is the attorneys' responsibility to order the reporter for trial. If neither side remembers to order the reporter, the trial might have to be delayed or moved to another date while the parties wait for the reporter to arrive.

An older court reporter will have small transcription machines with keys that look like small paddles, and paper that comes out with weird looking symbols.[4] Newer machines have the paddles but no paper at all, and are done on computer disk, so that's how your young reporter will work. What if one of these reporters hates your attorney character because he didn't pay her? She decides to change the words. Or if the reporter is just incompetent and can't read back a crucial part of the trial that took six months?

Even more newfangled is "real time," a process that only the wealthiest attorneys can afford. The court reporter hooks right into the attorney's computer and the attorney sees the transcript as it happens. This is very expensive. So while the high-powered attorney could be reading an instant transcript, your poor starving personal injury attorney will have to wait to get the transcripts printed. Is the court reporter in league with the rich attorney? Or does she know he's tampering with her

---

[4] For years, I used one of the last court reporters in the country who used shorthand. She was absolutely fantastic. I never figured out how she did it. If there are any left, I'd love to hear about them. But go ahead and insert pterodactyl comment here. You know you want to.

words? A seemingly simple thing like transcripts can engender some good writing material.

The counterpart to the court reporter is the videographer. Some depositions are videotaped as well as transcribed, so the jury can see the witness speaking, particularly if the witness won't be in the trial. If you have a screenplay, your story should use a videographer because then you'll be able to show the deposition visually in the story.

Notaries

Notaries witness and put their seal on signatures to verify that they obtained good identification from the person signing and that the signature is true, and certify copies of documents as being true copies. They can give oaths and perform wedding ceremonies. Banks, law firms, and copy centers frequently have staff notaries. Many lawyers are also notaries. Few notaries are full-time notaries.

Notaries are licensed by their state, and usually have to pass a test and post a bond that will pay for any damages they cause if they are negligent or dishonest. And there's lots of room for both. Did your dishonest notary put a piece of property in their own name? Did they notarize a document with lots of white space and turn it into a will in their favor? Or, do they know the document is a forgery?

A notary can justifiably lose their license by notarizing a signature they did not actually witness, but many do this anyhow. You see it particularly at busy real estate law firms. A notary who refuses to participate in this illegal practice could be a protected whistleblower in your story. Notaries can be witnesses to all kinds of fraud in your stories. They could be on the run, in witness protection, or a murder victim.

Unscrupulous notaries can use the Spanish translation, "notario" to bilk unsuspecting immigrants. The term notario can refer to a lawyer or someone of similar stature in some countries. Many notarios engage in the unauthorized practice of law here in the U.S. This comes up frequently in immigration fraud scams. Is your character an illegal immigrant who thought they were legal? Did the notario's scam get them deported? Might be a motive for murder.

Chapter 2 – Settings

Your settings will vary as much as your imagination and, like trial, the setting can be used as a prop to favor a witness, lawyer, etc. Small town courthouses will look drastically different than big city courthouses. Modern ones will be different from the very old. I'll try to give you a sense here of what they will have in common, and some of the items that may vary.

Courtrooms

Non-jury courtrooms can be as simple as a t-shaped table with some chairs. The judge sits at a desk. A longer table adjoins the desk, and the parties and witnesses sit on the sides.

Many judges do non-jury trials in their chambers. Most motions are also heard in chambers. The judge's chambers usually have a similar T-shape setup. The judge's desk has personal items, photos, memorabilia, awards, and usually a gavel or two. There are bookshelves with law books. Walls are filled with photos, artwork, memorabilia, honors, certificates, and articles about the judge. These items can tell about the judge's personality. For instance, I know a judge who used to have a ponytail who mounted the cut ponytail on the wall in a frame. These personal items can say a lot about your judge's personality. And don't think the attorneys don't pay attention to what is there. Attorneys will suddenly opine on the judge's favorite sports team or the judge's alma mater, to show the judge just what great guys they are, and just how much they have in common.

Courtrooms are usually not personalized. Many judges share courtrooms, and even those with assigned courtrooms usually keep the memorabilia in chambers. The courtroom will usually have an imposing symbol or motto over the judge's chair. My personal favorite is the not-meant-to-be-ironic, "We who labor here seek only the truth."

Courtrooms almost always have an American flag, and maybe a state, city or county flag. The judge's bench is raised in a jury courtroom so everyone has to look up. The idea is to create an imposing presence so the judge commands respect and the proceedings are dignified. Judges usually only wear robes in front of a jury.

The bench may be ornately carved or simple. It is usually big. Next to the judge's bench will be the witness box, usually just a wooden wall with a chair inside. This usually has a step up, but it is lower than the bench so the witness also has to look up at the judge.

Also next to the judge is a spot for the judge's assistant, clerk or bailiff, who handles the evidence as it comes in and deals with administrative issues as they arise. Most judges have their assistant or bailiff mark evidence and hold onto any admitted evidence. Lawyers are notorious evidence thieves, mostly accidentally. Witnesses also sometimes walk out of the box with evidence. Having a central person in charge of keeping track of exhibits works well to maintain control over slippery pieces of paper. Some judges make the attorneys keep track of the exhibits. This can have disastrous or comical results. I once had an opposing witness leave the box with a stack of exhibits, which neither lawyer caught until after lunch. We had to scramble to reconstruct the exhibits.

The jury box is on either side of the bench, usually against one of the perpendicular walls. Because civil trials usually have six jurors, the box will have six to twelve chairs, frequently in two rows with the back row raised. Sometimes the alternate juror's chairs will be separated from the group, sometimes they are mixed in.

Courtrooms can be tiny or large, acoustically sound or acoustic nightmares. My favorite has a large column in the middle so the lawyers choose between moving their tables where they can't see the jury or where they can't see the judge.

Counsel tables will be in front of the bench, and are either stationary in a larger courtroom or mobile in cases of tiny courtrooms with logistical issues. Judges usually have a preference as to where plaintiffs and defendants sit. Plaintiffs are more frequently on the judge's right, so on the left side of the courtroom walking in. But if the judge allows the sides to pick, then the first to arrive will pick the prime spot.

Spectator areas are usually behind the lawyers, but can be large or nonexistent. In the tiny courtrooms, I've seen spectators have to find chairs in other rooms or just a single chair sitting to the side or back of the room.

There will usually be a podium in the front of the bench for the lawyers to use, and it is usually movable.[5] The lawyers will move it around the room to position themselves where the jury can see them, or to make themselves less prominent so the jury focuses on the witness. Lawyers examining a favorable witness will position themselves at the end of the jury box so the witness will be looking toward the jury. When questioning adverse witnesses, or during cross-examination, they will move in front of the jury, increasing their prominence and making the witness look away from the jury.

Most judge's benches and lawyer's tables will be equipped with a water pitcher and disposable cups. Most trials have at least one water spill as a result.

Court reporters usually position themselves in front of the bench, near the witness box. They bring their machine, and are provided with only a chair.

Variables can be microphones, location of the bailiff (some have desks or chairs near the judge, some stand by the door, some have chairs in the back), décor, size, silencing devices at the bench used to muffle sidebar conferences from the jury, video or audio equipment, windows or none, view, lighting (some are surprisingly dark), amenities at counsel table such as lights and drawers, and size and ornamentation on doors.

Courthouses

Small towns may have a tiny courthouse with one judge; large cities may have courthouses that are huge, or multiple courthouses for civil, criminal, family, or other specialized courts. Whether large or small, most courthouses have some things in common.

The clerk's office is where lawsuits are filed, assigned numbers, pleadings and documents filed and docketed, certified copies provided, and files kept. There will be security at the door, mostly with a metal detector. All have an American flag somewhere.

---

[5] There's one courtroom I seem to get a lot. It has a giant pole in the center of the room. I always get there early, grab my favorite table, and move the furniture around so I can see the judge and jury. The room used to be a storage room, and now it's a courtroom. Ain't government grand?

There will usually be a conference room available for depositions and for lawyers to work. At least some form of law library is in most.

Variables are size, architectural design, amenities such as cafeterias, snack shops, wi-fi, computerized research, attorney lounges, juror rooms for jury selection pools, amount of clerk's staff, number of judges, size of law library, available rooms for attorneys, whether the courthouse has civil and criminal together, and décor.

Many courthouses don't have free parking. Some have none, and the lawyers and parties have to find pay parking lots. Others have meters or charge for parking with an attendant. There will always be parking for judges and staff, and there is usually some arrangement made for free juror parking. This can be made with an outside parking garage, or can be part of the courthouse parking lot.

Courthouses say much about the communities that host them. Palm Beach, of course, has a water view and state of the art facilities. If your story is in a specific locale, go and walk through the courthouse to get the local flavor. If the locale is fictional, then the courthouse is up to your imagination.

Law Offices

I talked about the variables among big, midsize, and small firms earlier. Some things all law firms will have in common. It will be important to know what should be present in any law office setting: phones, computers, desk, some private area for client meetings, at least some law books, and some access to a copier.

Other than that, the décor, amenities, staff, facilities, grade of building, shared or not, free parking or not, can vary as much as your characters and imagination allow.

Arbitrator/Mediator Offices

Many arbitrators and mediators have no offices at all and go to the locations agreed by the attorneys. If they have offices, there are some things that each will require.

A mediator has to have at least two private conference rooms for caucuses with each side and for the attorneys and clients to have private discussions. Phones may or may not be in the conference rooms. Usually at least one of the rooms will have a phone in case an insurance adjuster or other participant needs to appear telephonically. There will be some lobby or reception area for people not participating in the mediation. Most mediators have low overheads and few amenities.

Variables can be coffee/snack areas, receptionists, offices for the mediator with a computer and printer for printing agreements, wi-fi for attorneys, number of rooms if there are multiple mediators using the offices, and type of building.

Arbitrators need only one conference room, which should be relatively large so that multiple parties have room to sit, along with witnesses. They may or may not have refreshments. There will usually be a receptionist so that witnesses who arrive will not interrupt proceedings. Phones are usually available for witnesses appearing telephonically. Full time arbitrators usually travel around from location to location, and few have their own facilities. If they do, the amenities can vary as much as the personality of the arbitrator.

Government Offices

All government offices are utilitarian, cash-strapped, and short on supplies. Even the newest facilities become quickly out of date. Most use metal or cheap wood desks. Most have cubicles for at least some staff rather than offices. They become more and more crowded over the years as more staff is squeezed together into the same space. Computers are usually utilized years past the time they are outdated.

Other than these commonalities, government offices can reflect the town's personality. For instance, my town has a wild west theme that carries over to town hall. If you have a real locale, then go and look at the facilities. Otherwise, make your government setting as quirky as your story allows, within the reality of being taxpayer funded.

Court Reporter Offices

Court reporters usually have a warren of small conference rooms with coffee available and few amenities. Many rent offices from others or share with multiple court reporting operations. No court reporter can survive with high overhead. Most do their transcripts at home. Even large court reporting offices have staff doing billing and scheduling, but will have fewer amenities than law offices.

Some of the large firms will have teleconference capabilities, state of the art transcription, real time capabilities so that attorneys will see the transcript on their computers as it is being done, conference calling, speaker phones, and other high tech services. Videographers are not usually associated with court reporting offices. They usually bring their own backgrounds, lighting, and equipment to the deposition location for a videotaped deposition. Videotaped depositions will also have a court reporter that does a separate transcript.

All court reporters travel to location. Most depositions are done in a law office where the reporters attend, and reporters go to the courthouse for trials and hearings. Many have no offices of their own, and are completely mobile.

As long as your settings ring true for the community that is your story's location, you can let your imagination run free. Settings can be quirky or staid, utilitarian or fancy, modern or decrepit. Knowing what the settings must have to be authentic will add to your story's credibility.

Chapter 3 -Types of lawyers

The most basic breakdown of law, and therefore lawyers, is civil and criminal. But the types of civil practice are as varied as the law itself. The days of the general practitioner are almost gone. Most lawyers narrow their practice to a specific area in which they can develop mastery and have some level of comfort.

General practice is sometimes referred to pejoratively as "door law," meaning anything that walks in the door. This could be the lawyer in a small town representing people in all sorts of matters. Maybe there's only one other lawyer in town and they butt heads every day.

Oddly, most states won't actually let lawyers say they specialize in an area of law without some extra certification. This goes in the face of the way the practice of law actually works, but the Bar rules don't necessarily have to make sense. Lawyers can say they "handle" or "focus on" or "have experience in" certain areas, but not that they specialize. And don't even get me started about advertising rules.

Major Areas of Civil Law Practice

- Admiralty
- Antitrust
- Appellate
- Bankruptcy
- Business Law
- Civil Rights
- Commercial Litigation
- Condominium
- Construction
- Consumer Protection
- Elder Law
- Election Law
- Entertainment and Sports
- Environmental
- Family Law
- Governmental Law
- Health
- Immigration
- Intellectual Property
- International Law
- Labor and Employment
- Land Use and Zoning
- Legal Malpractice
- Military Law
- Personal Injury
- Probate/Estate Planning

• Real Estate	• Tax
• Securities	• Worker's Compensation

The thing most lawyers have in common is that almost all lawyers want to be former lawyers. Paul Newman played a perfect burnout in *The Verdict*. If your character is gung-ho and still believes in justice, they'd better be young. But an older lawyer writing a book or trying to pursue their dream of opening a bakery to escape the practice would be an interesting character.

Here are some of the major areas of civil law practice and what they are:

Personal Injury

This area covers all types of bodily injury and really is the subject of a number of subcategories. The major areas of personal injury law are:

- Medical Malpractice
- Products Liability
- Accidents

There are then subsets of all of these. Some lawyers handle only certain types of products, such as breast implants, asbestos, or pharmaceuticals. Some accident lawyers only handle aviation or auto accidents.

Personal injury lawyers are the lawyers everyone loves to hate, but they are, in a contrary view, heroes. They are the ones that keep bad doctors from killing more people, and who fight the corporate mentality of only fixing a product that hurts people if it costs them too much not to. While some are truly the ambulance chasers who go to funerals and hand out cards, this is the type of behavior that can get bad lawyers disbarred.

Most personal injury attorneys are crusaders who believe in trying to change the world. Some are in it just for the money, but few start out that way. No matter how you develop your personal injury lawyer character, they are always fun to write about because they can be flamboyant, arrogant, smart, and fantastic murder targets if you lean toward mysteries. And most trial lawyers of any sort are frustrated actors or entertainers. Remember when Supreme Court Justices Scalia and O'Connor sang opera? Trial lawyers perform in court as if they were on stage, and they frequently have bands, do community theater, or have other performing pastimes.

Commercial Litigation

Commercial litigators handle disputes involving businesses, such as contracts, partnership disputes, and unfair trade practices. Litigation means, very simply, a lawsuit. But a firm with a "Lawsuit Department" probably couldn't charge $700/hour. These are most commonly the folks who make the big bucks, work for the big firms, and represent businesses. Authors like to use these guys as foils for the underdogs. Or show them having attacks of conscience and giving up the Armani suits for a tiny practice in the sticks. Ha. That'll be the day.

Does your big firm character have to be a villain? Are they multidimensional? Can they be proud of their work and feel like they are helping their clients? Can they be secretly planning to start an art gallery or a banana farm?

Oh, sure, there are lawyers who consider themselves commercial litigators who are solo practitioners or in midsize firms. Could your small practitioner get overwhelmed taking on a too-big case? Some "boutique firms" with 10 – 40 lawyers handle only commercial litigation. But the vast majority of commercial litigators are of the Armani/Brooks Brothers/Ralph Lauren[6] crowd. You can have them travel to expensive places, buy fantastic clothes, or take a year's sabbatical. Characters with money can frequently be more flexible to write than poor ones.

Tax

Tax lawyers are the ones who advise corporations and individuals how to avoid paying too much in taxes and what taxes have to be paid. They sometimes are trial lawyers who practice in the United States Tax Court, a highly specialized court in Washington, DC. If you have a CEO character who is perpetrating some sort of corporate fraud, she probably needs a tax lawyer's help. Or maybe the tax lawyer uncovered a second set of books and has a moral dilemma.

---

[6] I'm an Escada/Prada/Coach gal, myself. Note I listed male designers. Litigation is still extremely male-dominated. Your litigator character is most likely to be male. If a woman, she should be surrounded by males in court.

Tax lawyers can also attend and help prepare for audits, prepare complex tax returns, respond to IRS inquires, and handle all aspects of the law involving taxes. If your character is in tax trouble, what will their lawyer be like? Tax lawyers frequently have an L.L.M., a degree that takes another year or two on top of the J.D. law degree. Many come from accounting backgrounds, and many are also C.P.A.s. So we're talking smart, bookish folks who like playing with numbers.

These lawyers tend not to be flashy, but many work for the big firms. Some firms have entire tax departments. Some tax lawyers are solo or small firm practitioners. If your character is an individual, they probably hired a lawyer with a tiny practice. The corporate CEO with a dozen tax shelters probably hired the big guns. Will your character follow their advice? End up in jail? Or will they claim the tax lawyer told them to do it?

Bankruptcy

Bankruptcy is what happens when the finances crash and burn. In today's economy, is your character facing bankruptcy? The two major types of bankruptcy lawyers handle personal and business bankruptcy. As the legal changes have recently made it tougher for individual bankruptcies, many bankruptcy lawyers are either moving into more corporate bankruptcy or moving into other areas of law. Did your character miss the deadline to file under the easier laws? Maybe the bankruptcy lawyer tells them they don't have a chance. Or maybe the bankruptcy laws will change back to favor individuals.

Is your character hiding money from the bankruptcy court? There are also bankruptcy trustees who manage the estate of the bankrupt corporation or individual. They are the ones who make sure all debts owed to the bankrupt estate are paid as the court orders. And they make sure all the assets are rounded up. Could the trustee get wind of some big hidden asset and ruin the villain's scheme to flee to Bermuda? Does the Russian mob have to stop the trustee before they get hold of the diamonds hidden in the safe deposit box?

Real Estate

Real estate lawyers handle the paperwork and closings for real estate transactions. Is your character buying a house? Are they a mogul buying a skyscraper? Then they probably have a real estate lawyer. Some also do landlord-tenant or other real estate trial work, but most would rather chew off an arm than go to court. If your character is being evicted or bought a house with toxic mold, they need a real estate litigator. Big firms have real estate departments that handle major deals, and your wheeler-dealer mogul probably has one of these gigantic firms handling the closing. Most real estate lawyers are from solo or small firm practices, and that's where the little guy goes. Your single mom character buying property for the first time probably has a lawyer from a small firm. Is the seller a big company with a big firm trying to take advantage? Or maybe the big firm is trying to bully the widow with the beachfront property into selling.

Probate/Estate Planning

Estate planning is preparing wills, trusts, living wills and other documents relating to how property will pass on death, how the person wants to be treated if incapacitated, and who will take care of children. Is your character dying of a horrible disease or going to Iraq? They probably went to a lawyer to make out their will. Or, did the billionaire leave everything to the bimbo? The probate lawyers will be representing the disinherited son.

Probate lawyers also frequently handle guardianships when a person is incapacitated mentally or physically. Did the designated guardian run off with the old lady's assets? Or is Mom suddenly forgetful but not acknowledging she can't take care of herself? Did Dad give all his money to the evangelist? Maybe the kids tried to get a guardian appointed when pop is still sharp as a tack.

Labor and Employment

Employment lawyers handle advice and disputes regarding work. Half your characters' waking hours or more are probably spent working. Are they having troubles? Is the boss hitting on them, or are they about to be fired? They may go see an employment lawyer.

Or is your book about a crusader fighting to change the justice system? Employee-side employment lawyers are usually true believers in crusading for justice, such as it is. They like to help people, and got into the law to make a difference. They refer to Management-side lawyers as "The Dark Side." They like to fight a stacked system, have mostly uphill battles these days, and are usually trying to push the edges of the law to expand employee rights. Management lawyers tend to think all employees are scum, and that all discrimination claims are frivolous.[7] Is your character being forced to defend a racist corporate president who hung a noose over an employee's desk?

Although your character may say they need a labor lawyer, many employment lawyers never touch labor, that is, union-related law. If your character tried to form a union and got fired for their troubles, they have a labor lawyer, not an employment lawyer. To a character facing an employment issue for the first time, they probably don't know the difference.

Did the secretary go to human resources to report a big shareholder fraud? Is your quiet bookkeeper spreading rumors that a coworker is a pedophile? Or are they an illegal immigrant working 80 hours a week and getting paid for 30? Employment issues can range from discrimination, whistleblowing, and overtime to breach of contract, defamation, and battery. Anything that happens in the workplace can be the subject of employment law.

Maybe your character is a seasoned personal injury attorney who thinks a sexual harassment case will be a breeze. There are so many loopholes in the law for management-side attorneys due to years of chipping away at employee rights, so having them handle their first employment case is a good way to get your lawyer character into deep trouble.

Admiralty

No, it has almost nothing to do with Admirals. Admiralty involves anything that happens on navigable waters, which can be oceans, rivers, and other large bodies of water. Accidents and assaults on cruise ships, and pretty much anything else that happens on these waters, is governed by admiralty. Was your lounge singer raped by her boss on the high seas? Most people are surprised that, when they go on a ship, they lose many of their rights to make claims under most U.S. laws. Admiralty

---

[7] I have to confess that my view of this area of practice is not entirely unbiased, as it is my own.

preempts all other laws when it involves navigable waters. So your character may go to an employment lawyer only to find out she has no rights. She may have to get an admiralty lawyer to fight for her.

Did your character find a great treasure at sea? The admiralty lawyers are the ones who will sort out the ownership issues.

Admiralty lawyers tend to be fun-loving sorts, mostly male, who like the water. Go figure. It's one of those weird areas of the law that other lawyers don't understand. I had an employment case involving an attack on a cruise ship, and I brought in an admiralty lawyer to be the lead counsel because you have to know what you're doing on these claims. They have all kinds of rules that other types of law don't have. Maybe your lawyer character filed a case not realizing admiralty law applied. Or maybe your character's case got thrown out because the other side brought in an admiralty lawyer who convinced the court the case was preempted.

Consumer Protection

Consumer protection lawyers handle consumer issues regarding automobiles, banking, and purchases of all sorts. Did your character buy a car that turned out to be a lemon? Have their identity stolen? Get ripped off by the wedding caterer who dumped them at the last minute for another job? Their consumer protection lawyer is probably someone who believes in crusading against the big guys. Consumer protection lawyers go up against firms that represent the giants, and like it that way. But maybe the giant figures out that there are a thousand other cases just like this one. Maybe the lawyer has to be bribed to give up the case. Do they take the money, or do they end up next to Jimmy Hoffa?

Condominium

Condo lawyers usually represent the Board of a condominium association, and advise them on proper procedures. They can also defend the association when it is accused of wrongdoing. No place is more like Peyton Place than a condominium. If you're thinking about a comedy, could it be set in a senior-only condominium? The lawyer character will have to have infinite patience and be able to stand long meetings. Does she snap and quit the practice of law to take up knitting?

Is she a witness for the prosecution testifying that the board member threatened the new president right before he turned up dead?

Family Law

Mostly covering divorce, family law also deals with custody, guardianship, commitment and other claims relating to families. If your character is getting a divorce, trying to regain custody, or claiming somebody needs to be put in an institution because they're a danger to themselves, they have a family lawyer.

Collaborative Law: The most cutting-edge type of family law is collaborative law. In this area, both lawyers sign an agreement that, if they don't settle the case, they'll drop out and let another lawyer handle the trial. The idea of collaborative law is that the parties need to work together to reach a resolution that benefits everyone and cut through the rancor of a contested divorce. Some states won't allow lawyers to agree to drop out at the end.

Do your characters think they can agree on everything, then change their minds? Does one seek out a collaborative lawyer, and the other want somebody who only handles contested divorces? Maybe one of them wants the collaborative lawyer to break the deal and handle the trial. Most collaborative lawyers handle only that type of law, and parties have to seek someone who handles collaborative divorces.

Parties in collaborative law agree to exchange full financial information, and to work in the best interest of any children involved. This would be a good place to have one of your characters holding back information about their bank account in the Caymans.

Uncontested divorces: Some divorces are uncontested, and lawyers will sometimes only handle uncontested proceedings at a low flat rate. Did your character pay their money, then find out the husband won't sign the papers?

Contested divorces: Contested divorces are the nastiest proceedings imaginable. Lawyers who handle these cases tend to be divorced or get divorced while practicing law, mainly because they know all the horrible things that can happen. They have to enjoy big nasty fights. Is your character's lawyer a jerk who likes creating trouble where there is none? Does your character fall in love with their lawyer while in a vulnerable state?

Elder Law

Elder lawyers handle wills, Medicaid eligibility, and other types of planning for retirees. The idea is to plan for disability, incapacity, and death so the heirs get their money, while also making sure the elderly person is cared for. Did your money-grubbing middle aged characters rush Mom off to the elder lawyer to make a grab for the money before the siblings get wind?

There are some elder lawyers who prey on older, wealthy clients to try to take as much away from them as possible. Did the greedy characters' plan backfire when the lawyer took all the money? Most elder lawyers have much patience and like to help the elderly. Did they help too much? Did the kids sue because they didn't get enough of the pie? Or maybe the lawyer uncovered the fact that the daughter supposedly caring for Mom is really out all day pursuing her modeling career.

Immigration

If your character wasn't born in the U.S., chances are they have used an immigration lawyer. Immigration law is heavy on filling out forms, and is supported by crews of paralegals who assist with the forms. Maybe your character hired a paralegal they thought was a lawyer. Or maybe he paid a phony lawyer who ran off with his money.

Immigration lawyers also might hire people or have in-house people to wait in the huge lines at INS[8]. Did the person who was supposed to be in line go to their boyfriend's house instead? Did the lawyer miss the important deadline because they couldn't get in? Immigration lawyers tend to be at least bilingual, and many are multilingual. Is your immigration lawyer from an interesting place? This could help her develop a niche practice handling the community of Croatian immigrants, for instance.

Immigration law changes completely about once every decade, so they have to stay up on current trends, and make sure the clients get into the system before changes go into effect. But maybe your character is lazy and forgot about the change taking place, causing their clients to miss out on amnesty.

---

[8] The United States Immigration and Naturalization Service. Which is now part of Homeland Security and really called U.S. Citizenship and Immigration Services. But everybody still calls it INS. Just like green cards aren't green anymore.

There are multitudes of predators in this area. Unlicensed practice of law abounds, and unscrupulous people will take large fees and then not file anything, or file for status that they know will never be granted. Is your character in Mexico where they can't sue the shyster because they got deported before they knew what was going on? Maybe their cousin wants revenge.

Great immigration lawyers help families stay together, help businesses bring in specialists from outside the U.S., and help entertainers and athletes from outside the U.S. gain entry. These lawyers have to be able to stand huge amounts of bureaucracy and red tape. Is your frustrated lawyer character rewarded in the end by being able to attend a citizenship ceremony? Does the Olympic athlete saved from oppression invite their lawyer to a front row seat?

Intellectual Property

Intellectual property involves copyrights (protection of creative work, such as books, articles, songs, screenplays, software, recipes, paintings, and sculpture); trademarks (the symbol or name of a company or entity that is used in its marketing and trade dealings); and patents (inventions and unique methodology, such as medicines, machines, and devices). Is your character a writer whose work was stolen? Did they invent something and need to find out whether they were first? Then they need an intellectual property lawyer. Many patent lawyers come from scientific or technical backgrounds, so if you're looking to write about a recovering geek, this could be a great profession for them.

Entertainment and Sports

These lawyers represent celebrities, but also represent beginning athletes, entertainers, and authors. Some serve as agents or managers, some do contract negotiations, some handle trials. Does your character like to be around the talented or famous? Are they a frustrated athlete, writer or entertainer? Then they might just be an entertainment or sports lawyer. This is one of the flashiest areas of law practice. Your character can drive a Ferrari, go to all the glamorous openings, and meet the gorgeous men or women they need if you're writing a romance or a spy novel.

Civil Rights

If your character cried, "You violated my civil rights!" then this is the lawyer they need. Whether your character was arrested based on a bogus anonymous tip or had their house broken into when the cops got the wrong address, civil rights issues can make for compelling stories. Did your character get arrested for staging a protest? Fired from a government job for wearing a Muslim hajib? Maybe the ACLU will step in.

These cases tend to be high profile and heavily covered in the press. If you're looking for a story that your reporter character can cover, you may want to think about civil rights. The government and private entities that get sued generally fight like cornered rats, so as a result, civil rights cases are long and drawn out and are usually the subject of numerous appeals. Is your character dying from their injuries after a police beating and time is running out for them? Or maybe they're sitting in a government prison in, say, some island without a lawyer or charges being lodged against them.

Many lawyers who do these cases handle them pro bono (fancy lawyer talk for free), and many others are paid only if they win by seeking fees to be awarded in court as the prevailing parties. These lawyers are the ultimate crusaders for truth, justice, and the American way. Is your lawyer character a crusader? Are they going broke from taking on a free speech case that dragged on for years? Many have successful practices doing other areas of law and also assist groups such as ACLU with civil rights cases, and some have practices devoted primarily to civil rights. Is your character a silk stocking lawyer suddenly thrust into the pro bono division of the firm as a punishment for turning down a date with a senior partner? Many criminal defense attorneys also handle the civil rights aspects of criminal proceedings, such as due process and false arrest issues. Is your criminal defense attorney character suddenly over his head with civil trial motions?

Environmental

Environmental attorneys deal with pollution, endangered species, clean water, and any issues involving protecting the planet. Or not, as the case may be. I don't know of any environmental attorney who goes into the practice intending to defend corporations but, other than government attorneys and those representing environmental groups, like the Sierra Club, for little pay, defense of polluters is the primary practice of most environmental attorneys. Did your character go to law school to save the world only to end up in a big firm environmental department representing a developer who wants to bury the burrowing owls? Did he start work for a corporation that sold him a bill of goods about how they just wanted to make sure they did the right thing, only to find out their job is to help them get around the law? Or maybe your lawyer admires the environmentalists until she does battle with an overzealous group trying to save the endangered red dandelion.

These tend to be folks who started out as idealists and who got practical when they realized there were few jobs for crusaders out to save the environment. Those Greenpeace jobs just don't pay as well as the big firms. Did your character start saving whales and switch? Or are they working for a Japanese whaling firm and crying every night?

Land Use and Zoning

Land use lawyers represent developers trying to change zoning from residential to commercial, from smaller density to multiple units, or other land use changes. These are the lawyer-lobbyists. They love politics, were usually involved in government in some aspect, and have figured out how to make their political involvement pay. They make the big bucks because millions ride on the results of these largely locally-decided issues. Do you have a character who used to work for a powerful state senator or county commissioner? They may become a lobbyist.

Land use lawyers get their firms to make campaign contributions, sponsor events, donate and buy at charity auctions, and buy those big sports arena boxes for entertaining. If you have a character you want to put in the middle of some powerful political players and people with money, you may want to put them in land use. They have big expense accounts for wining and dining the elected officials whose votes they court. Did they cross the line into bribery? Or did the firm tell them to take the Congresswoman to a Super Bowl game only to have your character end up indicted? They get to go to lots of fun events, but those events get old, and most of them would love to spend more time with their families. Maybe your character is getting a divorce because they don't spend enough time with the family. The events and meetings they have to attend tend to be on evenings and weekends, not leaving much time for family life.

Election Law

Vote fraud, voting rights, and hanging chads. You saw these attorneys by the dozens in the *Bush v. Gore* case and in the HBO movie, *Recount*. Other than in California, and government attorneys, I don't know any attorneys who do this full time. Most are lawyers who helped with specific campaigns who then volunteer[9] their time to handle any election-related issues.

Who does your character represent? A political party? A union? The candidate? There are usually teams of election law attorneys lined up for emergency issues on Election Day. Did your character write the manual for the candidate's legal team, then get shoved aside when bigger name lawyers started showing up? Did the elections department dump voters from the rolls right before the election? Did your candidate grab two hundred absentee ballots for people in nursing homes and vote for himself? Are zealous campaign workers blocking voters wearing buttons for the other side from getting into the polls? Did the opposing candidate throw up an ad at the last minute that claimed your character was a terrorist? This is a developing area of law and a great area for novels and screenplays.

Securities

Fraudulent investment schemes, shareholder issues, whistleblowing, stockbroker issues, and anything relating to securities (stocks and partnership interests primarily) are in this area of the law. These cases mostly go to arbitration (basically, a non-court trial that has a non-judge appointed to decide the case) before the NASD (National Association of Securities Dealers). That's right, the group that stockbrokers founded and are regulated by also decides whether your character's stockbroker did them wrong. Did your elderly character find out their broker did

---

[9] They expect to be rewarded later, usually with help on government contracts, government appointments, or merely being recognized in public when the elected official is out schmoozing.

dozens of trades without checking? Did your stockbroker character find out about an insider trade and spill the beans? Was your Muslim stockbroker fired after their training for "not fitting in?" Is the panel deciding your character's case stacked with lawyers who all did defense of the big stock brokerages?

Legal Malpractice

Legal malpractice lawyers sue other attorneys for negligence and wrongdoing. These are the most feared and reviled attorneys. Is your young lawyer character taking on a powerful attorney for failing to file a lawsuit on time? Maybe they're being threatened or bribed. Very few attorneys handle this area of practice. The few who do keep busy and can pick and choose their cases. Did the malpractice attorney turn down your character's case because they're sleeping with the lawyer who stole the trust money? These are attorneys who are proud of their profession and think bad lawyers should be out of the profession. They got into this area of practice because they hate the reputation the legal profession has and want to change it. But maybe your character is being pursued on a malpractice claim unjustly, or because they ticked off the President of the Bar.

Military Law

"You can't handle the truth!" Who doesn't remember that line from *A Few Good Men?* The U.S. Military has its own set of laws. They don't have to follow most U.S. laws that other employers follow. The military has their own criminal code and employment laws. These lawyers handle all types of law for service men and women. Did your female pilot suffer abuse from her co-workers, or did your character return home from Iraq and find that they'd lost their job? Military lawyers are busy now with USERRA claims – employers who refuse to reinstate service people when the come back from active duty, which is illegal. There are also lots of issues regarding lawsuits filed against active service people because you can't get a default judgment against someone in the active service. Did your character come back with war wounds only to find a million dollar judgment waiting for them? Or maybe a divorce decree? Misconduct or criminal behavior while in uniform are dealt with in military courts, not regular criminal courts. The rules truly are different here. Is your character in a military jail without any ability to sue for their civil rights?

International Law

These lawyers handle international deals. Multinational corporations have teams of international lawyers who deal with all the issues that come up in dealing with other countries. Did your character get caught bribing an official in Saudi Arabia? Is their business deal in Bosnia going south? International lawyers also sometimes handle international human rights issues, environmental treaties, and other issues that involve U.S. citizens' and corporations' dealings in foreign lands. Did the U.S. violate an Afghani prisoner's rights? Did the corporation that sent your character to the Antarctic have an oil spill they're trying to cover up? The internet has caused this area of law to explode. International copyright, trademark and patent issues are also rapidly developing for the big firms. Maybe your character has a blog and they're being sued in Spain for defaming a famous actress there. Or maybe they invented something that cures writer's block only to have it stolen and produced more cheaply in China.

Business Law

These lawyers draft contracts, fill out forms, and keep the corporate records. They set up corporations and partnerships, make sure it's the right kind of structure for the business's needs, and do everything but go to court for their business clients. Is your character starting their dream business? Maybe the lawyer gives herself half the business instead of charging a fee. Or maybe the partners argue over who is in control. Court is for the litigators, and corporate law departments like to stay far away from courtrooms. These lawyers tend to actually have lives. Is your corporate lawyer suddenly a witness in court because the deal they handled blew up?

Antitrust

There are some companies that like to squelch competition, and the law says they can't. That's what antitrust law is about. It's good to be a monopoly, and these lawyers try to keep it that way. Is your mom and pop store getting bullied by a big chain? Is the big tire chain cutting prices to drive the tiny garage owner out of business? The big AT&T split was part of an antitrust suit. Their recent re-merger will probably be another one down the road. Is your character caught in a battle of the titans? Do they have the smoking gun memo that talks about how the company plans to put their competitor out of business?

Appellate

Appellate lawyers handle cases where there's a claim that the trial court did something wrong. This area of practice is for the loners (because they spend so much time researching and working alone) and former members of the law review. Is your character smart but shy? She may be an appellate lawyer. Appellate lawyers like to be alone with their books and computers, and only emerge in public to make oral arguments before appellate courts. Could she be facing her first oral argument and be terrified? Is he claiming that a powerful judge did something wrong and getting pressure to drop the appeal? These lawyers sometimes also assist trial lawyers during trial by making sure that any appellate issues are preserved. Is your character helping with a trial for the first time? They could be scared or shy about being in court.

Health

These lawyers represent the hospitals, nursing homes, and doctors on all types of health-related issues. Is your character a doctor trying to switch hospitals only to be told they signed an agreement that they couldn't work for a competitor? Is your nurse character being accused of abusing a patient? Did the billing clerk uncover a Medicaid fraud scheme?

Government

Government lawyers represent state, local, and federal government entities. They are civil servants, have great insurance, and regular hours. Is your character a single father lawyer whose solo practice is struggling? He may decide to work for the government. Women lawyers work for government more than any other area of law because these jobs allow the lawyers to have real family lives and benefits. Is your big-firm partner character longing for better hours? These lawyers are as varied as the government entities themselves. No matter what kind of law your character does, you can probably find a government job where they would fit in. While they're working for the government do they uncover the memo describing how the Pentagon changed the statistics to support going into a war? Are they asked to expose a spy for political reasons? Is a powerful official trying to get them to lie under oath?

Worker's Compensation

Worker's comp lawyers handle workplace accidents. Employees injured in the workplace generally can't sue the employer, but instead have to file a worker's compensation claim. Did your character have a crane fall on him only to find out he can't sue? He needs a worker's compensation lawyer.

Odd or Unusual Practice Areas

There is no limit to the areas of practice that some lawyers handle exclusively. The show *John from Cincinnati* featured a lawyer who handles surfing law. Some of the more unusual practice areas I have heard of are pet law, Indian law, gaming, historic preservation, billboard law, karate law, marine mammal law, equine law, and missing persons. Imagine a lawyer who does shoe law, supernatural law, flower law or something else unusual. The writer has endless possibilities to use the imagination.

Chapter 4 – Legal Ethics

Yes. You read that right – legal ethics. Har de har. Go ahead. Get it out of your system. How about this one? Why do scientists prefer using lawyers over lab rats? There are some things lab rats just won't do. Are we done?

Yes, I know you think lawyers don't have ethics. But ethical gaffes in shows and novels about lawyers just make me steam. My favorite TV groaner is the one where the lawyer switched sides in the middle of the case. What the writer of that episode didn't show was the disbarment proceeding that would have taken place right afterward.

I'm going to talk here about some of the things you may not know about lawyers' ethical rules and how they may affect your stories.

Conflict of Interest

I didn't think it needed to be said until I saw it on a TV show. I'll say it again here. The lawyer can't switch sides in the middle of the case. It can never happen. The lawyer cannot handle a case against the interest of a current client. The lawyer cannot handle a case against the interest of a former client regarding the matter they handled for the former client. The lawyer's firm cannot handle one side of the case with the lawyer handling the other.

So, let's say your character is a homeowner whose house is sitting on a toxic waste dump. He goes to his deposition and decides that he likes the other side's lawyer better than his own. No matter how much he begs, no matter how much he offers to pay, your lawyer character can't take the case and represent someone on the other side of his existing client even if he withdraws. Your lawyer character can't even talk to this person without their lawyer present.

Let's say your character, Ida Mae, had her will done by a lawyer, then files a suit against Jones Company, can the lawyer who did Ida Mae's will represent Jones Company against her? Yes, unless the lawyer is still representing Ida Mae on something like a re-draft of the will. See the difference? Current client, never, ever. Former client, only if they are truly former.

How about if your character's title to real estate is at issue? Can the lawyer who prepared the title policy represent someone who claims the title is bad? No, even if the client is a former client, because the dispute is regarding something the lawyer handled.

What if the client consents? Well, then the lawyer character could represent somebody against the client's interests, but only if it didn't require them to reveal something against the former client's interest that was said in confidence. For instance, say your lawyer character represented two clients who worked for the same company and are claiming discrimination. Suddenly, they end up having to testify against each other because one knows the other punched the boss, giving the company cause to fire. Sometimes they will both agree to allow the lawyer to represent one of them. But if the lawyer knows something about the former client they wouldn't know if they hadn't represented them, they can't use that information against the former client. If the boss is in a coma after the punch you may have to write it differently than if the boss is able to testify.

Scope of representation

Can your character's lawyer do something the character specifically told them not to? No, no, no. Can they accept a settlement without getting the client to agree? No, absolutely not. So if the lawyer does this in your story, you'd better show them running from the Bar.

If the client tells the lawyer to lie for them or to help them commit a crime can the lawyer do it? No. Not without ending up in jail or disbarred.

Does the lawyer have to believe the client is a good person, believe in the client's religious, political or personal views, or think the client is moral? Heck no.

Fraud on the court

If the client tells your lawyer character they intend to lie on the stand, can the lawyer allow them to testify? No. If the client testifies falsely and the lawyer finds out later do they have to tell the judge? Yes.

If the lawyer in your story knows there's a case that would mean they'd lose their motion, can they fail to disclose it and hope nobody finds it in time? No.

Meeting with the judge or the opposing party

Is your lawyer character allowed to take the judge aside and tell her things about the case without the other side being present? No. Can the lawyer for the plaintiff meet with the defendant without the defense lawyer present? No. Neither side can meet with the judge or any represented party without the other side present.

What about key witnesses? If the disgruntled president of the company your lawyer character is suing calls the lawyer up and offers to provide secret evidence and to give a statement, should your character jump on it? No. Any officer or manager of the company is considered an agent with authority to bind the company. What does that mean? For all intents and purposes, somebody high up IS the company. If the company is represented, the lawyer can't meet with that person.

If the janitor comes to the lawyer and offers to testify against his employer, can the lawyer take his statement? Absolutely. Anyone lower to mid-level in the company can meet with either lawyer if they want. The company can force its employees to meet with the company lawyer, but meeting with the other side is either voluntary or done in a deposition with both sides present.

What if the former president offers to testify? It's a stickier situation. Most lawyers would call the former president for a deposition unless that former president is represented by other counsel. For instance, if your lawyer character gets that call, but the president volunteering to talk has their own lawsuit against the company, then the lawyer still can't speak to the president. What they have to do is get permission from the president's current attorney, or speak with the president in the presence of their attorney. Confused? Heck, ethics is a whole class in law school, so don't feel bad.

In fact, your lawyer character could be confused about their ethical requirements. They could hire another attorney to give them advice or get an opinion from their Bar Association before they decide what to do. Or they could guess, get it wrong, and end up in hot water.

Confidentiality

The lawyer has to keep all client communications confidential. Surely you knew that from watching TV court shows. But did you know there are times the lawyer can tell or even has to tell something the client told them not to disclose?

If the client character tells the lawyer they are about to commit a crime, the lawyer has to report the client. Same with bodily harm – if the client says they are going to beat somebody up or kill them, the lawyer has to go to the police. If the lawyer knows the client is a child abuser, they can't allow the child to be in danger and have to go to the appropriate agency.

Say your client character is suing the lawyer for malpractice. Can the lawyer tell the court about the client's confidences? Heck yes. The lawyer is allowed to defend themselves, and confidentiality is out the window.

Ending representation

If the client character fires the lawyer, can the lawyer still handle the case because they want to help? No. That is, unless the judge orders them to stay in. The judge can refuse to allow a lawyer to withdraw from the case in some circumstances, such as the middle of a trial.

If the lawyer character knows the mob boss client is using the lawyer to commit a crime, can the lawyer continue representing your mob boss? No.

If the lawyer is a drug addict and isn't in denial about it, or has gone off her manic depression meds and can't properly represent the client, can she continue representing your character? No.

If the client is a criminal but the lawyer's representation doesn't help them commit the crime, can the lawyer continue to represent your client character in a civil case? Yes, but they are also allowed to withdraw.

If the client insists on doing something stupid or unethical, can your lawyer client stay in the case? Yes, but they can also get out at that point.

If the client stops paying, is the lawyer stuck in the case? No, unless the judge says otherwise. They can withdraw with the judge's permission if a lawsuit is going on.

If the client refuses to obey a court order or provide information the lawyer needs, can the lawyer withdraw? Yes. They don't have to, but that is something that allows them to get out.

If the judge orders your lawyer character to stay on the case even though the corporate president client has threatened to kill the judge, refuses to pay the lawyer, and has fired the lawyer, does the lawyer get to withdraw? No. The lawyer has to obey all court orders. The lawyer can and should appeal such an order though.

Dealing with the other side

Can your lawyer character burn evidence they know goes against their client's case? No.

Can your lawyer character lie to the other side? No.

Can your lawyer character pay a witness to testify? No. The witness fee allowed is usually something from under ten dollars to around forty dollars. The only witnesses that can be paid are expert witnesses.

Can your lawyer character threaten to notify the police about a crime if the other side doesn't settle quickly? No. And that's extortion, so they'll go to jail for it.

Can the lawyer character threaten to report the other side to the Bar unless they settle? No. Still extortion.

Lawyer as witness

You think it would be fun to have a key witness in your story also be the lawyer. Can you have the lawyer walk from counsel table to the witness stand and call himself to testify? Well, maybe. I've actually seen it done. It was absolutely not a good idea because the lawyer's testimony ended up hurting his client. The only times it really happens is if the lawyer has won the case and is testifying about their own fees to get the court to make the other side pay the fees.

When else can it happen? It's allowed if the testimony isn't adverse to the client, and if the matter is supposed to be a formality or uncontested. Say the lawyer is the only person who can authenticate a particular piece of evidence, that is, say that the evidence is the real thing. The lawyer is probably allowed to testify. But things can go so wrong so fast if the lawyer is on the stand in their client's case.

Would it be fun to have your lawyer character testify, then have the other side turn it around to work it against the client? What if the lawyer testifies that the client did something based on their advice. Could the plaintiff's attorney get them to admit they would never have advised the course of action the client actually took?

Malpractice

Here's where the doctors have it good. If a lawyer realizes they did something wrong in a case, missed a deadline or failed to raise an issue they should have, can they sit back and hope nobody finds out? Nope. They have to tell the client. Do you think doctors have to disclose to patients that they sewed the sponge in during surgery? No, they don't. So your young lawyer could have to tell the elderly character they missed the deadline to file the lawsuit to get back the money the nursing home bilked from them. Does she do it, or does she move to Wisconsin and become a waitress?

Consequences

Now, of course, I've said lawyers can't do these things, but we all know they can. They aren't supposed to, but even lawyers break the rules. What happens if a lawyer is caught breaking an ethical rule? One of three things usually happens.

- **Disbarment** - where the lawyer loses their license to practice law. Sometimes a lawyer admitted in two states can continue practicing in the second state (but they have to tell the other state about the disbarment). So maybe the incompetent lawyer moves to New York after getting disbarred in California, leaving your bilked character frustrated with the system.
- **Suspension** - where the lawyer has to stop practicing law for a set period of time. It could be a week or a year. The Bar Association has lots of discretion in setting the penalty. Many times the lawyer will accept a suspension with the agreement they won't be disbarred. Is your character so angry when her crooked lawyer gets to come back to practice law and steal from another client that she takes matters into her own hands?
- **Reprimand** - where the Bar tells the lawyer not to do it again.

A public reprimand is published in the papers, done in court or a public ceremony, and the other lawyers get to kick sand in the reprimanded attorney's face. Well, I made up the last part, but a public reprimand isn't a picnic. A private reprimand means the lawyer is told quietly not to do it again, and they get to avoid the public humiliation.

So, if your characters do something that you know they aren't allowed to do, are you going to tell and show the reader the possible consequences, or do you hope the reader doesn't notice the inconsistencies? The show that had the lawyer switch sides mid-case lost me as a viewer forever. Considering how many lawyers there are, do you really want to take that risk with your writing?

Chapter 5 – How The Law Firm In Your Story Will Work

Each type of law practice has its own structure and billing practices. Your story can change any of this, of course, and the variety makes it interesting. But staying true to some basic structures will give your story credibility and realism.

Big firms

It used to be that a firm over 100 lawyers was a mega-firm, but now the ultra-large firms have thousands of lawyers worldwide and rake in billions of dollars. These firms have infinite resources. Even "smaller" big firms represent clients who have large wallets and can spend big dollars to defend against any lawsuit.

> With eighty lawyers, the firm of Whitney & Cable & White was the largest on the Gulf Coast. The firm had been hand-picked by Fitch himself, and it would earn millions in fees because of this selection. To earn the money, though, the firm had to endure the tyranny and ruthlessness of Rankin Fitch.
>
> When satisfied that the entire building was aware of his presence and terrified of his movements, Fitch left. He stood on the sidewalk, in the warm October air, and waited for Jose. Three blocks away, in the top half of an old bank building, he could see an office suite filled with lights. The enemy was still working.

In *The Runaway Jury*, John Grisham pits the large firm against a smaller plaintiff's firm to good effect. Readers enjoy David versus Goliath stories, and putting a new twist on them is always entertaining.

The show *Angel* had a law firm filled with supernatural demons that was great fun. Large firms have such variety and have so many employees that they have many potential uses to the writer. Whether villainous or heroic, background or a major part of the story, these firms can be used in any story involving a legal issue.

Large firms generally follow this structure:

The Lawyers

For purposes of this section, I am using the term "partner" even though most law firms now are corporations and the leaders are technically "directors." The more common terminology continues to be "partner" and associates are told whether or not they are on a "partnership track." Firms in your story can have either term used internally, but if you ask one of these attorneys outside the firm what their title is, they will usually call themselves partners.

Managing Partner: This is the top dog. The Managing Partner or Managing Director handles the major day to day issues at the firm, and can have powers ranging from assigning cases and staff, setting bonuses and pay structure, organizing firm events, approving expenses, hiring, firing, and having ultimate approval over which clients are accepted. Did your young attorney character turn down this guy's sexual advances? Is he now turning down all the business she tries to bring to the firm? This can make or break an attorney starting out, because rainmaking - that is, bringing in clients - will decide whether or not the young associate makes partner.

Management Committee: In very large firms, sometimes a committee takes over the role of the single managing partner, with responsibilities for certain functions split among committee members. So, say your character refused to sleep with a committee member. How would they torture her? One might refuse her new business. Another might refuse to approve her continuing education. A third might assign her to the worst secretary in the firm or the most obnoxious partner.

The committee meetings can be collegial or rancorous, depending on your story's needs. Does the committee in your story start throwing chairs? Or do they conspire to commit a crime? These meetings are usually mysterious to lower-ranking attorneys at the firm, and are the subject of much rumor and speculation. Are your young attorney characters guessing what's happening behind closed doors? They can be highly political. Is your committee member character suddenly on the outside of firm politics because they didn't want to refuse to hire black attorneys?

Senior Partner: This is someone with an ownership interest in the firm. Either they have been invited to buy into the partnership for a set amount, or they have been allowed to buy in with "sweat equity," that is, work they perform. Is your young lawyer passed over for partnership because a rich do-nothing paid their way in? Rainmakers – lawyers who bring in lots of clients – frequently make Senior Partner status without having to pay to buy into the partnership. Did your character do something slimy to take credit for bringing in a big client?

The Senior Partners usually have several Junior Partners or non-equity partners reporting to them. They get the top picks of offices, secretaries, and can bump any staff from any project supervised by lower ranking attorneys. Is your partner character benevolent or a tyrant? Do they torture or mentor the lawyers in their care? If the firm is young enough, there will be Name Partners, those partners whose name appears on the letterhead. These attorneys will have the highest status in the firm. Most huge firms have Name Partners who are now deceased, and thus much easier to deal with. But maybe your character wants their name on the marquee. Are they willing to kill for it?

Junior Partner: These are younger partners who have made the first cut, but either did not have to invest any money into the firm yet, or whose investment was much smaller. Is your junior partner character struggling to save their money to buy in? Are the senior partners making sure she'll never quite make it financially? What happens when she inherits enough money to buy in after all? These attorneys have slightly lower billable hourly rates, and they supervise associates and paralegals. They have minimum billable hour requirements, usually hefty, along with what are essentially quotas of how much business they have to bring in. Is your character overworked and underpaid? Do they take it out on the associates they supervise? Does the staff refuse to take them seriously, or do they treat the staff like dirt?

Associate: Read "slave" here. These are young attorneys, generally practicing 0 – 7 years, and they have no lives. Did your character think the hard work was over when they graduated law school? They have huge billable hour requirements, must attend firm functions, and must start to develop the ability to bring in business. Most big firms are "up or out" and those that don't make partner within a set amount of time are given the boot. Is your lawyer character sabotaging the competition by losing their files? These young attorneys have been the subject of a number of legal thrillers because they are just discovering the world of law so you can provide opportunities for terrific character development.

Associates can be divided into categories of regular and senior associates. Senior associates, generally made senior based on a given amount of time with the firm, can boss around the regular associates some, and may get to supervise some staff. Many associates share secretaries with other associates or with a partner. When they share with a partner, guess whose work actually gets done? I wonder, did a fist fight break out in your story over whose work was more important? Because I've seen it happen in real life.

These young attorneys rarely see court or a client, except to carry a partner's briefcase. Is your character longing for real work? Does solo practice start to sound appealing to them? They research and write the pleadings and memoranda, prepare the deposition questions, and then hand their work off to a partner who gladly takes credit. Their work is approved by a junior partner, who then passes it up to a senior partner, and all get a chance to put their billable hours into the matter. Does your character resent that they don't get to take credit for their own work? Enough to steal trust funds from the firm's biggest client?

Do associates in your story like to compete for who works the most hours? Do they brag that they spent the night, or put rumpled jackets on to let partners think they did? Is it a macho "let's see who can survive on the least amount of sleep" contest among these attorneys?

Law clerks

These are law students brought in to be wined, dined and overpaid to lure them into the associate/slave position. They are called "summer associates" and are told not to worry about those long hours. They have golf outings, boating trips, and parties thrown in their honor to distract from the fact that the associates live in the office. Sometimes the associates are even told to avoid giving work to or speaking to the summer associates so they don't get scared off. Is your character charmed by the trappings and fun, only to get lured into the slave job? Or does he find out the firm is really a money laundering operation and have to skip town? Law clerks usually rotate among the different partners to get a chance working for a variety of the departments and partners. Is he doing fine until he rotates to the cougar partner who will only give the male associates good evaluations if they put out? They handle research and writing, and get no client contact.[10] But maybe your law clerk character gets into trouble when she decides to meet with the big client and give bad advice.

The Staff

The big firms will have it all. Office manager, paralegals, process servers, messengers/runners, plenty of legal secretaries.[11]

Other big firm staff you could use in your story may include word processors, usually warehoused in a word processing department that handles overflow work for all attorneys; copying/fax departments, who do copying for the firm and who handle sending and receiving faxes; mailrooms who sort mail coming in and who put postage on outgoing mail and log it to the correct client; IT people who handle all the software and hardware glitches; AV people who handle video conferencing and all the audio-visual needs; bookkeeping departments who handle the billing and time records, along with managing the trust accounts; marketing people who prepare the marketing materials, attend community events, make sure the firm sponsors the right events, and deal with public relations (big firms don't advertise – they market); investigators; librarians; and receptionists who greet the clients and opposing counsel and get them coffee.

The Setting

What will the firm in your story look like? These firms like major metropolitan areas and big buildings. They will take multiple floors of the most prestigious buildings in town. The floors and counters are

---

[10] The no client contact part is the only way the summer associate job remotely resembles the associate/slave job. The summer associate who fails to pay attention to the fact that the real associates have rumpled clothing, red eyes, and have been served with divorce papers can be in for a rude surprise when they take that job offer.

[11] I talked about what they do and how you might use them in your story in Chapter 1.

marble or high-end tile. The paintings and artwork are real. The receptionists look like models. They have full size law libraries. The brochures are on the highest quality paper. Mugs and pens in the conference rooms are emblazoned with firm logos. Everything is first class. If the firm down the street has it, these firms must have it too. If you write your big firm with bold ostentation and modern furniture or, conversely, expensive but classic furniture and art, you will set the tone for your story.

Many of these firms have multiple offices and partners that don't know each other. Does your new associate meet someone claiming to be the Hong Kong partner who is really an FBI agent? Or is the lawyer in Brussels alone operating a scam to steal clients' money? Some scatter offices throughout a single state, some have offices in major cities around the U.S., and some have offices throughout the world. These firms tout their many locations on their websites and letterhead. D.C., New York, London, and Hong Kong are some of the must-have addresses for these firms. But did they overreach? Is the firm that looks so well-off desperate to get more money? Desperate enough to take on the Russian mob operation as s client?

The Billing

"Because I'm a lawyer and live by the clock, I checked my watch so that whatever happened could be duly recorded, if we somehow managed to survive. It was one-twenty. Mister wanted things quiet, and so we endured a nerve-racking period of silence that lasted fourteen minutes.

I could not believe that we were going to die. There appeared to be no motive, no reason to kill us. I was certain that none of us had ever met him before. I remembered the ride on the elevator, and the fact that he seemed to have no particular destination. He was just a nut in search of hostages, which unfortunately would have made the killings seem almost normal by today's standards.

In another masterful John Grisham story, *The Street Lawyer*, the character, a big firm lawyer, checks his watch for billable hour purposes during a hostage situation. This adds humor and tension at the same time to a thrilling story. These firms thrive on billable hours. The partners have hourly rates of $400 – 700/hour and up. Associates bill at $250 – 500/hour. Paralegals bill at $100 – 300/hour. Every dime spent on a case, from phone calls to research to copies to postage to faxes is tracked and billed to the client. If the attorney thought about a case in the shower, that time is billed to the client. Did your small company hire a big law firm only to get a whopping bill that bankrupts them? Associates have to bill every second of time they worked on the case to meet their billing requirements. Are your associate characters pressured to pad their bills? The partners have to slash associate hours to keep the clients happy while keeping their own hours intact, giving a writer ample opportunity to include conflict in the story. Is the associate angry because their hours are being slashed so the partner can meet his billable requirements?

Trial Preparation

These firms spend big dollars on trial preparation. They do videotape depositions, have exhibits blown up, hire experts and jury consultants, have multiple attorneys and staff sitting in on trials waiting for instructions, and spare no expense in their quest to beat down their opponent. Is your solo practitioner character up against a firm that has no limits on how much they can spend? Did the opposing side conduct mock trials in their own courtrooms for practice. Will they bury your small practitioner in motions and other paper? Did their appellate department bog the case down in appeals for years? Or, did your tiny law office win a David and Goliath battle, only to face revenge and ruin brought on by a corporation with infinite resources?

The Departments

These firms are organized in departments which handle particular areas of practice, as was discussed in Chapter 3. Some of the major departments the large firms will frequently have are:

- Appellate
- Bankruptcy
- Corporate
- Litigation
- Health Law
- Government Affairs
- Intellectual Property
- International Law

- Labor and Employment
- Land Use and Zoning
- Probate/Estate Planning

- Real Estate
- Securities
- Tax

Which department is your young lawyer in? Does she long to do real estate but get stuck in tax? Sometimes associates aren't given a choice. Assignments change and departments expand and contract. White collar criminal, technology, environmental, any area of expertise could develop into a department in your story. You can make it fun – have an Equine Law Department (don't laugh – a big firm just announced they were forming one). Or why not a Skydiving Law Department? The sky's the limit in your story.

Turnover

The lawyers in these firms come and go frequently. Mergers, splits, raids, layoffs, restructurings, and terminations all keep these firm rosters changing. It is sometimes hard to keep track of where these lawyers are at any given time. Did your young lawyer move firms only to cause a conflict of interest that cost the new firm their biggest client? I bet that lawyer character has a rough year. I just had a conversation with a lawyer who I first met at a large firm that was eaten by a larger firm. We were trying to figure out where some of his colleagues were now, and many have been to three or four firms in the past five years. There is little loyalty and much dissent at many of these firms, where law is just business. How many firms has your character hopped to? Do they sometimes forget which firm they're with? Do they forget what cases they have because they've moved too many times?

Midsize firms

"It's an impressive firm, Mitch," Oliver Lambert said, "and we're very proud of it. We're a close-knit fraternity. We're small and we take care of each other. We don't have the cutthroat competition the big firms are famous for. We're very careful whom we hire, and our goal is for each new associate to become a partner as soon as possible. Toward that end we invest an enormous amount of time and money in ourselves, especially our new people. It is a rare, extremely rare occasion when a lawyer leaves our firm. It is simply unheard of. We go the extra mile to keep careers on track. We want our people happy. We think it is the most profitable way to operate."

"I have another impressive statistic," Mr. McKnight added. "Last year, for firms our size or larger, the average turnover rate among associates was twenty-eight percent. At Bendini, Lambert & Locke, it was zero. Year before, zero. It's been a long time since a lawyer left our firm."

John Grisham took the traditional midsize firm structure and turned it into an exciting adventure in *The Firm*. The basic premise was simple – a firm whose offer was too good to be true turned out not to be what it seemed.

The players in the midsize firm are mostly the same as the big guys, only there are fewer of them. These firms generally have 10 – 50 lawyers, although under 100 can now be counted as "midsize". Midsize firms have similarities to the big firms, so I'll just deal with some of the major differences.

The Lawyers

Was the midsize firm in your book formed by partners who decided to split off from the big firm culture and emphasize quality of life? Does this sometimes mean quality of life for the partners, not the lowly associates? Is it now more difficult for the associates in your story to reach partnership level because of the smaller structure?

Law Clerks

Fewer law clerks mean more work for the associates. It also means fewer expensive summer events for the firm to sponsor. Did your law clerk character spend last year at a big firm doing spas and golf outings? Does he get a rude surprise when he's actually expected to work?

The Staff

These firms, at least the successful ones, run lean and mean. They have fewer in-house staff and use more outside services. Is the partner who used to be spoiled by the endless resources suddenly faced with the prospect of making his own copies? Does his secretary resent being sent out for his dry cleaning? Could an outside courier witness something illegal while he's waiting for a package?

Some staff will perform multiple functions, such as a paralegal/librarian, or a secretary/paralegal. Did your paralegal character come from a big firm only to find out she's doubling as a secretary? Is the secretary/paralegal/librarian leaving to go to a mega-firm for more money in the middle of the big trial?

The Setting

Some midsize firms use the same prestigious buildings as the big guys, and many more are in smaller buildings, or even in buildings they own. Maybe your midsize firm is trying too hard to compete. Is their overhead killing them? Or are they not quite keeping up with the Joneses? Does their office look a little shabby? Is your lawyer character feeling a little bit jealous of the big guys?

Much of what goes on in a midsize firm depends on what the founders were fleeing when they left their old firms. These firms vary too much to stereotype, and provide a wide variety of settings for the writer. Do the partners all like to fly and have a boutique aviation practice? Did they hate their big firm because it made them turn down a casino client? Is their gaming law practice thriving or did they just realize organized crime owns the casino?

The Departments

Boutique firms will handle only one area of law. Some midsize firms will have two to five departments in major areas, such as labor and employment, commercial litigation, securities, appellate, and corporate. Usually the areas will have an interrelationship. For instance, a firm that starts out handling only labor and employment will have a client ask for help on an unrelated lawsuit, and the commercial litigation department is born. Did the midsize firm in your story get into an area they don't really know how to handle? Or did an associate handle one sexual harassment case only to find themselves head of the new labor law department?

Midsize firms can have some pretty funky specialties. Animal law, maritime, U.S. Customs, Indian law, gaming law, anything you can imagine can spawn a law firm. I'd love to see a story involving a funny or unusual practice area.

Solo/small offices

The majority of lawyers still practice in solo or small firms. Fewer than ten lawyers is considered small these days, but most have one to five lawyers. If your character is in a solo or small practice, you have a great setup for a David versus Goliath story.

Small and solo firms usually have only one area of practice, or are general practices handling all types of law. These firms run very lean, with little or no staff. A solo practice, by definition, has only one lawyer. Are the big firm lawyers on the case repeatedly calling your character a "solo practitioner" to the judge to make sure he knows she's not one of the elite? Many solos have no staff at all. Small firms can have one or more named lawyer, and the rest are associates. Does your solo practitioner character do her own typing, filing, and cleaning? Is she in the office at all hours? Does somebody unusual show up late at night?

Some firms that deal with quantity of cases, such as collections, uncontested divorces, traffic, and other matters that require huge amounts of clients to be brought in, will have large paralegal staffs to process the paperwork. Is your character a paralegal who thinks the new case is just another routine matter only to find out she's representing a serial killer? Most have few secretaries and paralegals, and no other staff. Is the secretary taking out the trash or making a delivery when she sees a shooting?

The Setting

Tiny firms will usually be in small buildings, will share space with other firms, or will be in executive suites that share a common receptionist and conference rooms. Do the Armani lawyers show up and look like they don't want to sit on the chairs? Do they complain that the coffee isn't espresso?

Some solo practitioners buy small buildings to lease out to other lawyers. Did your building owner character lease out to somebody who is pretending to be a lawyer, but isn't? These offices can be luxurious, but most have less expensive trappings. Are they embarrassed at how shabby their office is?

Do the big guys try to charm away an associate in a small firm during a trial with their marble floors and lattes? Is he so charmed he's willing to sneak them some evidence? Many have a dedicated office space in their homes. Is your solo practitioner with a home office trying to fool the big firms into thinking she has a more luxurious setup? Does she hire somebody to answer phones to make it seem like she has an outside office? Is that person a psycho stalker?

Some small firm offices are shabby, some more upscale, but a successful small firm will keep the purse strings tight. (I once knew a guy who worked in the back of a restaurant.) Keeping unnecessary expenses down is crucial to survival. Did the small firm lawyer take on a case where they have to hock their furniture to pay for expenses? What happens if the case goes on too long?

The Billing

Solo and small practitioners usually have a mix of billing practices depending on the type of case and client. Contingency, partial contingency, mixed arrangements, and flat fees can all be part of the small firm's billing practice. Did your solo practitioner take on too many contingency cases? Are they stuck with outstanding cost bills? Clients can't afford huge expenses, so many firms require cost retainers in advance to make sure they aren't stuck with a bill for expenses. Did the lawyer get tempted and spend money out of the trust account?

Trial Preparation

Other than personal injury attorneys, solo and small firms run lean. Their clients can't afford expensive experts, jury consultants, or mock trials. Exhibits are usually normal size and discovery is done economically. These are the firms that represent ordinary people and small businesses. The differences between the tiny firm in trial and the big one, comparing the handmade exhibit boards to the computer models, the pricey expert to the side that couldn't afford the expert, can give you lots of conflict and drama. Is the expert torn apart by your character's brilliant cross-examination? Do his exhibits melt in the rain?

Turnover

Many solos are always looking to join a firm, but most of us like being on our own. Is your character being recruited to a big firm? Is she determined to stay independent? Small firms tend to run like families, and the staffs of small firms are treated as such. Did your solo practitioner trust the secretary a little too much? Is the trust money gone and the secretary in Brazil? Sure, there are abusive attorneys in every size firm, but most solo and small firms can't afford to keep advertising and training new staff, so they look for ways to keep good people. Does your solo start out abusive and learn to become a better human being? Or does an abused secretary come back one day from lunch and whack him on the head with a 2 x 4?[12]

Government practice

Ah, to be a lawyer who gets a salary, whose client has infinite money, and whose client's decision-makers have the attitude, "It's not my money." Welcome to government practice. Your lawyer character can have steady pay, no billable hour requirement, and great benefits.

Is your lawyer character suing a government? Suing a government is frustrating because government lawyers frequently don't care about the bill. These in-house lawyers need to make themselves useful, so they appeal everything, challenge everything, and never settle. Is your lawyer character getting frustrated and bankrupted by the endless case? While this is a gross oversimplification, governments rarely worry about the bottom line like corporations, and are more likely to litigate to the bitter end on principle.

Government practice has a form for everything, lots of bureaucracy, inexpensive furniture, and scarce supplies. Is the deposition set in a conference room doubling as a supply cabinet? Staff is underpaid and can be surly. Does the secretary refuse to give the new gung-ho government attorney his messages? Does she resent how young he is? Does she do everything she can to sabotage him? Many government jobs are considered to be for attorneys just starting out, a training ground, and turnover is high. Did your young attorney character commit to work two years in the state attorney's office then leave after six months to join

---

[12] This happened to a lawyer I knew. He deserved it.

a big firm? Does the old, politically powerful boss set out to destroy him? Some government offices are comfortable enough in pay and benefits to retain attorneys through retirement. Does the mild-mannered government lawyer in your story make more than the senior partner in the midsize firm who's trying to bribe him?

In-house counsel

These are the lawyers who refer the litigation out to the big firms, who watch the big firms' bills, and who handle primarily transactional law. Is the in-house counsel who sends out cases on a power trip? Does he require a little extra special attention from attorneys who expect to get work? The attorneys in large corporations usually have areas they concentrate on, such as contracts, employment, or zoning. Does your in-house labor attorney with the cushy job suddenly have to cover zoning matters due to a layoff? Small corporations have in-house counsel who must know enough about all the areas of law that come up with the company to know when they need to refer the matter to outside counsel. Did the in-house attorney draft a contract, thinking he knew what he was doing, and cost the small company millions?

What will your corporate legal department look like? The setting is going to be utilitarian corporate, in the same style as the rest of the corporate offices. If the corporate honchos like more upscale furnishings, the law department[13] will probably have some of the trappings as well. More often, you see the same generic steel or wood desks that everyone else in the corporate office has. Do they resent the marble and fancy art in the big firm that handles their business? Enough to start skimming from the company?

These attorneys worry about the bottom line. They are the ones who figure out the cost of settlement versus the risk of loss, and decide when or if to pay up. Is the president pressuring the legal department to settle the sexual harassment case against him? Many women are drawn to in-house counsel jobs because the hours are steady, the benefits and pay are good, and the jobs give them more flexibility to deal with family issues. Does the in-house counsel defending against the sexual harassment case uncover ten other women the president harassed?

---

[13] Or at least the General Counsel's offices.

Courts

The lawyers who work for judges are called "clerks" even if they are admitted to practice law. They apply for hotly-contested[14] clerkships during law school. These jobs allow the attorneys to see the inner workings of the courts, and they get to know the judges. Did one of the clerks cheat his way into the job? Is he creating more work for the other clerks? Is his dad so powerful he can't be fired? These attorneys are snapped up by the big firms when they finish their clerkships, so clerking jobs are extremely desirable. Is the law clerk being wooed by the firm who has a big case in front of the judge? Would they like just a little bit of inside information?

The clerks will draft the opinions for their judges to sign, research issues, and really do have great influence on the outcome of the case. Is the lawyer on the case somebody who turned the clerk down for a date in law school? Is the client paying for her slight?

Few state court judges can afford full time clerks. All federal judges have clerks who assist them. State court judges either have clerks who help all the judges, so they are very busy, or have interns who are unpaid law students working for law school credit. It is important to understand which kind of court you are writing about so you can get the atmosphere for your clerk character right.

Clerks sometimes have regular hours and sometimes work all hours, heavily depending on the personality of their judge. Is she sleeping in the office or working until three then leaving to play golf? In the federal system, clerks work first for trial judges, then the appellate judges get to pick the best and brightest of those. Is your character in a backstabbing war with the other clerks as they claw their way to the top? The Supreme Court then picks the best of the appellate clerks. The higher the judge, the more prestigious the clerkship.

The most interesting tidbit I have to offer writers about federal courts is that the proceedings are piped back to the office so the staff can hear. Few lawyers and almost no clients know that their microphones in the courtroom are piped back into chambers even when court is not in session. This means that, when the judge leaves the bench for breaks,

---

[14] Hotly contested because this is a great "in" to a big firm. Clerks, particularly federal appellate clerks, are much sought after in recruiting.

lawyers and clients have conversations they think are confidential that can be heard in chambers. Did your character confide in his lawyer that he hid some evidence? The whole court staff probably heard the confession.

At least, that's the way it is in one court I've been in. I had a bailiff warn me about that during a trial where the judge was treating me particularly harshly and he felt sorry for my client and me. He didn't bother to warn the other side, so who knows what they said in front of the microphone? Something overheard that shouldn't be would be a nice way to escalate conflict in the story. Did your character insult the judge? Confess he was secretly in love with the bailiff?

Chapter 6 – Pre-suit

One of my pet peeves in reading or watching stories about the law are cases that spring into court the day after the client meeting, which lasts two minutes. Cases can take weeks or even years before they get to court. At least age the characters a bit between the intake and the suit, for heaven's sake! Here's some of what goes on before a case even gets filed with the court.

The client meeting

Before the client even gets into the law office, they usually are pre-screened somewhat. Some attorneys allow staff to speak to the client to make sure the issue is in their area of practice before setting the appointment, some have clients come in to meet with paralegals or other staff and fill out a questionnaire before being allowed to meet with the attorney. Does your nervous character hem and haw trying to explain what her case is about? Does she even know whether she has a case?

Once the client comes in, most attorneys have a questionnaire that the client fills in to give some basic information. The questionnaire on this page shows some information that almost every civil attorney needs, no matter the type of case, that may help you with what kinds of questions your attorney character might ask, and what kinds of things a client might want to tell in your story:

INTAKE QUESTIONNAIRE

Name: _____Social Security No.:_____

Date of Birth: _____Place of birth: _____

Address: _____

Phone number: _____Beeper: _____

Fax number: _____E-mail address: _____

Person to contact if you cannot be reached: Name: _____

Phone number: _____ **Relationship:** _____

Individual or company that is subject of your dispute: _____

Address of individual or company: _____

Current employer: _____

Current position: _____
(Some of this information has an obvious purpose. The attorney needs to be able to contact the client, so having multiple ways to do so helps prevent clients from disappearing. Most of this information is also necessary on forms if there are any pre-suit requirements.)

Describe the issue that you have come to see us about: _____
(Your character may have more detailed questions relating to their particular area of practice. This is an all-purpose question that can cover a variety of cases.)

Have you ever been convicted of a felony? ___ Yes ___ No Date: ____
Crime: _____
(This is a question that can be asked in court for purposes of impeachment. It's best for your attorney character to know before that if the answer is yes.)

Have you ever been convicted of a crime? ___ Yes ___ No Date: __
Crime: _____
(If the crime involved dishonesty, even if it wasn't a felony, they can also be asked about it in court. Did your attorney character forget to ask this important question and find out about it in court?)

Have you ever been arrested? ___ Yes ___ No Date: ____ Crime:
_____
(This can be asked in depositions. Also, some clients have strange ideas about whether or not they've ever actually been convicted. Does your character think having their record sealed means it never happened? This kind of question usually flushes out the rest of the crime-involved issues that may come up in court.)

Disposition of arrest: _____

Have you ever filed bankruptcy? ____ Yes ____ No   **If yes, give the date of discharge, your attorney name, the case number, court name, state, and any other pertinent information.**
(This one's a killer. If the client is in bankruptcy, the attorney could violate a stay of proceedings that the bankruptcy court issues and end up in contempt of court. If the client has a claim they are allowed to bring outside the bankruptcy, they still have to list it as an asset in the bankruptcy court, and failure to do so could cause them to have their

case dismissed. Did your client character fail to tell the lawyer about their bankruptcy? Does the lawyer get thrown in jail as a result?)

If you filed for bankruptcy, did the actions that you are complaining about now occur before or while your bankruptcy was pending?
(If the bankruptcy is over and they did not list the claim, but the claim occurred before the bankruptcy was over, the client actually has to reopen the bankruptcy to disclose the claim. Did your attorney character win the case, only to have the bankruptcy court snatch the victory away?)

Has any court, judge, arbitrator, hearing officer, or other official ever made a finding that you committed fraud, were untruthful, or engaged in dishonesty? ____ Yes ____ No

If so, state the case number, date, and nature of finding:
(Any prior findings that the client was dishonest can come out in court and be used in court. Did your character lie in his divorce proceeding and get sanctioned?)

Have you ever been a party to any lawsuit? ____ Yes ____ No   If yes, give the date case ended, your attorney name, the case number, court name, state, and any other pertinent information.
(This is another one that comes up in court and in depositions. The lawyer also wants to know if the client is litigious, if they tend to sue their lawyers, or if they have made claims similar to the one they are making now. And the lawyer certainly wants to know if the client won or lost the prior case. If the client lost, the attorney needs to look at the case to figure out why. If it related to the client not being credible in court, your attorney character may decline even the best case.)

Do you have any judgments, tax liens, foreclosures, or other liens against you?
(If the client wins a judgment but has any of these, the entire judgment could be grabbed by a debtor, leaving the attorney and the client empty handed. Did your character forget to mention they had a million dollar IRS lien?)

Attach any other helpful information, documents to this questionnaire. Please do not provide your only copy of any document.

I HEREBY CERTIFY THAT THE INFORMATION PROVIDED IS TRUE AND CORRECT.
(Clients who won't say this should be dumped post haste. Their credibility and honesty with the lawyer is a first test of how they will be in court. Does the character in your book conveniently forget to sign? Does the lawyer realize later the client wasn't telling the truth?)

I UNDERSTAND THAT SMITH, JONES, AND CARTER, P.A. DOES NOT REPRESENT ME UNLESS A SIGNED RETAINER AGREEMENT HAS BEEN ENTERED INTO AND A RETAINER FEE PAID. I UNDERSTAND THAT PAYMENT OF A FEE FOR CONSULTATION DOES NOT OBLIGATE SMITH, JONES, AND CARTER, P.A. TO TAKE ANY ACTION ON MY BEHALF, AND THAT NO FURTHER ACTION WILL BE TAKEN WITHOUT A SIGNED RETAINER AGREEMENT AND ADDITIONAL RETAINER.

(Some unscrupulous clients will come in, get a free or moderately priced consultation, then claim they thought the attorney had agreed to file suit for them. They let the statute of limitations run out, then sue the lawyer. This is important to get right up front so there is no misunderstanding. I always make clients sign a retainer agreement spelling out what the services are that we've agreed to perform. Did your attorney get ambushed by pretend client who claims they thought the suit was filed four years ago?)

_____

Date/Signature

Once the intake form is completed, the attorney will meet with the client to ask questions to decide whether or not there's a case. Does your book have a scene with the initial attorney-client meeting? They will discuss what steps the lawyer might take, whether a negotiation, transaction, administrative proceeding, lawsuit, or other service, and the fees for the service.

The client will be expected to sign a retainer agreement that reflects the fee arrangement, any costs to be incurred, the extent of the relationship, and anything else that needs to be addressed at the beginning. Does your character get lots of information for free, only to decide not to hire the lawyer? Does the lawyer forget to get a signed agreement, so they end up not getting paid?

Fee Arrangements

We've discussed some of the potential retainer arrangements in prior chapters. Here's a description of the major types of fee arrangements and what they mean for your characters.

Contingency

A contingency fee is just what it sounds like. The contingency is winning the case. The fee is paid only if the attorney wins, and is based on a percentage of the recovery. Your character looking to hire a lawyer most likely thinks all lawyers work this way. Will they be surprised when they find out that the lawyers handling their type of case get paid by the hour? The maximum the Bar usually allows is 40%, although higher percentages can be done with court approval. I've never heard of that actually happening, but I assume it does from time to time. Does your client character offer to pay the lawyer half or more of the winnings? Does the lawyer get in trouble for saying yes?

Personal injury and medical malpractice cases are almost always done on a straight contingency. In those types of cases, attorneys will also frequently advance the costs of experts, court reporters, etc. because the clients usually cannot afford the tens or hundreds of thousands of dollars it can cost to bring those cases to trial. Does the personal injury character in your story spend everything they have on the case, like John Grisham had his lawyers do in *The Appeal*?

Many other types of cases are done on a contingency basis. However, many attorneys require their clients to pay for costs as they go along. Costs can bankrupt an attorney if they get out of control. Does your small firm have to hock the company cars and cash in the pension to pay for the expert witness fees?

"I thought *A Civil Action*[15] was pretty accurate (the families of children who died sue two companies for dumping toxic waste: a tort so expensive to prove, the case could bankrupt their lawyer)." Michael Massey, Florida Labor and Employment Attorney.

Erin Brockovich, a movie based on a true story, also showed how devastating costs can be to a small firm. Having a realistic portrayal of how much litigation costs can increase tension in your story.

Flat fees

These are set fees for a particular service. You see them commonly for divorce, immigration and bankruptcy. Other services that can involve flat fees are letter writing, contracts, forms, virtually anything that the lawyer can predict how much time will be involved. For instance, in my firm I charge flat fees for EEOC proceedings, certain administrative

---

[15] Indeed, *A Civil Action* is the number one book that lawyers and judges told me they enjoyed because it portrayed the civil justice system so accurately. It may go down in history along with *To Kill a Mockingbird* as a classic favorite for lawyers. *Mockingbird* was, of course, about criminal law and, for better or for worse, inspired many young people to take up law as a profession.

proceedings (a per day flat fee), services like letter writing, and some negotiations. Clients like these because they know exactly how much is involved. Does your lawyer character charge a flat fee only to find they spent way more time on the matter than they thought they would?

Hourly rates

These are just what they sound like. Rates depend on the attorney's reputation and experience. Most firms will get a retainer up front for some portion of the case, ranging between $1000 and $15,000 (upwards for expensive commercial litigation) and then bill after that retainer is exhausted. The other time hourly rates come into play is when a court awards fees after the case is over. I'll discuss that in the post-trial section. Did your character hire a lawyer on an hourly basis, then get socked with a $100,000 bill? Did your attorney character agree to take an hourly case only to have the client stop paying?

Retainer

You sometimes hear the term, "I have a lawyer on retainer." While attorneys usually refer to any fee paid up front as the retainer, a true retainer is paid to assure the availability of the lawyer's services rather than for any particular service. It can be a flat rate paid one time, or can be paid monthly. For instance, an organization once hired me to be available to their members who needed consultations from time to time. They paid me monthly, and I would consult with as many or as few members who needed advice that month. Sometimes I got paid less than the time I put in, sometimes more. The idea is to make sure it averages out. Does your lawyer character agree to a small monthly fee only to find out the client takes up all their time? Does the client have some forceful way to make the lawyer live up to the deal – or else?

I know one lawyer who, many years ago (he's now retired), had a very expensive verdict against a company. Legal ethics rules make it illegal to enter into an agreement with a lawyer that they won't file anymore suits against the company, so the company put the lawyer on retainer after the case settled to "consult" from time to time. To my knowledge, the lawyer never got called again, but always got paid his retainer. That way, he was conflicted out from suing his existing client. It's an ethically questionable but probably legal practice. Did your character get paid not to sue a company anymore? Do they get caught and risk losing their license? Or does a dream case they know they can win against the company walk in the door and have to be sent away?

Trust accounts

If there is a fee paid in advance either for costs that have not yet been incurred, or for fees that have not incurred, such as a retainer paid for a certain number of hours of work that haven't occurred, that money must be held in a trust account. Many settlements and other monies held for a client or for other purposes also go into the trust account. The lawyer can't use this money for operating expenses, or use one client's money to pay for anything else. Trust account violations are the number one way lawyers get disciplined. Bar associations have no sense of humor about these, nor should they. Did your lawyer character dip into the trust account? It's also a good way to start or end a character arc – a bad lawyer who rips off clients' money at the beginning who is redeemed or a good lawyer reduced to theft.

Here are some other variations on fee arrangements you may find useful in your story:

- <u>Hourly/contingency hybrid</u>: This is a combination. The hourly will be a reduced rate, ranging from, say, $50 - $150, and then the contingency is reduced to anywhere between 10% and 33.33%. Your client character could think they're paying a percentage and get a giant bill.
- <u>Partial contingency</u>: The client pays a flat fee, usually nonrefundable, up front. The rest is based on a contingency, ranging from 20% to 33.33%. Does the client character think the fee paid up front was all they have to pay? Do they resist paying the percentage?
- <u>Success fees</u>: These are more commonly used by lawyer/lobbyists. These differ from contingency fees in that they are usually a flat rate paid upon success measured according to the terms of the agreement. For instance, the agreement might say if the bill passes, the lobbyist will get a $10,000 success fee. Do your lawyer and client have different views of success?

Settlement discussions

One of the things writers frequently get wrong is what is allowed in settlement discussions. This is the number one thing that happens pre-suit.

The parties often talk to avoid the suit, so it's important for the writer to understand. What the lawyer cannot do is threaten to bring criminal charges, to go to the press, or to send damaging evidence to a spouse or boss. That is called extortion, and it's a crime. If your character does these things to gain advantage in a civil matter, he deserves to go to jail.

On the other hand, implied threats are frequently used. For instance, your lawyer character may say their client will pursue all their legal remedies, and that's allowed. If they say, "You know, the press frequently picks up on this type of case," it's (probably) allowed. There's a fine line the character will have to walk to keep it real.

Settlement discussions are confidential, and are almost never admissible in court. Judges don't even usually want to hear about them, other than sometimes just to ask whether the parties have discussed settlement. Sometimes judges will insert themselves into settlement discussions, but this is increasingly rare. So if your story has the parties telling the judge, "But they offered $100,000 when we talked about settlement before suit," your story can look amateurish. There had better be a good reason why this would be relevant to your case and appropriate. It almost never will be.

Demand letters

These are letters almost always sent out before the suit to try to get the party about to be sued to settle. They usually set out the potential claims, in summary or in great detail depending on the lawyer's style, and set out how much the potential plaintiff is seeking. These letters are usually what prompt a settlement discussion. The letters should never cross the line into extortion. Even a character who is inclined to cross the line into extortion is probably not stupid enough to put it in writing. This would be done verbally if the character has any sense at all. Comedic or stupid characters could well put the extortion in writing, but they should suffer some consequence for doing so.

Pre-suit requirements

Many statutory claims have requirements the parties have to fulfill before filing suit. These could be anywhere from a letter to a full hearing your character has to do before even being allowed to bring a case.

For instance, medical malpractice attorneys usually have to notify the doctors and hospitals about to be sued regarding the potential claims.

There could be a union hearing, a proceeding before a hearing officer instead of a judge, or another non-court process available. If those exist, the plaintiff will usually have to use them first or have her case dismissed because she failed to "exhaust administrative remedies." Did your lawyer character forget to use a procedure that was available to decide the case? Does your character have her case thrown out because she didn't go through a grievance she believed she'd lose because the hearing officer was in the company's pocket?

Cases against government usually require giving them an opportunity to resolve it prior to suit. Your character with claims has to send a letter telling the city what the claims are to give the city time to investigate. Did the lawyer in your story forget to send the letter? Is it too late?

Contract and many other cases will have a "condition precedent" that has to be addressed, frequently some sort of notice or some other step that has to happen before a suit can be filed. Your character's case can be dismissed due to "failure to comply with a condition precedent" to suit. Do they turn around and sue the lawyer?

Can you find a way to have your lawyer character win the case, only to have it snatched away due to their inexperience?

Chapter 7 – The Complaint

A lawsuit begins with a document called a "Complaint." This is one of the most important documents in the case. The jury almost never sees it, yet it puts the defendant on notice of the claim. The entire case can be thrown out based on technical deficiencies in the complaint. For instance, if a discrimination lawsuit doesn't say the plaintiff filed with EEOC first, the complaint could be dismissed. Does your lawyer character leave something vital out of the complaint?

What a complaint says

While different states and courts can handle it differently, every complaint has at least the following:

The Style: This has the name of the court, a blank where the clerk stamps the case number, and the names of the parties. Attorney characters will always call this "the style of the case," or "the style."

Jurisdictional allegations: This will usually look something like, "This is an action for damages that exceed $15,000." Or, "This is an action based upon (insert federal statute here.)"   The idea is to let the court know why you picked that court and assure the judge you are in the right court. The amount of money sought is probably the most common way a court determines whether it has the right to hear the case. Did your lawyer character file in the wrong court?

A description of the parties: "Plaintiff Joe Blow is a resident of Smith County, Utah and was at all times relevant to this action an employee of Jones Company." "Defendant Jones Company is a corporation licensed to do business in the State of Utah and at all times relevant to this action was an "employer" as defined by (insert statute here)." The idea here is to describe which county or court the case belongs in and why the plaintiff has an interest in the case. Does your complaint leave somebody out? Does your lawyer character forget to sue the property owner in a case over a piece of land? If they only sue the tenant, the case could be dismissed for "failure to join an indispensable party."

General allegations: These are numbered paragraphs describing briefly the facts that apply to all the counts in the Complaint. These can be as long or as brief as the writer's imagination. Sometimes complex facts require long explanations. Sometimes the facts can be described in one sentence. "Defendant owes Plaintiff $3000.00 that is due with interest since January 22, 2007 according to the attached account." Can you fit in some numbered paragraphs to describe the case to your readers quickly?

The claims: These are broken into "counts" if there is more than one. There will be "Count I – Breach of Contract"; "Count II – Trade Secrets Violations," etc. Each count will go into the elements necessary for that count. We'll talk about some of the more common types of claims that can be raised and what elements must be proven in Chapters 10 – 16. The judge and lawyers in your story will talk about "counts."

Ad damnum clause: Don't you love legal talk? This is, simply, what relief is demanded. "Plaintiff demands judgment for damages, injunctive relief, costs, and attorneys' fees against Defendant." Or whatever the relief is that is sought. These can be quite elaborate where there are multiple legal remedies. I dare you to fit in this term somewhere, maybe with a young lawyer trying to sound pompous.

Demand for jury trial: If the Plaintiff wants a jury trial, they have to ask for it in the complaint or it's waived. The defendant can still ask for it, but the Plaintiff loses the right to ask if it's not in the first version of the Complaint. Did your character forget to ask for a jury? A judge might award less money or be less sympathetic to the case. Or the lawyer may fear the judge will be too subject to influence if the other side is politically powerful.

Signature: The attorney, or plaintiff if they are unrepresented, must sign. They must type in their name, address and phone number. Many courts require fax numbers, email addresses, or both. The signature is considered to say that the party has a good faith reason to believe what they're saying is true. Did your lawyer character forget to investigate? Did they lie to make it sound more interesting and get caught?

Bar number: The attorney's bar number will go either in the style or the signature block. In over 20 years of law practice I have never figured out any use for this information. I assume it's just so you can check to see if they are licensed. Is your attorney character faking it? Maybe somebody runs the number and finds out.

Sample Complaint

IN THE CIRCUIT COURT OF THE 11TH JUDICIAL CIRCUIT, IN AND FOR DADE COUNTY, FLORIDA

CASE NO.

Jane Smith,
        Plaintiff,   Florida Bar no. 1111111

vs.

Dean Jones,
        Defendant.

_____/

COMPLAINT

Plaintiff, Jane Smith, sues Defendant Dean Jones, and says:

1. Plaintiff Jane Smith is an individual who resides in Miami-Dade County, Florida.
2. Defendant Dean Jones, Inc. is an individual who resides in Broward County, Florida.
3. The causes of action which bring rise to this Complaint accrued in Miami-Dade County, Florida. This is an action for damages which exceed $15,000.00.

GENERAL ALLEGATIONS

4. On or about November 10, 2008, Defendant published a flyer calling Jane Smith a "pedophile and a dope dealer."
5. The flyer was distributed throughout Smith's neighborhood.

6. On November 12, 2008, Smith's house was burned down in an arson fire.
7. Since the publication, Smith has been shunned by her neighbors, fired from her job as a neighborhood dog walker, and subjected to taunting and ridicule.
8. Smith is not now, nor has she ever been, a pedophile or a dope dealer.

COUNT I - DEFAMATION OF CHARACTER

Plaintiff realleges Paragraphs 1- 8 as if fully restated herein.

9. The knowingly and/or recklessly false statements made and published by Dean Jones were defamatory because such accusations held Ms. Smith up to ridicule, scorn and contempt.
10. Because the false statements impute conduct or characteristics incompatible with the proper exercise of Ms. Smith's lawful profession, and/or that Ms. Smith committed a crime, the statements constitute defamation per se.
11. The defamation by Dean Jones directly and proximately caused Ms. Smith's damages, including but not limited to, lost wages, humiliation, embarrassment, emotional distress, mental anguish, stigmatization, and loss of ability to earn money. The losses are either permanent or continuing and plaintiff will suffer the losses in the future.
12. The defamatory publications, if made with a qualified privilege, were made with malice and were excessively published, and were otherwise made under conditions which defeat the privilege.

WHEREFORE, Plaintiff demands judgment for damages against Defendant, and for such other relief as the Court deems just and proper.

COUNT II - FALSE LIGHT INVASION OF PRIVACY

Plaintiff realleges Paragraphs 1-8 as if fully restated herein.

13. The statements made and published by Dean Jones placed Ms. Smith in a false light.
14. The false light invasion of privacy by Dean Jones directly and proximately caused Ms. Smith's damages, including but not limited to, lost wages, humiliation, embarrassment, emotional distress, mental anguish, stigmatization, and loss of ability to earn money. The losses are either permanent or continuing and plaintiff will suffer the losses in the future.

WHEREFORE, Plaintiff demands judgment for damages against Defendant, for punitive damages should the court permit such damages to be pled, and for such other relief as the Court deems just and proper.

DEMAND FOR JURY TRIAL

Plaintiff demands jury trial for all issues so triable.
DATED: November 27, 2009.

Respectfully submitted,

Joan Doe, P.A.
123 Main St.
Miami, FL 33131
(305)555-1212

BY: _____
Joan Doe

Process servers

A summons goes with the complaint. The summons tells the person being sued when an answer is due and where to file it. It is usually served by a process server. If the complaint isn't served, or if there's a problem with how it is served, the complaint can be dismissed.

This part of litigation can be fun for your story. Most times, service of process is pretty uneventful. The fun part of service of process is where a character evades service. Evasion can be a minor plot device or a major part of a story. Think of comical creative ways the process server can sneak up to a door. Pizza or flower delivery is common. But how about something more unusual? Something creative involving snakes, smoke, dwarves - you get the idea.

What usually happens is that the process server knocks on the door or walks into the office, asks for the person being served, they come out, he says something to the effect of, "I have some papers to serve on you." The person says, "OK" and takes the papers. The end. Does your character calmly accept the papers or go berserk?

Service of process for an individual can usually be on any person over 18 who resides in the home. Live-in nannies count, daytime nannies do not. Did your character have a nanny accept a lawsuit, then throw it away? Do they have a judgment against them they have to challenge now? Guests cannot accept service for a resident of the household. Maybe the visiting in-laws can accept a lawsuit and decide not to tell your character. Many times, people won't open the door, thinking this somehow keeps them from being served. Not so. If the process server can provide an affidavit that they saw the person, that they then announced that they were leaving the papers, and left them in a prominent place, such as in the door or on the porch, that will be enough to constitute service. Did your character refuse to open the door? Do they think that means they haven't been served?

Corporations are usually served through a "registered agent" for service of process. The company will designate a person who agrees to be available to accept process during normal business hours. Corporations can also be served through officers, starting with the president. Did the tiny company your character started to pursue his dream have a secretary who accepted service and stuffed the lawsuit in a drawer?

Spending much time in court arguing over whether or not someone was served is usually a waste of time because they will be served eventually. Your character could have to spend money setting aside a judgment for bad service, or be a plaintiff who is having trouble getting service on a slippery character.

But what about if the character dies? Whether or not they were served could change the outcome of the case. What if the character disappears? If they disappeared and then their spouse is served at their home, is that home still the residence? These could be ways to develop your story.

Service can also be made by publication if the defendant can't be located. There are newspapers that publish these notices and they usually have to be published two or three times. Each state has a statute (law) that has to be followed strictly to accomplish this. Did your character move and get served by publication? Do they visit only to find a whopping judgment?

Where the suit is filed

This is usually an easy thing to figure out. Most cases arise in a particular county of a particular state, and state law applies. The case must then be filed in the county where the facts giving rise to the complaint arose. This would be where the accident occurred, the breach of contract happened, the employment was, etc.

Sometimes it's not so easy to figure out, and here's where your story could get interesting. If your employee character was sexually assaulted on a cruise ship that took off from California, but the assault occurred on international waters, there could be state law, federal law or international law that applies. Admiralty might force the case into federal court. If the state where the cruise line is located has a law on sexual harassment, and it applies to all employers in the state, the employee may be able to sue in state court.

Your story can spend some time having disputes over where a case should be filed. Some cases bog down for months or years arguing over where they should be heard. Defendants accuse plaintiffs of "forum shopping," which means trying to bring the case in a state where juries, judges, or the laws are friendlier. Plaintiffs do indeed try to find the most favorable court where the case can be properly heard. Did your character forum shop? Did they make the right choice?

Another issue, getting past which state and county, is convenience of the location. "Forum non conveniens" means that the majority of witnesses and evidence are in a different state or county than where the case was filed. Did your character file her suit, only to get moved to a place where everyone works for the company they are suing? Did the case move to a judge whose campaign had a fundraiser at corporate headquarters?

Sometimes the parties agree on venue, that is, where the case will be filed, in a contract. More and more, employers are sneaking these agreements into job applications, employment contracts presented after the employee starts, employment handbooks, and other "contracts" the employee had no opportunity to bargain. Sometimes you see these provisions in the fine print of consumer contracts, airline tickets, cruise tickets, and other purchased items. Your character can be surprised to find out they've agreed to file suit in Delaware when they live in Nevada.

Also more frequently, contracts and employment documents have arbitration clauses, meaning that the case never gets to court. Is it fair for an employment application your character didn't read to bind the employee to arbitrate the case in Bermuda? According to the courts so far, yes, it is. This could force your character into an interesting location, or force them to drop a case due to the expenses. If you're trying to figure out how to get your Iowa character to California, this is one possibility.

Standing – who can sue and be sued

This is one where, if you get it wrong in your book, you look really amateurish most of the time. The person who sues must be the injured party. The competing company can't sue to enforce your character's company's contract, unless the contract is actually with the competing company. The friend can't sue the person who hurt their friend. The character bringing the suit has to have an interest to protect. I see shows, mostly comedies, where somebody inappropriate sues and it gets my hackles up.

Similarly, the person or entity sued must be the one that caused the injury. Sometimes the laws say who can be sued. For discrimination, the supervisor is almost never personally liable. For overtime cases, the owner can be sued. Did your character think they couldn't be sued personally? Are they surprised when someone suing the company claims the company didn't hold regular meetings, so the owners aren't protected from liability?

Who can represent parties

This one drives me absolutely nutters when I see it in a story. Your character's neighbor, friend, boyfriend, cousin, waiter, wife, or boss cannot represent them, unless the person is a lawyer. The answer is simple. The party can represent themselves unless they are a corporation. A corporation has to be represented by an attorney. Anyone not representing themselves must be represented by an attorney. Their best friend can't show up and represent them, nor can their cousin who isn't a lawyer yet. Don't get this wrong.[16]

Jurisdiction – which court hears the case

This is usually a question of amount in dispute. Small claims courts hear claims under $1500 or $5000, or some other specified "small" amount.

---

[16] Yes, of course there are exceptions. If you really want to break this rule, do your research. There are some forums that allow non-lawyers to represent parties, but if you don't research it, you will almost always be wrong.

Don't have your character show up on *Judge Alex* with a million dollar case. There can be mid-level courts such as county courts or municipal courts, that hear cases that are over the small claims amount but less than the top level court. The top level court will usually be any claims over a certain amount, such as $15,000. How much is your character seeking? Do they file in the wrong court and get their case dismissed?

There can also be specialty courts, such as family courts, worker's compensation courts, and other courts having jurisdiction over only a particular type of matter. This will require some research to figure out if you want to place your story in a specialty court.

A case can be filed in, or removed to federal court, if it is between citizens of different states, or if there is a federal question such as a federal trademark claim. If there is "complete diversity," meaning all plaintiffs are from a different state than all defendants, then the case can be forced into federal court. The theory in this is that it used to be thought that out-of-staters couldn't get a fair shake against locals. That's still true some places, but in larger metropolitan areas, where everyone doesn't know everyone else, these cases are usually safe for non-locals. What's more likely is your character gets stuck in a federal court with an issue the federal judges hate, such as disability discrimination. Did your character think she was filing a simple county court case that could get decided in a few months? Does it, literally, turn into a federal case, making the suit drag on for years and extremely expensive?[17]

These days, in many areas of the country, plaintiffs try to figure out creative ways to stay out of federal court. In employment cases, for instance, some federal courts can be extremely unfriendly because they have so many employment cases many judges think all employees' claims are frivolous. And federal court can also frequently be drastically more expensive because they have requirements that are easier for large firms, but which cost small firms huge amounts of time and resources. The system is skewed to favor the wealthy corporate party because of the expenses involved. Does your character end up spending thousands of dollars just on extra copies of exhibits for the juries and complying with the court's electronic filing system?

---

[17] There's a good reason for the expression "he made a Federal case out of it." Federal court is a bureaucratic nightmare and can bog your characters down for years.

Defendants can force cases to federal court even if state courts are also allowed to hear them, and plaintiffs can try to get it moved back. For instance, if the company in your story claims diversity (those are the out-of-staters), the plaintiff character can try to figure out a citizen of their state to add as a defendant, such as a corporate officer. If it's federal question, there is a requirement that the case be seeking over $75,000. Did your character spend lots of time avoiding specifying the amount of money they are seeking, or even concede that damages won't be over that amount, to avoid the dread federal court?[18]

---

[18] I would never do this, of course. I live for the honor of appearing before the Federal Bench, Your Honor.

Chapter 8 – Responses to the Complaint

One of the biggest complaints lawyers have about the way lawsuits are portrayed is the failure to capture just how long it takes. A year or more will pass before a case gets to trial, much of it taken up with responses to the Complaint and discovery, which we'll discuss in the next chapter.

"Hollywood always gets it wrong. They can't help themselves. Of course, in my own novels, I try to get it right, but those are always the parts where the editor says, 'Can't it move faster than that?'"

Brad Meltzer, bestselling author of, *The Tenth Justice, Dead Even, The First Counsel, The Millionaires, The Zero Game, The Book of Fate* and, *The Book of Lies*.

In this chapter, we'll discuss some of the motions that get filed to try to knock out a complaint, the answer to the complaint, and some common defenses.

Motion to dismiss

This is a motion that attacks what is said in the complaint, either in whole or in part. A motion to dismiss can be granted "with prejudice," meaning that the complaint cannot be amended. Dismissed "without prejudice" means it can be amended to fix the problem. Does your character lose a motion to dismiss and think the case is over, only to find out it's just the beginning?

The most common issue raised is "failure to state a claim upon which relief can be granted" (in some states, called "failure to state a cause of action"). This means that some vital "element," that is, part of the claim, is missing. We talked about elements of the claim in Chapter 7. Sometimes the error can be corrected. Did your attorney character omit a required part of the claim, or fail to attach an exhibit? If the case is about a contract, the contract has to be attached. The motion would be granted with leave to amend to attach the missing contract. Frequently, lawyers realize the opposing counsel is right, and they agree to amend. Your character can be unduly distressed by this, or even fire the attorney, thinking that the attorney has done something wrong. In truth, needing to amend is quite common.

If the complaint can never be amended to state the claim, then the complaint can be dismissed and the case thrown out. This can happen where the attorney is trying to push the law in a new direction, or is arguing something that the courts have never decided. Does your character have a unique situation? Does he argue that the sex discrimination laws should apply to his housing discrimination case because if he were a woman married to his male partner, the landlord wouldn't discriminate? This motion could bring an abrupt end to the legal case, causing him to take matters in his own hands. The dismissal would be "with prejudice," meaning the complaint can't be amended.

A motion to dismiss can also be for "lack of jurisdiction." That is simply whether the court is the correct one. There can also be lack of personal jurisdiction – the party was not served, or the court has no right to hear cases against that party. For instance, state courts can't hear cases against the U.S. Government or its agencies. Did your character file a small claims case against the federal government? Did the government force her into federal court?

The motion to dismiss can be for "improper venue" location is wrong or "forum non conveniens" (the location is less convenient than another location). Did your character's case get abruptly moved across the country? Can he afford to continue so far away?

Some defenses, that is, reasons the defendant should win even if everything the plaintiff says is true, must be brought by a motion to dismiss. If those defenses aren't raised in that motion they are waived. Those defenses are 1) lack of personal jurisdiction; (2) lack of subject matter jurisdiction; (3) improper venue; (4) insufficiency of process: (5) insufficiency of service of process; (6) failure to state cause of action; and (7) failure to join indispensable parties. Did the plaintiff serve your character by leaving the lawsuit with the maid? Does your character find out after they lose that they could have had the case thrown out?

Sometimes the judge can correct a minor error with an "amendment by interlineation." This means, simply, that the judge crosses it out and writes in the correct allegation. For example, it's commonly done with a minor typographical error, particularly when the case is already set for trial and the amendment doesn't change the substance of the claim. Does the big firm file a motion to dismiss at the last minute to try to get the trial date moved? Your lawyer character can ask the judge to amend by interlineation and keep the trial date.

Motion to strike

This is used to attack impertinent, scandalous, or harassing allegations. Say your character insists on putting into the complaint that the defendant is of loose morals, but the case is for breach of contract. Or the case is about discrimination but the complaint says the defendant is also a pedophile. The judge could strike this type of allegation without dismissing the complaint.

Motion to remove

If the complaint is filed in state court, the case can be removed to federal court[19] if there's a federal question or diversity (the out-of-staters) within 30 days after the complaint is served by filing a motion to remove.[20] Do your characters have a comical dance where defendants offer to not remove if only the plaintiffs will stipulate that damages won't exceed $75,000, and plaintiffs respond that they will agree to removal if the defendants will admit that damages if they win will exceed $75,000?

If removal can't initially be granted, but grounds for removal becomes apparent within one year after the suit is filed, the defendant may remove then. Does your character decide to add a claim for overtime? Does that simple little addition turn it into a federal case?

Answer and affirmative defenses

The answer will address each paragraph in the complaint. The defendant will admit, deny, or state that they unable to admit or deny because they are without knowledge.

The answer will have the style of the case at the top, and will then look something like this:

---

[19] The darling locale of corporations and the defense bar these days.
[20] See Chapter 7 pp. 83-85

ANSWER AND AFFIRMATIVE DEFENSES

Defendant Jane Doe answers the Complaint of Jim Rowe as follows:

1. Paragraph 1 is admitted.
2. Paragraph 2 is denied.
3. Defendant is without knowledge of the allegations of Paragraph 3 and is unable to admit or deny.
4. Defendant admits the first sentence of Paragraph 4 and denies the remaining allegations.

You get the picture here. Don't have your characters give a long explanation of each paragraph.

Next will be the affirmative defenses, which are an "avoidance" of what's in the complaint. Defenses can be any number of reasons why the complaint, even if true, should still not result in a judgment against the Defendant.

They will look something like this:

Defense no. 1: Count 1 for fraud in the inducement fails to state a claim upon which relief can be granted.

Defense no. 2: Plaintiff cannot recover under any counts because such recovery would violate the Fair Labor Standards Act.

Defense no. 3: Plaintiff cannot recover due to unclean hands.

Defense no. 4: Plaintiff is barred from any claims raised herein by its own breaches of contract.

Defense no. 5: Plaintiff's claims are barred by the Economic Loss Rule.

Defense no. 6: Plaintiff has failed to mitigate damages.

Defense no. 7: Plaintiff's claims are barred by the doctrine of waiver.

Defense no. 8: Plaintiff's claims are barred by the doctrine of estoppel.

Defense no. 9: The Court lacks subject matter jurisdiction over Count II.

Any defenses that are not raised are waived. Your character could lose her case even though she had a valid defense because the lawyer didn't raise it in the answer, and then didn't amend. Did the lawyer fail to raise "accord and satisfaction," that is, that the defendant already paid the money she thought she owed and the other side accepted it? Maybe that could be the beginning of a malpractice story.

Counterclaim

In many cases, the Defendant has claims against the Plaintiff. These are raised in a counterclaim, which would be part of the answer. The pleading would then be titled, "Answer, Affirmative Defenses and Counterclaim." Counterclaims can be any claims that could be raised in a complaint. Does your character sue, only to find he has some claims against him he has to defend?

Mandatory counterclaims must be raised in response to the complaint, or they are waived. A counterclaim is mandatory if it is part of the "same transaction or occurrence" as the complaint. For instance, if the complaint is for breach of contract, claims for Plaintiff's breach of the same contract would be part of a mandatory counterclaim your character would have to raise in the case. If your character's complaint is for discrimination relating to an employee being fired, and the employer wants to claim that the employee stole trade secrets when they left, the counterclaim is mandatory because the claim is about the employment.

Permissive counterclaims are ones that can, but aren't required to, be raised in the same case. For instance, if the John Smith sues your character for breach of a contract, and John Smith was also in an auto accident with your character, the claims on the auto accident could be either raised in same or a separate lawsuit. Could your character end up defending against two different cases?

Reply

Most states have pleading called a reply if an affirmative defense requires an "avoidance." Essentially, a reply states a defense to a defense. In a defamation case, for instance, if the affirmative defense is "qualified privilege," that the statements were allowed, the reply might say: "The defense of qualified privilege is not valid due to excessive publication of the defamatory statements." What does that mean? I'll talk about it more in the section on defamation in Chapter 10, but it means that the statements were made to people who had no right to hear them.

You could use a reply in your story if you had an attorney who was handling a case outside their state and they didn't know they had to file a reply. Did your plaintiff lose the case on a defense they had an avoidance to but failed to raise?

Chapter 9 – The Authorities

Your character may spend time doing legal research, or you may need to do some research for your story. Entire law libraries are devoted to only a small portion of the legal authorities that exist on U.S. law. I'll address some of the major authorities that your character may need for your story in this chapter.

Rules of Civil Procedure

Every state and the federal courts have their own rules of civil procedure. These rules tell the lawyers how things work in that court. Everything the lawyer needs to know about when things are due, motion practice, the pleadings allowed and required, discovery, and trials is in these rules.

If your character is taking a civil procedure class, they may refer to it as "Civ Pro." When citing rules of civil procedure, the format will usually be something like Fed. R. Civ. P. 56. When the lawyers refer to a rule, they'll usually just say, "Rule 11."

Most states base their rules on the federal rules. However, when the federal rules are amended, it takes awhile for the states to catch up. Did your lawyer character assume the rules in a different state were the same as the federal rules and get the case dismissed?

Each type of court will have its own rules. Bankruptcy courts, criminal courts, family courts, appellate courts, all have their own rules, and the lawyers need to know the rules of the court where they are practicing. Not knowing the rules of the court[21] is a good way to have your lawyer character embarrass herself.

Courts can have their own local rules on top of the main rules. For instance, each federal court has its own local rules. These can address minutia such as the font for briefs, how documents need to be stapled,

---

[21] The federal rules were recently amended, so having the character cite the wrong rule number or an outdated rule could be fun for your story, or cause some conflict or humiliation.

how many copies of a document to submit to the court, the color of a binder[22], and other requirements that individual courts have. Is your lawyer character who is practicing out of his usual locality humiliated by not knowing the rules? The rules can give an advantage to the local players.

Some judges have their own rules, usually done by Administrative Order. Judges can have rules they impose in addition to the rules of civil procedure and the local rules on things like how to set hearings, how long hearings can last, what documents they want to review before hearings, deadlines on submitting items not addressed in the other rules, such as jury instructions, and any number of details. Did your lawyer character draw a crazy judge who makes lawyers refer to him as "Your Excellency"?

Rules of Evidence

The rules of evidence address what kinds of evidence can be used in a trial. They can also be used in some hearings, and may affect what discovery is allowed. The law school class is simply called, "Evidence." Lawyers will cite these rules in a brief as something like, "Fed. R. Evid. 5." In court, lawyers will usually refer to these rules by the type of rule, such as the "hearsay rule."

I'll deal more with these rules in the section on objections at trial. It is important for your lawyer character to understand how they will admit each piece of evidence. For instance, if it is hearsay (simply, an out of court statement offered to prove its own truth), then the evidence may come in under an exception to the hearsay rule. Is your law clerk character frantically researching the rules of evidence and case law about those rules on an unusual piece of evidence, into the wee hours?

Case Law

The U.S. is under a "common law" justice system.[23] That means case law is used as "precedent" and each case builds on other cases.

---

[22] Yes, color. Your tax dollars at work. And if it has the wrong cover color or font, the clerk will return it with a rejection notice. After resubmission, it has to be re-docketed, and re-filed.

[23] This is as opposed to a civil law form of justice system. Every state in the U.S. other than Louisiana is also under a common law system. Louisiana follows civil law, except with respect to federal law, which it must apply under the common law system. If your story is based in Louisiana, you'll need to have an understanding of how civil law works. France also has a civil law system, which is why Louisiana ended up with this form.

If there is no case law on the issue, it's called a "case of first impression." This can happen where the issue is unique, or where the court is interpreting a new statute. Can you think of a unique issue for your lawyer characters to argue?

Where your character has a case addressing the same issue, they'll refer to it as a "case on point." Your character might say, "Your Honor, in a case exactly on point, the Eleventh Circuit stated . . ."

Case law is written in Reporters. Each type of court or court region has its own reporters. Reporters are cited by the volume number, abbreviation of the reporter, then page number, followed, in parentheses, by the name of the court and the date. For instance, in the Southern Reporter, a case on page 822 of book number 82 of the second series, decided by the Third District Court of Appeal in 1986 would be cited: 82 So. 2d 822 (Fla. 3d DCA 1986).

The way to write these citations is in a book referred to as the "blue book."[24] Sometimes the local rules or rules of civil procedure will tell lawyers the way courts want lawyers to write out citations. Some localities have customs as to the citation format of specific authorities. Otherwise, following the blue book is considered the preferred format. Does your judge give a lawyer from out of state a hard time about her citations? It could be a way to show she's an outsider.

In court, your lawyer character might argue something like, "Your Honor, in *Smith v. State*, which I'm handing you right now, the third district addressed this exact issue. You'll see on page 282 of that case that the court held that a statement made to the police is absolutely privileged and can never be the subject of a defamation action."

What lawyers mainly learn in law school is how to find and argue about case law. They may distinguish the facts of the case. "My opposing counsel makes much of *Smith v. State*, but the facts in this case are quite different. You'll see that *Jones v. Smithers* is directly on point. In that case . . ."

Ways a lawyer character could get into trouble in your story might be failing to tell a court about a case on point that is against the position

---

[24] *The Bluebook: A Uniform System of Citation* is the most commonly used style guide for citations. It is compiled by the Harvard, Colombia, and University of Pennsylvania Law Reviews, along with the Yale Law Journal. Its cover is, not surprisingly, blue. Lawyers aren't that creative with names.

they are arguing, misrepresenting what a case said, failing to shepardize[25] the case to find out whether the case was overruled or otherwise is no longer a case that can be argued as "good law," or failing to find a case on point that the other side finds.

Cases are the center of the U.S. justice system. If your character is in court, he'll probably have to argue about cases in your story.

Treatises

Treatises are the books lawyers and judges write about the law. They are never binding on the judge, but can be used to persuade judges to decide a case the lawyer's way. There is no end to the topics treatises cover. From general topics such as civil procedure to very specialized topics such as environmental law, labor relations, and taxation, there is a treatise for almost every area of law. Does your character pull out an article from the *Complete Handbook of Surfing and Other Awesome Sports Law*?

The other way to get information on how scholars view a legal topic is to look at law review articles. Some are for specific areas of practice, such as the University of Miami's *Entertainment and Sports Law Journal*[26]. Most law schools also have a general law review, put out by the top students[27] in the school. Law review membership is done either by top grades or by submitting written work product. These students write and edit articles on legal topics on top of their studies. Lawyers and professors can also submit articles for publication in law reviews. Is your law student character on law review under a deadline, and still studying for exams?

Legal magazines, such as the *ABA Journal*, also have articles on legal topics that staff and lawyers write for lawyers about current topics of interest.

In your story, you could have an attorney researching a treatise, have a law student writing an article, or have a funny name for a treatise to give your story comic relief. How about "Barking Mad" for a journal on dog law? "Air Heads" for aviation?

---

[25] Shepard's is the service that allows attorneys to find out whether a case is good law or has been overruled. It also allows the attorney to find every reported case where the case they are utilizing has been cited.

[26] A blatant plug for an excellent journal. I used to be on the Editorial Board, but I'm otherwise completely unbiased.

[27] Geeks, nerds, gunners, yeah, you got it. And I was one of them, so I can make fun.

Statutes, ordinances and regulations

Statutes and ordinances are, simply, fancy words for laws.[28] A regulation is a rule that interprets a law. For instance, Congress may pass an environmental statute, and then the Environmental Protection Agency will pass regulations interpreting the statute. Courts have to follow the statutes, but do not necessarily have to apply the regulations. Does your judge character say they believe the regulations conflict in some way with the intent of the state legislature?

A state statute cannot conflict with federal statutes. A county ordinance cannot override a state or federal statute. Certain areas of law, such as foreign policy, are reserved solely for the federal government.[29] In your story, does the state pass a law allowing bigamy? Does Congress race to pass a law to make it illegal? What happens to the characters who got married while it was still legal?

Statutes can override existing case law. For instance, if Congress is ticked off that the Supreme Court interpreted the law of negligence in a particular way, it could pass a statute that would change the law, just not retroactively. Did the Supreme Court in your story rule that the don't ask don't tell regulation in the military is illegal? How long will it take Congress to introduce a bill to make it legal again? What happens to the character who thought it was safe to come out?

---

[28] Federal and state governments generally pass statutes. County commissions and city councils/commissions generally pass ordinances. Government agencies generally pass regulations.
[29] Although don't tell that to the Miami City Commission, which likes to periodically try to engage in foreign policy, particularly relating to Cuba and Haiti.

Chapter 10 – Torts

A tort is, simply, a wrongful act upon which someone can sue for damages[30].

Negligence

> "I thought the portrayal of Jann Schlictmann in *A Civil Action* was right on. The book captured the fear, hubris, excitement, and eventual anti climax that comes with winning a big PI case against a corporate defendant. The book had perfect pitch."
> **- David Auslander**, Miami personal injury attorney.

Most personal injury cases (PI cases to lawyers), many business to business cases, and most malpractice cases are based on negligence. Negligence is, very simply:

- **A.** Someone had a legal duty to do something
- **B.** They breached that duty
- **C.** Someone was harmed by the breach

So why are there entire sections of law libraries covering various aspects of negligence law? Because nothing in law is simple.

The problem with negligence is it can apply to just about every type of injury. Economic, personal, emotional, and any imaginable injury. Jury instruction forms have versions for professional negligence, negligence of a child, contributory negligence, all types of traffic negligence, railroads, products liability, landowner, and negligent violation of a statute, and they have multiple levels:

- **ordinary negligence** – this means, simply, failing to use reasonable care.
- **gross negligence** – consciously or deliberately disregarding the need to use reasonable care.

---

[30] And not a delicious pastry.

- **criminal negligence** – failing to use reasonable care resulting in harm or likely harm to someone in violation of a criminal law (such as criminally negligent homicide). Because this is, by its nature, criminal, not civil law, it won't be addressed in this book, but it's a term you may hear or your characters might throw around.

There are specific types of negligence:

- **products liability** – relating to the sale of products
- **malpractice** – relating to providing professional services
- **negligence per se** – relating to violation of a law or ordinance
- **negligent infliction of emotional distress** – most states don't allow, but this relates to the duty not to cause emotional upset, such as to a relative who witnesses a child's death but isn't in danger themselves.

Negligence is also the way that the very richest of the mega-rich lawyers get that way.

Torts is a complicated subject – a full year class in law school. But I can give you a jump start for your writing. Here are some basics.

The Basics of Negligence

"Negligence is the failure to use reasonable care. Reasonable care is that degree of care which a reasonably careful person would use under like circumstances. Negligence may consist either in doing something that a reasonably careful person would not do under like circumstances or in failing to do something that a reasonably careful person would do under like circumstances." Fla. Std. Jury Instructions. Did your character do something that wasn't careful? He could have tried to jump his motorcycle over a car only to land on a pedestrian.

- What if both parties are negligent? When both sides are negligent, it's called **contributory negligence**, which affects the amount of money recovered. Did your character hit the bicyclist because she was on her cell phone having an argument? But did the bicyclist also cut in front of her without signaling? Some states consider this a complete defense to negligence. In those states, the bicyclist would lose their suit.

  Some states have juries assign negligence, and then it's called **comparative negligence**. If a jury says the driver defendant was negligent, but finds the bicyclist plaintiff 10% negligent and they award $100,000 to the bicyclist, the judgment would be reduced to $90,000. If there are multiple defendants, or unnamed parties deemed negligent, then the damages get apportioned among them and they only have to pay their share.

Say the bicyclist also sues the cell phone company and the jury decides the cell phone company was 50% negligent. The cell phone company would pay half of the judgment. In some states, as long as the defendant was more than 50% negligent, they would be responsible for paying the whole amount. So if the driver convinced the jury to blame the cell phone company 51%, the driver might not have to pay anything.

- **The last clear chance doctrine** says that, if the defendant was negligent after the plaintiff was negligent, then even if the plaintiff was contributorily negligent, they can still recover. In other words, say your character was driving while talking on the cell phone. They aren't paying attention. A kid runs out in front. They have to slam on the brakes and stop suddenly. Had they been paying attention, they could have stopped more quickly. The person behind them is busy yelling at their passengers, so he slams into the back. Even though the cell phone talker was negligent, the person behind had the last clear chance to stop the accident.

- **Assumption of the risk** is where the victim knows of a risk and voluntarily, well, assumes it. For instance, smokers who ignored the surgeon general's warning are having this defense raised. Sky divers are frequently deemed to have assumed the risk that they will break a leg or worse. Motorcyclists who drive without a helmet, drivers without seatbelts, bungee jumpers, you get the idea.

- Then there are **immunities**.

  Parent-child and spousal immunity prevent family members from suing each other, mainly to prevent insurance fraud I believe (the official reason is to "preserve family harmony").

  Sovereign immunity prevents a lawsuit from being initiated without the sovereign's (government's) consent. They pass statutes to waive all or part of their sovereign immunity. These statutes are very specific and require many hoops for plaintiffs to jump through before they can sue, and they also contain limits on amounts of money for recovery. If your character was hurt by a government, sovereign immunity can stop them from suing.

If there's one case that is a fantastic example of how negligence is applied, it's the McDonald's coffee case.

The Infamous McDonald's Case

This case is a classic example of tort law, and how to apply both negligence and products liability.

> "In my view, the misrepresentation of that [McDonald's coffee spill] case did more to hurt the reputation of lawyers than anything else in the past 20 years."
> - **David Auslander**, Miami personal injury attorney.

For decades to come, I expect to see mistaken references in movies, TV, novels and the press about the McDonald's coffee case from writers who didn't have the good sense to buy my book. Here's what really happened in *Liebeck v. McDonald's Restaurants*, which resulted in a $2.9 million jury verdict, so you can get it right.

Stella Liebeck, riding in her grandson's car, received coffee at a drive through window. Her grandson, the driver, pulled forward so she could add cream and sugar. She put it between her knees and tried to remove the lid. The entire cup spilled into her lap when she took the lid off. Her sweatpants held the coffee next to her skin. She suffered third degree burns across her groin, inner thighs and buttocks.

A vascular surgeon determined that she suffered full thickness burns over six percent of her body. She was hospitalized for eight days, during which she underwent skin grafting and debridement treatments (surgical removal of tissue) on her inner thighs, perineum, buttocks, genital and groin areas.

It turned out that McDonald's had received more than 700 claims by people burned by its coffee over ten years. These claims included similar third degree burns.

McDonald's admitted it kept its coffee between 180 and 190 degrees Fahrenheit to maintain optimum taste. Other competitors sold coffee at much lower temperatures. Your coffee at home is around 135 to 140 degrees.

McDonald's own quality assurance manager admitted that they knew a burn hazard existed with any substance served at 140 degrees or above and that McDonald's coffee was not fit for consumption because it would burn the mouth and throat. He testified that the company required that coffee be held in the pot at 185 degrees, plus or minus five degrees. He also testified that, even though it knew burns would occur, McDonald's had no intention of reducing the "holding temperature" of its coffee.

A scholar in thermodynamics testified that liquids at 180 degrees will cause a full thickness burn to human skin in two to seven seconds. At 155 degrees, the extent of the burn decreases exponentially. At 155 degrees, the liquid would have cooled and given Liebeck time to avoid a serious burn.

McDonald's also admitted it knew that customers intend to drink the coffee immediately while driving. They admitted its customers were unaware they could suffer third-degree burns from the coffee and that a statement the cup was not a "warning" but a "reminder" since the side location of the writing would not warn of the hazard.

A McDonald's executive testified that McDonald's knew its coffee sometimes caused serious burns, but hadn't consulted burn experts about it. He said McDonald's had decided not to warn customers and that the company did not intend to change its policy.

The Wall Street Journal quoted a juror as saying the trial was about, "callous disregard for the safety of the people."

The company tried to convince jurors that the deep burns this woman suffered, and others had suffered before her, didn't matter, because they were rare. The jury apparently didn't agree.

While Liebeck had offered to settle for $20,000, McDonald's wouldn't settle. The jury awarded $200,000 to compensate Liebeck for her medical expenses. That amount was reduced to $160,000 because the jury found Liebeck partially at fault for the spill, to the tune of 20%. They awarded $2.7 million in punitive damages, or two days of coffee sales for the company. The court reduced the award to $480,000.

After the trial McDonald's dropped its coffee at the same location to 158 degrees Fahrenheit. The parties ended up settling.

This is a great example of why products liability suits are so important, and why they make good stories. They involve David v. Goliath stories, callous indifference, and the cold corporate calculation of how much it will cost them for an injury or death they know is likely to occur.

When you write about the McDonald's case, get it right.

Assault

Your character is slapped. He cries, "I'm going to sue you for assault!" He can try, but that wasn't assault, that was battery. Assault is putting someone in fear of an unwanted or harmful touching.

And yes, even lawyers interchange the two terms. Sexual assault is actual unwanted sexual touching, but it really should be called sexual battery. Sometimes it is, and sometimes it isn't.

Elements of Assault
An actor is subject to liability to another for assault if

    A. He acts intending to cause a harmful or offensive contact with the person of the other or a third person, or an imminent apprehension of such a contact, and

    B. The other is thereby put in such imminent apprehension.
Restatement (2d) of Torts

Assault is, more correctly, when the robber points the gun at your character but doesn't shoot; where the bully balls up his fists and threatens to hit the class geek, but doesn't; where the boss throws the stapler at the secretary but misses; or the driver who deliberately drives too close to your character the bicyclist, then laughs when the bicyclist swerves and falls.

The tricky part of assault is that:

1. The person committing the assault actually had to intend that the person would fear the contact;

2. The person did really fear they were about to be hit; and

3. The victim and perpetrator were close enough that it was actually possible.

For instance, let's say your character receives a phone threat. While the person making the threat intended to cause fear, and your character was really afraid, your character also wasn't anywhere near the danger. The phone threat is a crime, certainly, and may be another tort, but it's not assault.

Battery

A battery is any harmful or offensive touching. Your character doesn't have to be hurt at all to be the victim of a battery. The guy who gets in your character's face and yells while poking her in the chest is committing a battery.

Snatching something out of someone's hands or off their body is a battery. An example would be grabbing a necklace off your character's neck or knocking books out of their hands.

Elements of Battery

An actor is subject to liability to another for battery if:

A. He acts intending to cause a harmful or offensive contact with the person of the other or a third person, or an imminent apprehension of such a contact, and

B. A harmful contact with the person of the other directly or indirectly results.

Restatement (2d) of Torts

The problem in tort law with a battery where nothing but emotional distress occurred is the money damages. If the person was severely injured and incurred medical expenses, it's much easier to get that big bucks jury award. The incident of snatching the necklace may result only in "nominal damages,"[31] a personal injury attorney's worst nightmare.

Battery also requires an intent to either harm or cause fear of harm. The person who falls and bumps into your character (as annoying or clumsy as they may have been) is at most negligent, unless the fall was on purpose.

---

[31] Just like it sounds. A token award, like $1 or $100.

False Imprisonment

False imprisonment is a temporary detention against the person's will. It can be brief, such as a bear hug, or it can be lengthy, such as actually putting someone in prison. All false arrests are false imprisonment, but your character doesn't need to be arrested to be falsely imprisoned.

My favorite personal false imprisonment story was when I had a client who became sick during a deposition. I announced to opposing counsel that we were adjourning the deposition and it would have to be continued. It had gone on for hours. My opposing counsel announced we were not leaving, stood in front of the conference room doors, balled up his fists, and blocked our exit. This was not only false imprisonment, but assault. I asked him, while the court reporter was still typing, if he was blocking the door. I told him to move. He wouldn't budge. I figured I was about to be hit, but I reached behind him, carefully grabbed the handle, and pushed the door open so his receptionist could see and hear what was happening. He finally stepped aside. Does an attorney try to keep your character from leaving by blocking the door or putting her in a headlock?

Elements of False Imprisonment

An actor is subject to liability to another for false imprisonment if:

   A. He acts intending to confine the other or a third person within boundaries fixed by the actor, and

   B. His act directly or indirectly results in such a confinement of the other, and

   C. The other is conscious of the confinement or is harmed by it.

Restatement (2d) of Torts

False imprisonment doesn't have to be by physical force. Threats coupled with the ability or apparent ability to carry out the threats is enough. For instance, where the security guard accuses your innocent character of shoplifting and orders him to go into a back room to be interrogated or be arrested, that is probably enough to be false imprisonment.

The restraint does have to be total. That is, the victim can't be blocked from only one exit. If the stalker stands in the hallway, but your character can simply turn and go the other way and leave, it's not false imprisonment. If the stalker stands in the hallway and says, "Don't move or I'll shoot," and your character believes him, it's false imprisonment even if it turns out that the bump in the jacket was only his finger instead of a gun.

If the detention is under lawful authority, it will never be false imprisonment. Say a state attorney with a grudge against your character issued an arrest warrant without any probable cause. The officer character who arrests with the warrant won't be liable for the false imprisonment, but the state attorney will be.

There has to be an actual intent to confine or detain the person. The comic character who accidentally locks his friend in the bathroom won't be liable for false imprisonment. But if the comic character intends to lock his friend in but instead locks his boss in, the mistaken identity is not a defense.

If your character is willingly confined, it will never be false imprisonment. If they voluntarily commit themselves to a mental institution, make their friend lock them in so they won't eat chocolate, or participate in bondage[32], they can't sue for false imprisonment.

Unlike many intentional torts, the defendant can have good intentions and still be liable for false imprisonment. The friend who locks up the drug addict for their own good, the officer who really believes the arrest was justified, and the doctor who involuntarily commits the patient can still be held liable if the detention is found to be unlawful or unjustified.

If your character is confined but doesn't know it, such as being locked in their room while they are asleep, then there is no false imprisonment.

Slander/Libel

Both slander and libel are within the category of defamation of character. And it's really so much easier to call it defamation. Because if the count in the complaint is mislabeled "slander" when it's libel, or vice versa, then the case can be dismissed. Lawyers get these terms mixed up all the time, and laypeople even more so.

Here's the difference: Slander is defamation through the spoken word, and libel is defamation in writing.

---

[32] Mink-lined cuffs or not.

Whether a published statement is something for which your character can actually recover money depends on who made the statement, your character, and the circumstances of the publication. It's published if it's said to a third party. If it's only said to the person being insulted, it won't be defamation.

If the defamation is of a public figure, such as a celebrity, politician, person accused of a high-profile crime, then the speaker must have made the statement with malice in order to be liable. Malice would mean that the speaker character knew the statement was false or made the statement with reckless disregard as to its truth or falsity. If the defamation is by the media, then the plaintiff character will have to show that the speaker was negligent in making the statement. If the defamation is by a private person against another private person, then the speaker's good motives will be a defense.

Elements of Defamation

A. A false and defamatory statement concerning another;

B. An unprivileged publication to a third party;

C. Fault amounting at least to negligence on the part of the publisher; and

D. Either actionability of the statement irrespective of special harm or the existence of special harm caused by the publication.

Restatement (2d) of Torts

If the speaker's primary motive is ill will or to harm the victim, then they may be held liable for defamation even if they might otherwise be excused due to a "qualified privilege." A qualified privilege (the conditional right to say it) exists where the statement was made to people who have a legitimate interest in the information. An example would be investigating sexual harassment in a company.

Some communications are considered absolutely privileged, and can never be the subject of a defamation case, no matter how knowingly false. Statements made in a legal proceeding are absolutely privileged, which means they will never be considered defamation if said in a lawsuit. For example, if your character threatens to sue a witness in a lawsuit for defamation, they might be surprised to find out the witness is immune. Other matters that may be considered absolutely privileged could be statements made to police, to administrative agencies, and by government officials in the scope of their employment. I say "may" because this can vary by state and can be fact-specific. Does your character file a police report against a stalker? Does the state in your story protect him, or can the stalker sue?

Sometimes the law will assume that the defamation victim's reputation was damaged. Statements that are incompatible with the person's ability to work in their profession, and statements about criminal activity are within this category, called "defamation per se." Did someone falsely accuse your character of insider trading or of being a thief?

Otherwise, the person must prove money damages, which may not be easy. Unless they lost a job or suffered some economic damages, they may still not be able to win a defamation claim. Most employment cases involve statements inconsistent with the person's ability to work in their profession, so most are within the purview of "defamation per se." Did a neighbor falsely accuse your character of being gay? Even though it's false, your character may not be able to sue.

Statements of opinion are not defamation, such as, "I think he's a jerk." But simply saying, "In my opinion, he's a pedophile," doesn't cut it. It's still defamation if it's false. If it's true, it will never be defamation.

Trespass

Trespass to land is what we normally think of when we think of "trespassing." If your character enters property she doesn't own when she has no right to be there, she can be sued for trespass.

Trespass can also be on a person, but it's called assault or battery.

The most interesting development in the law of trespass is "trespass to chattels." Chattels is, simply, stuff. The textbook definition is that a person "intentionally uses or intermeddles with non-real estate property (called personal property) in the possession of someone else without permission."

Elements of Trespass to Land

A trespasser is a person who enters or remains upon land in the possession of another without a privilege to do so created by the possessor's consent or otherwise.

Elements of Trespass to Chattels
A trespass to chattels occurs when one party intentionally uses or intermeddles with personal property in rightful possession of another without authorization.
Restatement (2d) Torts

For example, trespass to chattels could be sneaking into a file room and peeking at files, or stealing something. The liability attaches if "the chattel is impaired as to its condition, quality, or value." Restatement (2d) of Torts at §218(b). So if the mere fact of looking at a file impairs its value, then there's a trespass. If, for instance your character sneaked a peek at the *Harry Potter* ending before the book was released, they trespassed on a chattel (the book) even though they didn't take it. When they thought up this tort, they never anticipated the computer age. While this was a little-used tort until recently, bulk emails have been the subject of suits over trespass to chattels. AOL sued bulk emailers for using them as a server, saying that the emails damaged AOL's reputation and goodwill, and won. In these cases, the chattel is the computer itself. Spyware, spam, viruses, and other computer nemeses can all constitute a trespass to chattels. Now computer trespass is also a crime, but since criminal law isn't our subject, it's important for you to know that your hacker character can be sued for their trespass into a corporation's computer network.

Privacy
Privacy is, simply, the right to be let alone. There are several types in tort law. I'll address a few of the more common.
- **False light.** This is similar to defamation, except that the statements can be true and still be the subject of a false light claim. The idea is that the statement had an implication of something false, such as linking your character to a murder by stating that they were in the room with the victim, without also stating that the character was attempting to save the murder victim.

Elements of False Light Invasion of Privacy
One who gives publicity to a matter concerning another that places the other before the public in a false light is subject to liability to the other for invasion of his privacy if:

A. The false light in which the other was placed would be highly offensive to a reasonable person, and

B. The actor had knowledge of or acted in reckless disregard as to the falsity of the publicized matter and the false light in which the other would be placed.

Restatement (2d) of Torts

- **Appropriation of likeness.** Another type of invasion of privacy can be "appropriation of a likeness," that is, using someone's picture in an advertisement or using someone's name without their consent. If the use involves someone who is newsworthy and the advertisement is a promotion of the news story, then it's allowed. If the person consents to the use then it's allowed, such as entering a name in a contest, then having the name announced as the winner. Does your character's Facebook picture end up on the front of a cereal box?

- **Right to publicity.** The right to publicity is recognized in many states, and applies to using a celebrity's image, such as face, look-alikes, voice or voice imitators, in a way that they normally would profit from. Vanna White sued Samsung and won when they advertised having a blonde robot flipping cards on a game show. Bette Midler sued Ford and won when Ford's advertising agency used a backup singer who could imitate her voice to sing a song after she turned them down for an ad. Does your rock star character get embarrassed when a toy company develops a bear that uses his catch phrase?

- **Intrusion.** Intrusion would include taking someone's property, such as letters, and using them; using telephoto lenses to photograph someone in public; harassing someone in public (think paparazzi); doing something on property that exceeds the consent to use the property (such as photographing a restaurant for a news story without permission); opening mail; or electronic eavesdropping. Your character can go through the murder suspect's garbage on the curb or in the dumpster because there's no expectation of privacy, but peeping in windows is a trespass.

- **Constitutional privacy protections:** Some states have statutory or constitutional privacy protections, along with the common law tort protection. How much privacy does your character have?

Intentional vs. unintentional torts

Assault, battery, false imprisonment, defamation, and trespass are intentional torts. The person committing an intentional tort does not need to intend the specific tort, the specific harm, or the specific victim. For instance, if your bully character intended only to scare his victim by swinging a bat and missing, but in the backswing hits another victim, he is liable for the battery on the other victim.

Negligence is an unintentional tort, which means that the person didn't need to intend to commit the careless act. Even if the elderly woman didn't mean to run the red light when she hit the gas instead of the brake, she can be negligent. If she gunned the car on purpose to hit a bicyclist, then she's crossed over into the area of intentional torts.

The reason it matters is that insurance won't cover an intentional tort as a general rule. Therefore, if the lawyer character wants to make sure that the million dollar insurance policy can cover the claim, they will always allege some sort of negligence. On the other hand, punitive damages can only be awarded for intentional torts.

If your character is engaging in an inherently dangerous activity, such as a tiger rescue preserve, then they are liable if the tort (the wrongful act) occurs, even if they were not at fault.

On the other hand, if the victim consented to the tort, or the tort was necessary, such as in a rescue to save the person's life (like using CPR), then the victim cannot complain about the tort.

If an employee is acting within the scope of their employment (while performing their duties, such as a janitor sweeping up garbage), then it is the corporation that will be liable for negligence, and the employee is probably immune from liability. Intentional torts, on the other hand, are almost never considered within the scope of employment. If the janitor took the broom and hit someone over the head with it to steal her purse, then the employer is probably not liable. That is, unless the employer knew he was likely to do that because he had done something similar before.

In *The Tortelli Tort* episode of *Cheers*, Carla jumps on a guy's back and starts beating his head against a bar. Sam pulls her off and stops it.

The guy says, "Listen Sam, you're legally responsible for the actions of your employees. You know that don't you?" Indeed, Sam admits she had "a history of being abusive with customers." Abusing customers wasn't part of her job duties. But Sam knew of her inclination to be abusive. While the guy ends up dropping the case in the story, that was a good thing for Cheers, because the company was probably liable. If an employer knows an employee is inclined to commit wrongful behavior, the employer will be liable.

Causation

What caused your character's injury? The test in tort law that will be the most difficult for juries and your lay[33] characters to understand is causation. The concept of "proximate cause" is complex.

- First, there is the "but for" test. But for the fact that your character ran the red light, she would not have been hit.
- Then there is "proximate cause," which decides who really is at fault. Whether or not the risk was foreseeable is the main question here, and is not so easy. For instance, if your character throws a rock at someone, it is foreseeable that someone may be hurt with the rock. But because injury was foreseeable, they are also liable if the rock misses, hits the tree branch behind the intended victim, and knocks a mango on the head of an innocent passerby.

  Proximate cause is an act which sets off a continuous sequence of events causing the injury. Think Dr. Seuss's, *Because a Little Bug Went Ka-Choo* where one bug's sneeze caused pandemonium in an entire town. But generally it is the last negligent act which causes liability.

- If someone else's negligence or intentional tort intervenes to cause the injury, then even if the first act of negligence set off the series of unfortunate events, the last actor will usually be the one liable. If your character who ran the red light and got hit by the other car then gets out to help the person who hit her, who is only shaken but not hurt, but is interrupted by the stalker ex-

---

[33] Slap yourself if you guffawed, you naughty person. Lay refers to "non-lawyer." A layperson is a non-lawyer.

boyfriend of the injury victim, who then shoots the shaken car wreck victim, who is liable? Well, even though the stalker would not have caught up with the victim but for the character who ran the red light, it is the shooter who is liable.

Who gets sued is not necessarily the person most at fault. A creative personal injury lawyer could come up with a way to sue if your character is a billionaire anywhere near an accident. Personal injury lawyers look for the best theory against the person with the deepest pockets, that is, the person with the most money. That will usually be a corporation or someone with insurance.

Damages

Damages are the money value of the losses that a judge or jury awards. The losses have to have been reasonably foreseeable, and not speculative. Compensatory damages are those that compensate for the actual loss, such as medical expenses and lost wages.

Damages can also be awarded for future injury that is reasonably certain to occur in the future, whether future lost wages, medical expenses, or emotional distress. If your character is a paraplegic, they are reasonably certain to have medical expenses and lost wages in the future. If your character is suing for a lost job, but they already got a better paying one, then they would only get back wages, not future lost wages.

- **Compensatory damages:** The most usual are out of pocket expenses, such as medical expenses, lost wages, auto repairs, and property damage. In personal injury, there is also a damage award for loss of a limb, loss of life, scarring, or other permanent injury. How does your jury figure out what an arm is worth? Juries face this question every day.

  But compensatory damages get harder when you add in pain and suffering, inconvenience, loss of enjoyment of life, mental and emotional distress, aggravation of an existing condition, and my favorite, loss of consortium (loss of a child's or spouse's companionship, solace, love, affection, and services[34] – ahem).

The trick to damages, besides how to place values on the invaluable, is to figure out which damages are unforeseeable or too speculative to allow. For instance, if the accident victim character lost their job and had to move out of town to a less expensive area as a result, the moving expenses probably weren't foreseeable. If a new business in your story is claiming lost profits when they've never seen a profit, then the lost profits are probably too speculative to calculate.

- **Punitive damages** are those which punish someone who commits an intentional tort to act as a deterrent to future bad behavior. Punitive damages are really hard to get and your lawyer character will have to show that the corporation whose product caused the injury either demonstrated a reckless disregard of human life or safety, such a lack of care that they were consciously indifferent to the consequences, entire lack of care showing a wanton or reckless disregard to the safety and welfare of the public, or such reckless indifference to the rights of others as to be the equivalent to an intentional violation of those rights.

Going back to the infamous McDonald's coffee case, the reason the testimony of their own people was so damaging was it showed that they knew about the dangers, knew other serious injuries had occurred, and they just didn't care. Say your auto company's risk manager character admits that they sat with a calculator and figured out how much the wrongful death cases would cost them. They realized that one out of ten thousand of their radiators would cause a chain reaction that caused a gas explosion. But the cost of replacing them was cheaper than the cost of paying the compensatory damages. Or where the company president character admits that he knew there was a chance the toy could catch fire, but really, it was going to happen so few times that he didn't think to make the $1.00 per toy fix.

---

[34] Yes. It's exactly what you're thinking. Which can make for some fun testimony. But it's also spousal services like the honey-do list, driving the kids to soccer, and picking up dry cleaning.

Punitive damages are why Pintos don't explode anymore, and why companies don't lock their workers in 120 degree sweat shops with no chance of escape from fires anymore. And yes, they can be abused. So they can cut both ways in your story. Your small business owner character can be ruined by punitive damages awarded when something utterly unexpected happened.

Chapter 11 – Cases About Employment

Your characters most likely spend half their waking hours on their job, so employment law may come up in your story. Employment law is one of the most interesting areas of law because it is in constant flux. It is a relatively new area of the law, and it changes constantly based upon the political winds and the changing judiciary. It's a great area to include in your story in big or small ways because almost everyone is an employee. I'll try to touch on some of the major areas of employment law.

The first subject is discrimination.

Discrimination

I'll bet you didn't know that small companies are allowed to discriminate based upon sex, religion, national origin, age, disability, and pregnancy. Federal law on most categories of discrimination only covers employers with 15 or more employees. The chart on this page tells which states have laws for which size employers. Is your sexually harassed character working for a small company? Is she surprised to find out she has no legal protection?

The exception to this would be race discrimination under 42 U.S.C. § 1981, which covers only race, color, ancestry, and ethnic characteristics discrimination, in hiring, promotion, discharge, hostile environment, and retaliation. It has no minimum number of employees. Does your small company think it's allowed to discriminate? Does your character surprise them by suing under this law?

STATES THAT DEFINE "EMPLOYER" AS HAVING DIFFERENT NUMBER OF EMPLOYEES THAN 15 *

States Covering Employers With 1 or more Employees
AK, MN, CA (sexual harassment only), MT, HI, ND, IN (age only),VT MI, WI

States Covering Employers With 2 or more Employees
KY (sex only), WY

States Covering Employers With 4 or more Employees IA,NY (pregnancy), KS, OH, NM, PA

States Covering Employers With 5 or more Employees
CA,ID, DC, VA (more than 5, less than 15)

States Covering Employers With 6 or more Employees
IN, NH, MA, OR, MO (2 for discriminating against for refusing to have abortion)

States Covering Employers With 8 or more Employees
KY, TN, WA

States Covering Employers With 10 or more Employees
GA (sex only)

States Covering Employers With 12 or more Employees
WV

States Covering Employers With 20 or more Employees
AL, AR, LA (25 for pregnancy)

* The ones using 15, mirroring the Federal law, are: AZ, CT (25 for seeking political office), DE, FL, GA (disabilities), KY (disabilities), MD, MN (disabilities), NC, NE (25 for age), NV, OK, SC, TX, UT

The vast majority of discrimination claims follow these guidelines:
Prerequisite to suit: The employee must file a charge of discrimination with the Equal Employment Opportunity Commission (EEOC within 180 days from the date of discrimination. Where the state has its own agency that takes discrimination charges, the deadline is 300 days. Did your character file her charge on time?

The EEOC will then decide to ask the parties if they want to mediate to try to resolve the problem, or send it straight to the investigator. Do your characters decide to mediate to try to settle their discrimination claim?

If it goes to the investigator, it goes to the bottom of a pile of thousands of cases. The investigator will send out a list of questions to the employer, along with the charge. The employer will answer in what is called a "Position Statement." The employer will be given extensions to respond, which can cause the process to drag on about a year. Your employee character could get impatient with waiting and start a website attacking her former employer.

Once the position statement is issued, the employee will then have to respond in 10 days. Whether or not the employee's attorney is hospitalized, on vacation, or kidnapped, the EEOC hates to give charging parties much of an extension, usually giving 7 – 10 days. For example your character could be vacationing in Hawaii and have to scramble to get their response in on time.

99.9% of the time[35], the EEOC then issues a "Notice of Dismissal and Right to Sue." This form says they are unable to determine whether or not there was discrimination. Employers' attorneys call this a "no cause letter" because EEOC used to make a finding in them that the employee did not have cause for the charge. What it really meant was that the evidence was disputed and they couldn't decide either way. It paves the way for a lawsuit. Does your character get a dismissal letter and think they've lost because they misinterpreted its meaning? How depressed are they?

The other possibility is a "cause" finding, which means EEOC found the employee had cause to bring the discrimination claim. The only thing most employees get out of this, besides a moral victory, is "conciliation." Conciliation used to be where EEOC told the employer they'd better try to resolve the case with the employee. Otherwise, it would go to the EEOC's attorneys, who might sue on behalf of the employee[36]. Now a cause finding has almost no meeting, and it has little practical effect. Conciliation rarely settles cases now, and EEOC takes on very few lawsuits for discrimination victims. Does your character get excited about their big win, only to find out they still have to sue?[37]

Suit for non-harassment discrimination: Most suits for non-harassment discrimination fall within the category of **"disparate treatment."** This means that the employee was treated differently than similar employees under the circumstances. In these cases, the employee will have to prove:

---

[35] Maybe a slight exaggeration, but I'm betting not by much.

[36] Employers know the chance of that happening are slim to none. EEOC doesn't even bother to make the threat much now because employers laugh if they do.

[37] The other thing the employee with a "cause" finding gets is a review by the EEOC's attorneys. EEOC can bring a lawsuit on behalf of the employee, but this almost never happens. They limit suits to areas where they want to make new law, crack down, or clarify an area of confusion in the law. Getting a case brought by EEOC is fabulous for the employee because it's free. Your character shouldn't hold his breath.

1. **They are in a protected category**. Protected categories are race, age, sex, religion, national origin, pregnancy, color (meaning shade), and disability.

2. **Different treatment.** They were treated differently than someone else in a different category under the same circumstances, or they were turned down for a position or promotion they were qualified for and it was given to a less qualified person. For example, two employees are Junior Managers. One is male, one is female. When the promotion comes up for Senior Manager, the male is given the promotion even though the female had more seniority and education. Is your character the only person in his position in the company? Does the employer argue there is nobody to compare him to so they can't have discriminated?

3. **Compliance with administrative requirements** (filing with the correct agency, such as EEOC).

The employer will have to come up with a so-called "legitimate reason" for the action they took. This doesn't have to be a good reason, just one motivated by something besides discrimination. For example, the employer in your story could claim the legitimate reason for firing an employee was that she didn't get along with supervisors.

Then, the employee has to prove that the "legitimate reason" was really "pretextual" (phony), and the real reason was discrimination. Was she failing to get along with her supervisors because they were sexually harassing her?

This "shifting burden of proof" could come up in your story if the lawyers are discussing what has to be shown at trial. This was originally established in a case your characters will refer to as *McDonnell Douglas*.[38] If the judge, the lawyers, or the characters are discussing the trial, this is the terminology you will need. Your character could be frustrated by how confusing the law has become.

A term you may use in discrimination cases is "mixed-motive." For instance, your employee character may have been fired for reasons other

---

[38] If you really must know, it's <u>McDonnell Douglas Corp. v. Green</u>, 411 U.S. 792 (1973). If you find a way to use the actual cite in a fiction book that gets published, I'd love to see it. I can't imagine how you can keep your editor from snoring over this.

than the pregnancy. If the lawyer proves pregnancy was a "substantial or motivating factor," but not the only factor, then it's still a discrimination case. Once the employee shows discrimination was a factor in the employer's decision, the employer will have to show that it would have made the same decision even if she weren't pregnant.

Confused? Trust me, your employee character will be, and chances are your lawyer character may be as well.

Disparate Impact

This applies to employment practices that seem neutral, such as promotional testing, height, weight, or education. Even though the practice appears fair, it may have a discriminatory impact on a particular group of people. This is how weight and height requirements were eliminated for police and fire departments, for example. Does your character have to sit for a promotional test? Do the males do much better than the females even though the questions seem OK? There may be hidden test biases that affect a woman's ability to test well on the exam.

These cases are proven through statistics. Once the plaintiff shows the practice has a negative effect on a minority, the employer can then show that the practice is "reasonably job related" and "justified by business necessity." Then the employee has to show the employer refused to use another means of doing the same thing with less of an impact. Here's an example. Your employer character gives a multiple choice test that seems neutral, except no Hispanics pass. The employer says, "but I have to be able to test the employees' knowledge before promotion." The employee then shows that essay tests would accomplish the same thing, but have less of an impact on Hispanics.

The prerequisites to a discrimination lawsuit are a nightmare. Some statutes require filing with an agency, some do not. Deadlines vary, agencies vary, and messing these up can cost the plaintiff the right to bring a lawsuit. Did your character lose the right to file a righteous case because she missed a deadline?

If your character has a discrimination case, you'll need to know the lingo. Title VII is what they'll call the most common federal law against discrimination. The main discrimination statutes other than Title VII are the Age Discrimination in Employment Act (ADEA), the Americans

With Disabilities Act (ADA), Equal Pay Act (EPA)[39], the Rehabilitation Act (basically, ADA for the federal government), the Older Workers Benefits Protection Act (OWBPA), and the Pregnancy Discrimination Act (which nobody actually refers to much because it's an amendment to Title VII).

Here are just some of the many differences among the statutes:

Statute	Employees	File with	Deadline for filing	Suit deadline
Title VII and ADA	15	EEOC[40]	180 days or 300 days (depends on state)	90 days from receipt of right to sue letter
ADEA and ADA	20	EEOC	180 days or 300 days (depends on state)	90 days from receipt of right to sue letter
EPA	15	EEOC, but not a pre-requisite to filing suit	180 days or 300 days (depends on state)	2 years, 3 if violation is willful

Some cities and counties have ordinances covering smaller employers. Does the employer tell your character that they are perfectly within their rights to discriminate against pregnant employees, for instance, only to find an ordinance to the contrary?

Federal employees have a completely different set of rules, under most of the same statutes. They have 45 days to see their "designated EEO counselor." This is a co-worker trained to handle intake and investigation of discrimination issues. There is an entire investigative process that circumvents the EEOC (agency that investigates discrimination claims). Does your post office worker fail to see his EEO counselor within 45 days and lose his ability to bring his discrimination case? Does he go postal?

Each statute also has different remedies, definitions, and requirements. Lawyers who dabble in this area of practice can get into

---

[39] Lawyers love to talk in jargon. But be careful. An employment lawyer's EPA is the Equal Pay Act. An environmental attorney's EPA is the Environmental Protection Agency.

[40] The United States Equal Employment Opportunity Commission, the agency that investigates most discrimination issues.

difficulties pretty quickly. Does your lawyer character get into trouble by dabbling in employment law and missing a deadline?

If your story involves discrimination, just remember, these cases are never simple or straightforward. Judges - federal judges in particular - love to throw them out. Many judges assume all these cases are frivolous. Does your character draw a judge that hates employment cases? Does your character get justice? If not, does he try to change the law? Or does he take out some vigilante justice?

Harassment

Believe it or not, harassment is not illegal. Many people wrongly believe that creating a "hostile work environment" is illegal. A boss can be abusive, arbitrary, and hostile, as long as it's not because of the employee's race, age, sex, religion, national origin, color, disability, pregnancy, or to retaliate because of whistleblowing. For example, your character might think she has a great case because her workplace has a hostile environment. She could be surprised to find out that working with jerks isn't illegal.

Sexual harassment

Sexual harassment where a supervisor hits on a subordinate is called "quid pro quo" sexual harassment, and it is illegal. This is where the supervisor either offers a job, promotion or job benefit in exchange for sexual favors, or retaliates against someone who declined sex. And yes, this still happens, more often that judges or juries believe. Is your middle-aged mom character surprised to be propositioned at work?

The other, more common, type of sexual harassment is creating a "hostile work environment" due to the person's gender. While this usually brings images of workplace porn and sexual jokes, these are pretty rare. Instead, women (or men) are singled out for treatment that people of the other gender do not receive. They can be nitpicked to death, stereotyped, disciplined unfairly, or made miserable. Is your female character being targeted for abuse by her supervisor? Does she realize she is being sexually harassed?

Harassment based on other protected categories is also illegal.

Other discriminatory harassment

Discriminatory harassment based on race, age, religion, national origin, etc. is illegal. This type of illegal harassment can go from the overt, such as use of the N-word or nooses hung over desks, to more subtle differing treatment. Does your character suspect the reason her boss hates her is because she is Middle-Eastern?

Reporting it

The Supreme Court, in its "infinite wisdom," says employees have to report harassment and give employers a chance to correct it if the employer has a written policy. Most employers have these now. Does your character realize she has to report it first before suing? Does your small company have no policy and lose a key defense?

The problem with reporting harassment is that many employers retaliate even though retaliation is illegal. Being afraid is no excuse. If your employee character quits without reporting harassment, they probably lose their case, no matter how bad it was.

Another major problem with proving sexual harassment is the confusing standard of "severe or pervasive."

Severe or pervasive

For harassment to be illegal, it must have been "so severe or so pervasive that it altered the employee's conditions of employment." Pervasive means that it had to happen a lot. Severe means one really bad incident is enough. Many judges and lawyers get confused and think both are required. Is your character raped? Does the judge think she has to have been raped multiple times for the employer to be liable?

> "It's called the nuts and sluts defense. Either you're nuts
> and you imagined it or you're a slut and you asked for it."

North Country, screenplay by Michael Seitzman, based on book by Clara Bingman and Laura Leedy Gansley, *Class Action: The Landmark Case that Changed Sexual Harassment Law*.

Other than some obvious fictionalization and ignoring "the rule"[41] at the end, *North Country* shows a pretty accurate picture of the

---

[41] "The rule" means witnesses can't sit in on a trial or deposition.

humiliation sexual harassment plaintiffs go through and how witnesses will lie to save their jobs.

> "Who is Sammy's father?"
> "I don't know who Sammy's father is."
> "Is that because you've had so many sexual partners?"
> "Objection. The Plaintiff's sexual history is irrelevant, Your Honor."

In this passage, *North Country* shows how, still today, a sexual harassment victim's sexual history can be used against them to cause humiliation. In federal court and many state courts, this type of questioning is barred, but some states still allow it.

The current legal climate is that sexual harassment is pretty much legal. Behavior such as rape, groping, calling at home for dates, overt sexual comments, and other drastic behavior is dismissed as an "isolated incident" excusing employers from liability.

Sexual orientation

It is still legal in this country to discriminate and harass on the basis of sexual orientation. The states that make it illegal are: California, Connecticut, Hawaii, Illinois, Maine, Maryland, Massachusetts, Minnesota, Nevada, New Hampshire, New Jersey, New Mexico, New York, Rhode Island, Vermont, Washington, and Wisconsin. Cities and counties that sometimes pass ordinances against sexual orientation discrimination.[42] Is your character living in South Carolina, where it is legal to fire him for being gay? Does he have to hide his orientation, or does he fight for equality?

Maybe your story can change this sad state of the law.

Disability discrimination

Disability discrimination is illegal under the Americans With Disabilities Act, the Rehabilitation Act, and most state anti-discrimination laws. These cases are not easy. By the last statistics I heard, 90 - 96% of these

---

[42] A great source for the current state of these laws is http://www.lambdalegal.org.

cases were losing in Federal Court. Unless the disability is obvious, many people, including judges, believe employees are faking to get special treatment. Does the employer in your story think your client is faking her fibromyalgia?

A disability must "substantially limit a major life activity," other than work, and thousands of cases exist where lawyers disagree over what this means. Congress recently passed amendments to fix some of the problems with the way the courts have interpreted the ADA. The employee must be able to perform all the "essential duties" of their job, either with or without an accommodation (something that helps them do their job). Does your employee character think he should be granted light duty after being injured? Is he fired because he could no longer perform all his job duties?

Accommodations your employee character might request could be larger computer monitors, special desks or chairs, changed hours, or other accommodations not deemed a hardship to the employer. Does the employee in your story ask for a changed work schedule, only to have her employer claim the schedule would be a hardship?

Employees who don't fit in the "disabled" category are still protected from discrimination if the employer regards them as disabled, or if they have a history of a disability. Does your injured character get fired because the employer thinks they're going to be too slow after an injury?

Both mental and physical disabilities count. Does your character with severe depression ask for time off to adjust his meds? Does the employer hold the depression against him?

Even if the new legislation manages to fix some of the problems with this law, disabled employees will continue to have rough time in the courts, I predict. Until attitudes change, 90% of these cases will likely still be thrown out of court.

Workplace bullying

While general harassment is legal in all states, some states have pending legislation on workplace bullying but right now it's legal. It will be up to the states to decide what bullying is and when it will be illegal. Since 2003, 13 states have introduced workplace bullying laws, none of which have passed.[43] Is your character bullied? Do they have to take tae kwon do classes instead of going to a lawyer?

Whistleblowing

This is a great, sexy area for any story. Whistleblowers make great heroes or victims. Remember *Silkwood,* the true story of a nuclear power plant whistleblower? In general, whistleblower laws prohibit employers from terminating, and sometimes from disciplining or harassing, an employee because they objected to, reported, or refused to participate in illegal activity. Did your character witness something illegal? Some whistleblower laws also protect employees who report unethical or improper activity, but most require that there be a violation of a law. Does your character report something unethical (but not illegal) and mistakenly think the law protects them? The remedies, requirements, and administrative hoops are the subject of entire treatises, so I'll just draw your attention to some of the major whistleblower laws to jump start your research.

The federal whistleblower laws are:

The OSHA–enforced laws: govern protection of workers for complaining to employers, unions or the Occupational Safety and Health Administration (OSHA), or other agencies about unsafe or unhealthy conditions, some public safety hazards, and some securities fraud. Does your employee find something unsafe for workers?

Sarbanes-Oxley: is the most famous whistleblower law. It protects employees of public corporations who report violations of securities rules and laws. Does your character find out the CEO is lying about revenues to shareholders?

The Whistleblower Protection Act: protects Federal employee whistleblowers.

Military Whistleblower Protection Act: protects whistleblowers in the U.S. military.

False Claims Act (FCA): enables a citizen to file a lawsuit in on behalf of the U.S. Government for fraud by businesses that use federal funds. "Qui Tam" (lawyer talk for this type of case) prohibits employer retaliation for

---

[43] A site that tracks the status of these laws is http://www.bullybusters.org/.

attempting to report fraud against Medicare, Medicaid, FDA, GSA, HUD, USDA, U.S. Postal Service, NIH and the military, but not the IRS. Does your character uncover millions in Medicaid fraud?

States that have whistleblower protection laws:

California	Maine	New York
Connecticut	Michigan	North Carolina
Delaware	Minnesota	Ohio, Oregon
Florida	Montana	Rhode Island
Hawaii	New Hampshire	Tennessee
Louisiana	New Jersey	Washington

Does your character think he's protected if he reports some illegal activity? Does he live in Kansas where he's not protected?

States that offer whistleblower protection to government, but not private employees:

Alaska	Louisiana	Oklahoma
Arizona	Maine	Oregon
California	Maryland	Pennsylvania
Colorado	Massachusetts	Rhode Island
Connecticut	Minnesota	South Carolina
Florida	Missouri	South Dakota
Georgia	Montana	Tennessee
Hawaii	Nevada	Texas
Illinois	New Hampshire	Utah
Indiana	New Jersey	Washington
Iowa	New York	West Virginia
Kansas	North Carolina	Wisconsin
Kentucky	Ohio	

OSHA enforces these anti-retaliation laws:

- Occupational Safety & Health Act (OSH Act), 29 USC § 660(c)
- Surface Transportation Assistance Act (STAA), 49 USC § 31105
- Asbestos Hazard Emergency Response Act (AHERA), 15 USC § 2651
- International Safety Container Act (ISCA), 46 USC App. § 1506
- Energy Reorganization Act of 1974 (ERA), 42 USC § 5851
- Clean Air Act (CAA), 42 USC § 7622
- Safe Drinking Water Act (SDWA), 42 USC § 300j-9(i)

- Federal Water Pollution Control Act (FWPCA), 33 USC § 1367
- Toxic Substances Control Act (TSCA), 15 USC § 2622
- Solid Waste Disposal Act (SWDA), 42 USC § 6971
- Comprehensive Environmental Response, Compensation, and
- Liability Act (CERCLA), 42 USC § 9610
- Wendell H. Ford Aviation Investment and Reform Act (AIR21), 49 USC § 42121
- Sarbanes-Oxley Act (SOA), 18 USC § 1514A
- Pipeline Safety Improvement Act (PSIA), 49 USC § 60129

Defamation

Is a former employer saying something false about your character? Some states have statutes protecting job references, but even then, the employer generally cannot give out knowingly false information. A false statement in your story that the employee was a thief, child molester, or sexual harasser, made when giving a reference, will probably not be protected. Defamation is covered in more detail in **Chapter 10 p. 106-08.**

States with statutes protecting job references from defamation claims

California (sec. 12940)	New Jersey (34:19-1)
Florida (Fla. Stat. §768.095)	New York (CLS Exec sec. 296)
Hawaii (663-1.95)	North Dakota (sec. 34-02-18)
Louisiana (La. R.S. 23:291)	

Unemployment

If an employee worked for the company long enough, and this varies by state, then if they are terminated without cause, they will probably qualify for unemployment, which is what the state pays employees who have lost their jobs. A cruel employer could contest your character's unemployment claim to keep them even more destitute.

Unemployment hearings are also a great way to obtain free discovery for their discrimination case. Because both the employers and employees are frequently unrepresented, unemployment hearings could be used for comic relief, tension, or exploration of the facts in your story. For example, your lawyer character could get to ask questions of the HR person without the company lawyer being present. The HR person could admit they were looking for a younger image when they fired your 50-something character.

Unemployment hearings are conducted by referees or other government employees who may not even be lawyers. If you're bored with judge characters, maybe you could have an unemployment referee in your story instead. They hear all kinds of interesting sob stories about people being fired and the excuses employees give. Remember *Night Court*, the comedy about the motley characters who got arrested at night? How about doing your own screenplay with a new twist and calling it *Unemployment*?

Wrongful Termination

Most states are "at will" states[44], meaning that an employee can be fired for any reason or no reason at all. No good reason or cause is required. Only two states, Arizona and Montana, require that employers terminate only for "just cause." Does your story show a brave politician trying to get some rights for employees in her state?

Is your character shocked at the concept of "at will" employment? Did he believe that his employer had to have a reason to fire him? Did he find out the truth - that the employer can walk into the office in a bad mood and fire people with few consequences? Did your employee character get fired because his boss didn't like his shoes that day?

Most states have some exceptions to the at-will doctrine, such as prohibiting retaliation for making worker's compensation claims, objecting to illegal activities or discrimination, testifying under subpoena, and serving on jury duty. Did your character get fired for testifying at an unemployment hearing?

Your characters' rights will almost entirely depend on what state they are in, so some research on that state's laws will lend authenticity to your story.

---

[44] Many people (including lawyers) will say, quite knowingly, that their state is a "right to work state" instead of "at will," as if this means the employer can terminate for no reason. This makes no sense, does it? "Right to work" means the employer cannot require the employee to join a union to work. "Right to work" states are AL, AZ, AR, FL, GA, ID, IA, KS, LA, MS, NC, ND, NE, NV, OK, SC, SD, TN, TX, UT, VA, and WY.

Non-compete Agreements

Enforcement of non-competition agreements, that is, agreements not to work for a competitor for a particular period of time, varies wildly from state to state, from Florida, which allows the most restrictions on employees, to California, which allows none.

Employers can't form monopolies by preventing competition, so they have to be careful if they want to limit their employees after they leave. Non-compete periods usually range from 6 months to three years. The employers have to show that the restrictions are reasonable and made for a legitimate reason.

If the customers voluntarily follow the employee to their new job without being solicited, many courts will allow this. However, employees may not be allowed to ask customers to follow. Does your hairdresser character want her clients to follow her to a new salon? Does the old salon sue to stop her?

Non-compete agreements are also considered valid if there is some other legitimate reason, such as protection of a confidential process or trade secret. An example of this would be where your character has access to the company's secret computer program. If information is publicly available, then the employer can't protect it. Did the employer put the so-called secret program on their website? It's not secret anymore then. Or, for example your salesperson character could generate leads through cold-calling the phone book. Because anyone can get a phone book, the employee will probably be allowed to use it.

Some states allow employers to present these agreements post-hire, and the employee has to either sign or lose their job. Most states, fortunately, don't allow such agreements without additional money or benefits. Does your employee move from Minnesota to Florida thinking she has the job of a lifetime, only to have to sign a two year non-compete? Does her job last a month because the employer just wanted to take a competing sales person out of circulation?

NON-COMPETE AGREEMENTS BY STATE

States With Statutes Authorizing Enforcement:
Connecticut (Chapter 35 (trade regulations) and Chapter 916 (injunctions)
Florida (Fla. Stat. 542.33)
Georgia (O.C.G.A. 10-1-372 (deceptive trade practices))

Hawaii (H.R.S. sec. 482B-2 (trade regulation))
Indiana (Burns Ind. Code Ann. 24-1-1 (trade regulation))
Kansas (K.S.A. Chapter 50 (unfair trade and consumer protection))
Louisiana (Title 23 (labor and worker's compensation))
Michigan (Mich. Comp. Laws 445.766)
Minnesota (Minn. 325C (uniform trade secrets))
Missouri (431.202)
Oklahoma (15 Okl. St. sec. 219A)
Oregon (Ore. Rev. Stat. 51 sec. 653.295)
South Dakota (S.D. Codified Laws 53-9-11)
Texas (Tex. Bus. And Com. Code sec. 15.51)
Wisconsin (Wis. Stat. 103.465)

States With Case Law Authorizing Enforcement:

Arkansas	Maine	Ohio
Arizona	Nevada	Pennsylvania
District of Columbia	New Hampshire	Virginia
Idaho	New Jersey	West Virginia
Illinois	New Mexico	Wyoming
Iowa	New York	
Kentucky	North Carolina	

States That Don't Allow Non-Compete Agreements to be Enforced:

Alabama	Delaware	Tennessee
California	Massachusetts	
Colorado	North Dakota	

States That Only Allow Restrictions Regarding Clients With Whom Employee Had Personal Contact:
Nebraska

States That Have Not Decided On Enforceability:

Alabama	Montana	Utah
Maryland	Rhode Island	Vermont
Mississippi	South Carolina	Washington

Sources: www.ama-assn.org/ama/upload/mm/46/model_physician_aug.pdf; **American Medical Association Annotated Model** *Physician Employment Agreement; Lexis legal research)*

If a former employer character wants to torture the ex-employee, usually a letter goes to the new employer threatening them with a lawsuit. The employee is fired, then has to fight the agreement with no money. Few can afford to fight these restrictions.

While non-compete agreements can be properly used to keep an employee from walking off with a confidential customer list, a secret process, or truly trade secret information, they are often used these days to force involuntary servitude.

For example, your employee character could feel trapped in a humiliating job, but feel afraid to leave because he has a non-compete agreement. Is it enforceable? You could have a new employer decide to stand by him and fight, or have him left to fight alone and penniless.

Trade Secrets/Confidentiality

All states prohibit theft of trade secrets by employees. What is a trade secret depends on the state. Almost all states protect secret processes. Many protect customer lists. If information is public, it will not be a trade secret or confidential. For instance, if the customer list is on the company website, it's not secret. However, the KFC secret recipe is, without a doubt, a trade secret.

Thriller stories frequently involve employees walking off with secret formulas, lists, or company documents. If a competitor would pay for it, then it will probably be a trade secret. It will be important for the story, and the level of tension, to make sure you let the reader know that there are potential consequences for stealing trade secrets, such as a lawsuit, money damages, and in some cases even criminal penalties.

Wiretapping/Privacy

The plot device most likely to get me to turn off the TV or shut the book is having someone secretly record a conversation. Doing so illegally is a crime. The question if you want to use this device is whether the state has "one party" or a "two party" consent. One party consent simply means that, if any party to the conversation agrees to be taped, it's okay. Two-party consent (also called all-party consent) requires every person who participates in the conversation to agree to be taped.

Here's how these laws apply to your story. In a two-party/all-party consent state, the employee cannot go into a disciplinary interview with a secret recorder to tape the employer's sexual harassment or admission of bribery. In a one-party consent state, as long as the employee is in the conversation they can tape it. Your character can't stand in the shadows and tape a conversation they aren't participating in to eavesdrop on what is being said. Placing a bug or hidden tape recorder in a room and leaving is always illegal unless there is a court order.

The following states require consent of all parties to a conversation (two party consent) in order for the conversation to be recorded:

California	Maryland	New Hampshire
Connecticut	Massachusetts	Pennsylvania
Delaware	Michigan	Washington
Florida	Montana	

Illinois — By statute. However, in practice the courts of Illinois allow most individuals and businesses, not law enforcement, to use one party consent.

States that allow one party to consent are:

Alaska	Maine	Oregon
Arkansas	Minnesota	Rhode Island
Colorado	Mississippi	South Carolina
District of	Missouri	South Dakota
Columbia	Nebraska	Tennessee
Georgia	Nevada	Texas
Hawaii	New Jersey	Utah
Idaho	New Mexico	Vermont
Indiana	New York	Virginia
Iowa	North Carolina	West Virginia
Kansas	North Dakota	Wisconsin
Kentucky	Ohio	Wyoming
Louisiana	Oklahoma	

Federal law, the Electronic Communications Privacy Act, has some exemptions. If a phone line is recorded for customer service, for use as a 911 line, or by court order, then the recording may be allowed. However, there are many suits over these exceptions.

So don't make me turn off your show or shut your book. Please get this right.

Family and Medical Leave

If an employer has 50 or more employees, and the employee has worked at least a year, they are entitled to up to 12 weeks of unpaid leave. Leave can be for a serious medical condition of themselves or their spouse, child or parent, birth of a child or adoption. They can also be entitled to go to doctor's appointments or treatments for such conditions. They must be reinstated to the same or an equivalent position on their return. Does your father character get fired after taking time off for the birth of his child?

Does your employer lull the employee character by encouraging or allowing a longer leave? Are they fired when they get to 12 weeks and one day? Are they allowed to return from leave and get reassigned to the midnight shift? If the position has been the subject of a real job elimination, the protection ends. Is your character told her job was eliminated while she was on maternity leave?

Conclusion

Because employment law varies from state to state, and is mostly by statute, it constantly changes. It is the source of dispute and struggle, a dream for writers. Because your characters spend half of their waking hours at work, these workplace struggles can be used for an infinite variety of purposes in your stories.

Chapter 12 – Professional Malpractice
Medical Malpractice

"The very best ever is 'The Verdict' because the overall feel of what the Plaintiff's attorneys do and how difficult it is, how defense lawyers work, preparing experts, was well done. Unfortunately, none of my opposing counsel has ever sent a female associate to seduce me. Of course, I don't look like Paul Newman either."
-**Frank Glinn**, Miami medical malpractice attorney.

Medical malpractice is a great story subject. Doctors are highly educated and highly paid. They make people wait hours to see them. They double book patients, act like demi-gods and make mistakes. On the other hand, they are heroic, mostly got into medicine to try to help people, and save lots of lives. There's a good reason why there are dozens of medical shows on TV. Few areas of the law involve life and death as much as medical malpractice.

There is no question that top medical malpractice lawyers make more money than you or I. Some of my best friends are medical malpractice attorneys. They are also the reason why, whenever I fill out my intake in a doctor's office, when I have to list "profession," I write "Employment attorney," instead of just "attorney." Doctors hate these guys, and some refuse to treat their families or them. Does your medical malpractice attorney character have trouble finding a doctor to treat her? Does she have to lie about her profession?

Med mal (lawyerism for medical malpractice) cases are extremely, extremely expensive to bring to trial. Scott Turow, in *Personal Injuries* gets the sheer gut-wrenching cost of these cases just right when he writes a wonderful story about lawyers gone bad and a corrupt civil justice system.

> "We didn't have anything to take care of, not to start
> with. Mort and I had been bumping along on workmen's

comp and slip-and-fall cases. Then about ten years ago, even before Brendan was appointed presiding judge over there, we got our first real chance to score. It was a bad-baby case. Doc with a forceps treated the kid's head like a walnut. And it's the usual warfare. I got a demand of 2.2 million, which brings in the umbrella insurer, so they're underwriting the defense. And they know I'm not Peter Neucriss. They're making us spend money like there's a tree in the backyard. I've got to get medical experts. Not one. Four. O.B. Anesthesia. Pedes. Neurology. And courtroom blowups. We've got $125,000 in expenses, way more than we can afford. We're into the bank for the money, Mort and me, with seconds on both our houses."

Medical malpractice is controversial, and that's what makes for great drama.

Medical malpractice can consist of many types of claims. The issue is whether the doctor or medical professional used the skill and treatment that is considered acceptable under the circumstances. These cases, by necessity, require another professional to testify that the doctor, hospital, or nurse did not do things correctly. Could your character be a doctor who testifies against another doctor? Is he still popular at the golf course? The only exception is in cases of obvious mistakes, such as leaving a piece of equipment inside a surgical patient. In those cases, the doctrine of *res ipsa loquitur* (the thing speaks for itself) means expert testimony isn't needed. Can you think up something unusual, like an MP3 player, that was left in your character?

Here are some of the major areas where you may explore malpractice in your story.

- **Drugs:** Examples of areas where there might be a malpractice claim involving prescription drugs would be where your doctor character prescribes the wrong dosage of medicine, uses it for an improper purpose, or fails to disclose that the treatment is experimental. Pharmaceutical companies can be liable for failing to warn of dangers or side effects. Did the drug cause your character to run down the street naked?
- **Diagnosis:** Incorrectly diagnosing a condition or failing to diagnose is a huge area for medical malpractice claims. Did your

character's x-ray show a malignant tumor the doctor didn't notice? If too much time passes and the cancer isn't treatable anymore by the time the tumor is discovered, there may be a malpractice claim.

- **Informed consent:** If the medical professional fails to disclose all the risks, or worse yet, to obtain consent to a procedure, then the claim could be for negligence or even battery. Did your character remove the leg of a patient admitted for swine flu?

- **Breach of warranty or contract:** Most doctors aren't dumb enough to promise results. If the plastic surgeon in your story promises perfection and fails to deliver, then they could be held liable for a breach of warranty or breach of contract as well as negligence.

- **Licensing/training:** If a doctor or hospital in your story fails to assure that staff are properly licensed or kept up training, then they may be liable for the failure if someone is injured as a result. Your story could have an unlicensed nurse wreaking havoc by giving the wrong medicines and treatments.

- **Impairment:** If a medical professional is impaired, whether by drug/alcohol use or some physical or mental impairment that kept them from performing competently, there may be a negligence claim or even recklessness that could result in punitive damages. Does your surgeon character drink before operating? Think of Jack on *Lost* and how the writers have used his addictions to add dimension to one of the best series on TV.

- **Understaffing:** If a hospital or nursing home does not have adequate staff to handle the patient load, they could be liable if someone suffers an injury under the inadequate care. Did your chief nurse warn the nursing home owner she needed more staff? Did the Alzheimer's patient wander off while they were busy dealing with a heart attack patient?

"If Dr. Salisbury did not puncture the aorta with the rongeur, could not have, as you have testified, what might have caused it to rupture?"
"We call it spontaneous aortic aneurysm."

In *To Speak for the Dead*, Paul Levine shows that he researched the medicine and the law when he wrote his legal thriller on a murder connected to a medical malpractice case. Medical malpractice litigation involves expert testimony on the specifics of the medicine. You don't need to be an expert, though, when you write. A good place to start on your medical research is another book in this series, *Body Trauma, A Writer's Guide to Wounds and Injuries* by David Page, M.D. Dr. Page details much of what you need to know about how the body works and what can go wrong with your character's body.

Expert testimony makes medical malpractice cases expensive. Other factors can make them even more difficult.

Many states have passed tort reform bills that relate to medical malpractice claims. Some shorten the statute of limitations or create pre-suit requirements. Your character could miss a key deadline or fail to jump through a pre-suit hoop and end up with the client's case dismissed even if medical malpractice occurred. Some require an expert to certify that negligence occurred as part of the suit. Many states cap (set a maximum amount that can be awarded for) non-economic damages (such as the value of the person's life or limb, loss of enjoyment of life, pain and suffering, and loss of consortium). Many states cap punitive damages, and some cap all damages. For example, your character could be stuck with a $100,000 maximum award for her daughter's care when the hospital turns her into a quadriplegic. How does she afford the millions in medical treatment? Does she end up seeking government assistance?

Medical Malpractice Jury Instructions
A. Negligence (physician, hospital or other health provider):
[Negligence is the failure to use reasonable care.] Reasonable care on the part of a [physician] [hospital] [health care provider] is that level of care, skill and treatment which, in light of all relevant surrounding circumstances, is recognized as acceptable and appropriate by similar and reasonably careful [physicians] [hospitals] [health care providers].

B. Negligence (treatment without informed consent):
Negligence is the failure to use reasonable care. Reasonable care on the part of a [physician] [(name other health care provider specified in '768.46(3))] in obtaining the [consent] [informed consent] to treatment of a patient consists of . . .

... when issue is whether consent was obtained irregularly
obtaining the consent of the patient [or one whose consent is as effective as the patient's own consent such as (describe)], at a time and in a manner in accordance with an accepted standard of medical practice among members of the profession with similar training and experience in the same or a similar medical community.

... when issue is whether sufficient information was given
providing the patient [or one whose informed consent is as effective as the patient's informed consent, such as (describe)] information sufficient to give a reasonable person a general understanding of the proposed treatment or procedure, of any medically acceptable alternative treatments or procedures, and of the substantial risks and hazards inherent in the proposed treatment or procedure which are recognized by other [physicians] [(name other health care providers)] in the same or a similar community who perform similar treatments or procedures.

Florida Standard Jury Instructions

Tort reform

Tort reform is the push to end or reduce medical malpractice lawsuits. Some tort reform applies to all tort claims, but much more applies to medical malpractice claims. Tort reform is hotly contested and provides a platform for rich, emotional writing on both sides. It is a wonderful story topic.

Your story could be the doctor who is faced with a malpractice suit that is emotionally devastating to him; a low income hospital that faces economic ruin as a result of a malpractice claim; a family demolished by the loss of a beloved member; or of a patient suffering from a ruinous injury.

This is a controversial topic, and it's important to define the pro and con elements

Arguments in favor of tort reform

Tort reform advocates argue that there are too many frivolous lawsuits clogging up the courts and creating a system that is too expensive. Insurance costs are too high. Plaintiff's attorneys make too much money.

Doctors have to shut down their medical practices in areas with expensive insurance or runaway plaintiff's bars. Is your doctor character struggling to keep her practice open?

Advocates for tort reform also claim that government has the power to regulate doctors, and if government chooses not to do so, the courts should not be allowed to create laws by imposing new rules.

Tort reform supporters point to high punitive damages awards (money awarded to punish the evildoer), high non-economic damage awards (money for things like pain, suffering and emotional distress), and high attorney's fee awards as evidence of a "runaway system." For example, the hospital in your story could get smacked with a multi-million dollar judgment for emotional distress and punitive damages judgment for leaving the surgeon's reading glasses in a patient's intestines. Do they have to cut down on some staff as a result?

Because losing plaintiffs will rarely have to pay the attorney's fees of the winning defendant, tort reform advocates argue that there is little disincentive for filing frivolous suits. This could be the doctor in your story who faces huge legal fees.

Tort reform advocates argue that tort claims cause job losses, which in turn cause reduced safety and more injuries to the populace. For instance, your character could be hurt because the hospital in your story had to cut back on nursing staff after a big injury case. Maybe the hospital had an outdated x-ray machine that malfunctioned because they couldn't afford to replace it.

Arguments against tort reform

Tort reform opponents argue that there are adequate safeguards in the current system. They believe that juries are the fundamental basis of our justice system and should be trusted. Judges have the right to set aside outrageous verdicts, and judges can throw out baseless suits before they get to trial. Your character could have his big verdict against a hospital for operating on the wrong hangnail thrown out because the judge thought too much money was awarded.

Litigants and their attorneys can and are sanctioned for filing frivolous suits, and do have to pay the fees and costs of these cases. There are also many states that have settlement statutes that allow defendants to make formal settlement proposals. For instance, a defendant might offer to pay $5000 to settle the case in your story, and if the plaintiffs turn them down and win only $3000 at trial, may still have to pay the fees of the defendant even though they won. Does the lawyer in your story win the trial and then face having to pay tens of thousands of dollars in fees and costs to the other side?

Opponents also argue that the tort system is the only way to keep companies, doctors, and professionals on their toes, resulting in higher levels of safety for all citizens. The argument is that capping (setting maximum amounts on) damages and other tort reform measures actually increase the dangers and number of deaths and injuries. For example your character could get injured because the hospital cut back on nursing staff to save money after tort reform was passed because the hospital figured the staff cost more than the money that could be awarded.

Opponents also point to the Ford Pinto case, the notorious case where the accountants did the calculation of the cost of paying wrongful death cases versus the cost of fixing the car, without calculating the value of a human life. By capping non-economic damages like pain, suffering and emotional distress, and capping punitive damages, they say, companies will go back to making such callous statistical analyses instead of deciding that one lost life is not worth the profit. For instance, the lawyer in your story could uncover the accountant who calculated the value of a human life. Does anybody try to stop the accountant from testifying on who gave his instructions?

Legal and Other Professional Malpractice

Legal and other professional malpractice claims are handled under the general principles of negligence that were discussed in Chapter 10.

Examples of legal malpractice would be missing a deadline, failing to inform of a statute of limitations, failing to secure witnesses or evidence, failing to disclose or withdraw due to a conflict, or acting to the detriment of a client. Did your character's lawyer miss the deadline to file her lawsuit?

In extreme examples, the lawyer can be found to have breached the client's trust and confidence (fiduciary duties), or committed fraud, such as stealing client money or self-dealing. Did your client character win a big judgment only to have the lawyer steal all the money?

Professional Malpractice Jury Instructions

Reasonable care on the part of a [lawyer] [architect] [(name other professional)] is that degree of care which a reasonably careful [lawyer] [architect] [(name other professional)] would use under like circumstances. Negligence may consist either in doing something that a reasonably careful [lawyer] [architect] [(name other professional)] would not do under like circumstances or in failing to do something that a reasonably careful [lawyer] [architect] [(name other professional)] would do under like circumstances.

Florida Standard Jury Instructions

Other professionals frequently sued for malpractice are architects, accountants, and contractors. Did the architect in your story design a building where all the windows fell out?

Plaintiff's attorneys first look to see whether the professional has liability insurance. Many, such as architects, have insurance requirements. If there is no insurance, most plaintiffs' attorneys will decline the case because they won't have a readily available source of funds to pursue. Did the contractor who built the staircase that fell and killed two people get away without a lawsuit because she didn't have insurance? How do the families get their justice?

Any professional malpractice case can make for a great story. The single mom whose house collapsed when it was built badly; the corporation facing ruin because the accountants colluded with a corrupt CEO; or the professional who faces ruin due to the malpractice claim all make for great drama in a story.

Chapter 13 – Business to Business

"[Writers] are in the business of entertainment and are therefore unable to realistically show the hundreds if not thousands of hours that go into preparing a complex commercial case for trial. I always think of [litigation] as a jigsaw puzzle with pieces missing, a scavenger hunt where there is no list of what you are looking for and a game of chess in which the other side is using a variety of legal weapons to frustrate your discovery process. Good lawyers work very, very hard. They labor over the details. They are meticulous. The process is a marathon in which there are a series of sprints. The media can show flashes of all of these aspects but cannot capture the entirety of the process."

-Michael Higer, Miami Commercial Litigation Attorney

Trademark/Copyright

This should be near and dear to every writer's heart. Stealing creative work should be punishable by death, but all our justice system can do is offer money.

Trademark

A trademark is used to identify a unique product or service. It can be a logo, design, name, word, phrase, symbol, or other indication. An individual, organization, business or other legal entity can have a trademark. A service mark identifies services instead of products (for example, a law firm name).

Your character could coin a name that becomes a verb. Does their e-book company's name, Zerbit, become the verb for downloading books? Do they become flattered when people start to say they have to zerbit the bestseller, only to realize that they're letting their trademark be lost? If the name becomes synonymous with the product or service, then the trademark has become "genericized" and it is no longer enforceable.

Keeping a trademark from becoming "generic" is why you can't call all tissue "Kleenex," and you can't say you Xeroxed something. If you do this in your story, expect a letter from a high-priced lawyer. Some famous trademarks that lost their enforceability are Allen wrench, Aqualung, aspirin, cellophane, crock pot, dry ice, escalator, granola, heroin (originally registered by Bayer as a pain reliever!), jungle gym, kiwi fruit, lanolin, laundromat, linoleum, spandex, tabloid, touch-tone, thermos, trampoline, yo-yo, zip code, and zipper.

A trademark is determined by the concept of "first use," that is, the entity that first used it in the marketplace. Did your character come up with a great name only to find out they weren't the first?

Types of marks include:
A. **Fanciful or inherently distinctive marks**. These would be made-up words, like Haagen-Dazs, Microsoft or Lexis that had no meaning before they were used.
B. **Arbitrary marks.** Words that are used out of normal context, such as Apple for a computer or Comet for a cleanser.
C. **Suggestive marks.** These suggest the product or quality of the product, and appeal to the consumer's imagination. Mustang for a fast car, Coppertone for a sun product.
D. **Descriptive marks.** These are terms that connect a dictionary definition and a product or service directly related to that meaning. These terms are not registrable or enforceable unless they are connected to some registrable phrase. Red isn't a registrable term because it describes a color. A purely descriptive name could become registrable if it becomes recognizable for a particular product or service through years of advertising, such as "Holiday Inn."
E. **Generic trademarks.** These are the least likely to be registered. For instance, "subs" is a common term for submarine sandwiches. Miami is a geographic indicator that anyone can use. But, "Miami Subs" is a registrable name. "Red Apple" would not be registrable in connection with actual apples.

Emblems of nations (like the U.S. flag), the Olympic Games, and some other organizations are not going to be registrable. That means they are protected by law from being used to represent commercial products. If you want to have your character organize the Beer Olympics, you'd better also have them get a letter from the International Olympic Committee telling them to stop.

Factors in determining confusion

1. The similarity of the respective parties' marks;
2. The similarity of the parties' marketing methods;
3. The similarity of the parties' channels of distribution for their goods or services;
4. The level of sophistication of the prospective purchasers for the respective parties' goods or services, and the degree of care used in purchasing such goods or services;
5. The source-designating strength of the mark sought to be protected;
6. Where the second-comer's goods or services differ from the first-comer's, the likelihood that prospective purchasers of the second-comer's goods or services would expect the first-comer to have expanded its marketing or sponsorship into the second-comer's field;
7. The extent of overlap in the parties' geographic markets and whether the prior user is known by its mark in geographic markets in which it does not actually sell its goods or services;
8. Whether the second-comer intended to copy the first-comer's mark in order to cause confusion or deceive; and
9. The degree of actual confusion that has surfaced as a result of the two parties' respective marks.

Restatement (Third) of Unfair Competition

Deceptive names, immoral/scandalous names, and names of living people who don't consent also can't be registered. Does your character try to call his bookstore Rowling's Reads? He can expect a lawsuit.

Of interest to my readers will be that names of characters and series titles can be registered. While copyright law doesn't protect titles, trademark law may well protect them if they are distinctive. One-shot characters and titles aren't registrable unless they have a secondary meaning. *Magic Treehouse*, one of my daughter's favorite series, is certainly registrable. For instance, if you have a main character named Sneadly Snellman, his name can't be registered. But if your book becomes a series, or the Sneadly Snellman doll becomes a hit, then you can trademark the name. *Harry Potter* is, needless to say, a trademark. An individual book title is not registrable as a trademark or a copyright. Your story can have the same name. The story itself is, however, copyrighted. But a series title, like *Star Wars*, will be registrable as a trademark.

While a mark does not have to be registered, it does have to be registered before it is enforceable under the law. Does your character try to sue for trademark infringement before he's registered the mark? He'll lose if he sues under the trademark statutes. There are common law trademark protections that can be used to protect unregistered marks. If the mark was used first, then it is protected even if it hasn't been registered. However, it must be registered before it can be enforced.

Once there is a trademark, whether registered or not, the owner can demand that it not be infringed, that is, they can keep someone else from using it.

There are two general ways that a trademark can be infringed.

- **Confusion:** This is where the consumer thinks the product is associated with the owner of the original mark, or if the consumer believes they are purchasing the other product. For instance, your character couldn't register, "Koka-Cola." Although actual confusion isn't necessary, it would certainly be evidence of the likelihood of confusion.

- **Dilution:** If a mark is so strong that it is associated in the public mind with a particular product, it is enforceable even where there is no likelihood of confusion. For instance, your character couldn't open a company called, "Pepsi Computers."

The big statute in the U.S. on trademarks is the Lanham Act, which tells how to register marks, what is registrable, and how to enforce against trademark violations. Individual states also provide trademark and service mark registration and protection. Does your character have a mark that is known only locally? They might have some protection under their state's laws.

Remedies include mostly injunctive relief (prohibiting the use of the mark), money damages in some cases, and attorney's fees (my favorite).

If your character is starting a new business, you may create a problem for her by calling the business, "Computers 'R Us,"[45] or "Kentucky Fried Frog Legs." That can start lots of trouble for her. Or, have her start a company with a unique name and then have a giant come in and steal it. Does she have a restaurant called Liver and Onion Palace, but it's purely a local joint? A national chain could come in, use the name in other states, register it as a national trademark, and try to make her stop using it. Could she afford to fight them?

Copyright

Ah, the writer's favorite law. Just by writing something, it is copyrighted. It doesn't have to be registered. If your character sat at the computer and typed the words, they own a copyright. And copyright infringement has criminal penalties along with financial penalties. A recent example of fictional copyright infringement is the television show *Californication.* A teenager stole David Duchovny's novel and claimed it as her own. Now, you'll have to watch to see what he does about it. But I desperately want to see the girl go to jail in the show. Or is that purely a writer's bias?

All creative works are protected. These include paintings, drawings, plays, novels, broadcasts, software, music compositions, recordings, choreographic works, photographs, architectural works, and non-fiction works. What is not protected under the copyright laws is any "idea, procedure, process, system, method of operation, concept, principle, or discovery, regardless of the form in which it is described, explained, illustrated, or embodied in such work." As an example, say your character writes a story using voodoo curses and posts it in his writer's colony for critique. Another member of his writer's colony is also writing a children's story about voodoo curses. The idea of using voodoo curses in a story is not copyrightable. This is why you see so many copycat TV series.

The expression of an idea is what is protected. For instance, a scientist who discovers the cure for the common cold who writes down the process for the cure can protect the writing. The process is not

---

[45] Never, ever, mess with the "Toys 'R Us" people. They don't play, in spite of their fun-sounding name.

copyrightable (it is probably patentable). Did your character discover the cure for all cancers? She can patent the process and copyright the paper where she writes about it.

Similarly, facts will never be protected in copyright law. The president's birth date, the elements of a negligence claim, the way copyright law works, will never be copyrightable. However, my description of how copyright law works will be protected.

A great example of a protected copyright is, "Happy Birthday to You," a song that everyone sings. If a restaurant sings it to patrons or if you use it in your book or movie, you will have to pay a royalty to a subsidiary of AOL/Time Warner. It brings in over $2 million in revenue per year.

Copyrights generally last the life of the author plus either 50 or 70 years. There are circumstances that extend this.

Copyrights can only be transferred from the creator in writing signed by the creator. That is why your publishing contract may transfer your copyright to your publisher. Otherwise, you own it.

Defenses to Copyright Infringement Claims

Even if your character owns a copyright, there are certain ways it can be used legally. If they sue to enforce, they may encounter defenses to their claims.

Fair Use

"Fair use" basically means that part of the work is quoted, with attribution, for scholarly purposes or commentary/criticism. Fair use is often misunderstood. Even if you think you're doing an author a favor by mentioning the work, you may well not be protected by "fair use." Examples of fair use are, "quotation of excerpts in a review or criticism for purposes of illustration or comment; quotation of short passages in a scholarly or technical work, for illustration or clarification of the author's observations; use in a parody of some of the content of the work parodied; summary of an address or article, with brief quotations, in a news report; reproduction by a library of a portion of a work to replace part of a damaged copy; reproduction by a teacher or student of a small part of a work to illustrate a lesson; reproduction of a work in legislative or judicial proceedings or reports; incidental and fortuitous reproduction, in a newsreel or broadcast, of a work located in the scene of an event being reported." 1961 *Report of the Register of Copyrights on the General Revision of the U.S. Copyright Law.*

The fair use doctrine is why I can use quotes of books and movies as examples of how authors got particular parts of the civil justice system right. If, however, the use damages the value of the work, such as giving away the *Harry Potter* ending or quoting the most important part of a work such that it makes the purchase of the work no longer necessary, that's not fair use. When a newspaper quoted only 300 words from Gerald Ford's memoir, but they gave away the reason he pardoned Nixon, which is why everyone was buying the book, it wasn't fair use.

Factors in determining fair use
1. The purpose and character of the use, including whether such use is of commercial nature or is for nonprofit educational purposes;
2. The nature of the copyrighted work;
3. Amount and substantiality of the portion used in relation to the copyrighted work as a whole; and
4. The effect of the use upon the potential market for or value of the copyrighted work.

U.S. Copyright Act.

Failure to defend the mark

Unlike trademark law, you don't need to defend your copyright to keep it. You can't lose it just because others are using it. You don't have to put a copyright symbol on the copyrighted material or register it. Failing to do either is not a defense to its enforcement.

Derivative work

If your story is based on another work, it's a "derivative work" and will belong to the original copyright owner. A good example of this is fan fiction. You can parody a work, but you can't do the sequel. Even if you don't make money from the use, it can still be a violation.

Remedies

Remedies for copyright violations include statutory damages, actual damages and attorney's fees. However, statutory damages and attorney's fees are available only if the work is registered with the copyright office within 3 months of publication. Otherwise, only actual damages and profits are recoverable. Did your character lose the right to get some money damages because he failed to register his copyright when he self-published?

If you're writing about a writer, and many of us do, or about an artist, chef, choreographer, or architect, copyright law may come into play.

Patent

Patent law protects inventions. The idea itself is not patentable – it must be a completed product or design.

There are two types of patents: **utility patents and design patents.**

Utility patents are for anyone who invents or discovers a new and useful machine, process, composition of matter, article of manufacture, or a new useful improvement on any of the above. Does your character invent a personal helicopter? A **design patent** is for the invention of a new, original, and ornamental design for an article of manufacture.

Utility patents last twenty years from the date of application, and begin when the grant is made. Design patents last fourteen years from the date of application, and also begin when the grant is made. Right now it takes over two years to process a patent application, which is why you see so many new products marked, "patent pending." Is your character's patent about to expire? Or are they waiting for the patent to get approved?

To be patentable, the invention must be "non-obvious." Obvious changes can be things like substitution of materials or change in size. For instance, your character can design a bigger diaper bag because hers just won't hold enough diapers for twins. But the size change is probably obvious, a logical extension of a design that exists. She'd have to come up with a truly clever innovation to earn a patent.

The U.S. Patent and Trademark Office processes patent applications. This is a complicated process that involves multiple reviews, challenges, amendments, and very specific scientific requirements. While having an attorney is not mandatory, unlike applying for a trademark or copyright, patenting is not for the faint-hearted. In the television show *Medium*, the main character's husband, Joe DuBois was working with an investor to launch his new design. The writers managed to use the patent process to create an interesting storyline.

Also unlike trademark and copyright, patent holders can prevent others from making, selling or using the patented item. Even if the infringer independently came up with the invention, they will not be able to use it. Did your character invent a fantastic product that is worth billions, only to be the second in line for the patent? If they believe they invented it first, then they may be able to challenge the patent application and prove they thought of the design first.

In an infringement action, that is, an action claiming someone else is using the patented item, the patent holder can get injunctive relief (a court order to stop the use), along with damages and attorney's fees. If sued, your character could claim that the patent was not original, was obvious, or is not otherwise allowed to be patented. If your character was second in line for the patent, she may have to argue that her beloved invention was obvious or unoriginal.

Let's say your character is an inventor who invented a flying car that only uses solar power. He could have his invention stolen on the way to file with the patent office and have someone else claim to be the first inventor. Patents can be useful in your sci fi, medical fiction, legal drama, or middle grade novel about a science fair.

Unfair Trade Practices

False advertising, deceptive pricing, price fixing, falsely representing quality or newness, or disparaging a competitor's product by false means can be unfair trade practices. For instance, if your character the water bottler claims that his water is the only water that is lead-free in the country, another water company or a consumer could sue for unfair trade practices.

States that have passed the Uniform Deceptive Trade Practices Act
Colorado (1966 Revision) - §§ 6-1-101 to 6-1-115

Delaware (1964 Act) - Del. Code, Title 6, Subtitle II, Ch. 25, Subchapter 3, §§ 2531-2536
Georgia (1966 Revision) - §§ 10-1-370 to 10-1-375
Hawaii (1966 Revision) - §§481A-1 to 481A-5
Illinois (1964 Act)
Maine (1964 Act)
Minnesota (1966 Revision) - §§ 325D.43 to 325D.48
Nebraska (1966 Revision) - §§ 87-301 to 87-306
New Mexico (1966 Revision) - N.M. Statutes, Chapter 57, Art. 12
Ohio (1966 Revision) - Ohio Revised Code, Title 41, Ch. 4165
Oklahoma (1964 Act) - 78 §§ 51 to 55
Oregon (1966 Revision) - §§ 646.605 to 646.656

The Uniform Deceptive Trade Practices Act describes what rights consumers and other businesses have if they are the victim.

Your character wouldn't necessarily have to sue if they were the victim of unfair trade practices. They might file a complaint with the Federal Trade Commission, which enforces the Federal Trade Commission Act. It also enforces antitrust laws, that is, laws which prevent companies from preventing fair competition.

Examples of practices that keep competition from being fair are:
- **Collusion:** basically, ganging up with competitors to the detriment of consumers. A good example of this is when major league baseball owners tried to restrict players' salaries. Cartels like OPEC, essentially, groups of the same type business that get together and make decisions about how to run the industry, are illegal in this country because of collusion issues. Do your characters who own cloning factories try to set the pricing for replacement hearts so they can keep the French cloning factories out of the U.S. market? If their customers suffer higher prices or lower quality, they may have the U.S. Attorney's Office knocking on their doors.
- **Dividing territories:** competitors split up by region. If Ford decided it would take the area east of the Mississippi and let General Motors have west, that would be illegal.
- **Conscious parallelism:** an unspoken agreement among competitors that they all raise prices when one does.

- **Bundling:** when you have to buy several products together or get none at all, that's bundling. Sometimes this is legal, particularly when consumers get a choice as to whether to buy the bundled products or individual products. Making the purchase of one popular product conditional on purchasing another, less popular product is "tying," which is illegal. For instance, Microsoft was sued for tying Windows to Internet Explorer. That's why your publisher can't tell Barnes & Noble that they have to buy your book if they want to buy *Harry Potter*. Voiding a warranty if the product is serviced outside the company is illegal tying in many states.

- **Monopolies:** forcing competitors out through unfair practices. Just because only one business can survive in a particular market doesn't make it a monopoly. But doing things like predatory pricing to keep competitors out will be illegal. Is your card shop owner character being undercut by a huge chain store to try to put him out of business? Think *You've Got Mail*, and you get the idea.

- **Bid-rigging:** competitors agree not to bid against each other, agree to hire each other as subcontractors to share the spoils, bid deliberately high or with inappropriate terms, or take turns being the successful bidder. Does your architect character bribe a competitor not to bid on a building design?

- **Price-fixing:** just what it sounds like. Competitors set minimum prices, agree on set prices, agree to set advertisements at the same price, or limit discounts. Do your donut shop owners get together once a week to decide on the price of a glazed?

- **Predatory pricing:** the opposite of price fixing. Setting prices artificially low to drive competitors out. If Lexus decided to corner the car market by selling cars for $100 until all other car manufacturers were out of business, that would be illegal.

Your small business owner character could face any of these anti-competitive behaviors when a big competitor comes into town. Or your grandma consumer character could be victimized as a consumer by this type of practice. Your big CEO could be falsely accused of trying to drive others out of the market, causing him to become an alcoholic. See – you didn't think antitrust law could be fun.

Contract Law

Life is full of contracts. Almost every major life decision involves a contract of some sort. There are entire courses in law school on contracts, so this is just a brief discussion. But your characters will frequently encounter a contract of some sort in your story. Some basic knowledge of how contracts work will go a long way toward assuring the authenticity of your story.

Contract Basics

A contract is created when there is an offer, an acceptance of that offer and consideration.[46] In order for a contract to be enforceable, it does not have to be in writing. That being said, having it in writing sure helps. Lawyers like to say that a verbal contract is worth the paper it's written on. But then, we're easily amused.

Offer: An offer is an expression of being willing to enter into a contract on certain terms, so that all that is required is an acceptance. An oral offer could be your kid character saying, "I'll shovel your sidewalk for $7." Presentation of an employment contract, real estate contract, or other written contract is usually an offer, because all that needs to be done is acceptance by signature. A job offer is usually not a contract.

Acceptance: Acceptance means that all the terms are accepted. If the offer was, "I'll shovel your sidewalk for $7" then a simple, "OK," will do. The kid can start shoveling, and upon completion they have to be paid. If the response was, "I'll think about it," or, "maybe," that's not an acceptance. If the response is, "OK, if you'll do it for $5," that's a counteroffer. A counteroffer is a rejection of the offer, not an acceptance.

Counteroffer: This is a new offer that can be accepted or rejected. If rejected, the original offer does not have to be put back on the table. That is one of the perils of negotiation. If the character who said, "I'll think about it" tries to accept two days later, the offer can be withdrawn. For instance, if there was a blizzard and prices went up, the kid's offer might not be good anymore. Similarly, if the homeowner said, "No," and then the blizzard occurs, they can't go back and say, "Now I accept" and have an enforceable contract.

---

[46] I have to dedicate this section to Professor Richard Hausler, the best teacher I ever had. Bar none.

An offer can be accepted anytime before the offer is withdrawn. If the offer is accepted by mail, the acceptance is effective as soon as it is placed in the mailbox. This is called the "mailbox rule." If the offeror withdraws the offer after the acceptance is mailed but before he receives the acceptance, there is still a contract. Did your character get a book contract in the mail? Does she sign it right away, mail it back, then have the publisher call to change their minds? She still has a contract.

Consideration

Consideration is, simply, both parties changing their circumstances. This change of circumstances can be anything of value to the parties. For a contract to purchase an item, the price is the consideration. Both parties have to get something out of the contract, and it must be something of value.

Consideration can also be refraining from some action. I'll agree not to sue you if you'll pay me money is one of the most common agreements in law – it's called a settlement agreement. Continued employment can also be consideration for a contract. Does your character offer her assistant that he can stay in the job for another month if he organizes her files? She may have a valid contract, so she might not be able to fire the assistant after only a week.

What Isn't Consideration

Gratuitous promise is one without consideration, and is not enforceable. For example, if your character promises her deadbeat uncle that she'll give him her computer when she gets a new one, he can't enforce that if she doesn't. But if she tells him she'll give him her computer if he paints her house, it's enforceable.

Past consideration is no consideration. If it already happened, such as a character saying, "I'll give you my computer since you already painted my house," it's not enforceable.

Pre-existing duty also won't constitute consideration. "I'll finish writing my book by the contract date if you book me for the Maui Writer's Conference," sadly, won't work where you already are under contract to finish. Even if your editor makes such a promise, you can't enforce it. That's really so depressing, isn't it?

On the other hand, if your editor says, "I'll only pay you $1 for your manuscript now that I know you've turned down all the other publishers," when you already signed your six figure contract, they won't get away with it. You can still produce the manuscript, and when they publish it, they have to pay the amount in the contract, not the $1.

The exception is where the parties modify the contract. Most contracts say they can only be modified in writing signed by both parties. If that's what they say, then that's the only way they can be modified. Otherwise, they can be modified by agreement of both sides. Does the employer in your story tell your character he works for minimum wage now? Not if your character has a contract saying otherwise.

Defenses to the Formation of a Contract

Defenses to the formation of a contract (meaning the contract isn't valid) include being a minor, insanity, impairment such as Alzheimer's or Parkinson's that would cause dementia, duress (but it has to be pretty extreme, literally having a gun held to the head or something about as bad), undue influence (taking advantage of a position of power over the person, such as parent/child, doctor/patient, attorney/client), and statute of frauds (certain kinds of contracts must be in writing signed by both parties). For example, did your character sign a contract to buy fifty $100 light bulbs while she was in the beginning stages of Alzheimer's? Her family could try to get her out of it by saying she wasn't mentally sound to enter into such a contract.

Defenses to the Enforceability of a Contract

Defenses to the enforceability of a contract (the contract exists, but can't be enforced) are:

- **anticipatory breach** (you breached first)
- **mutual mistake** (we both thought the cow was barren, but when I realized she was pregnant, I changed my mind about selling for that price)
- **frustration of purpose** (for example, the government enacts a law after the contract to buy auto parts from China is executed saying buying from China is now illegal)

- **impossibility** (the house under a purchase contract burns down so it no longer exists to be bought)
- **illegality** (contracts to commit a murder)
- contracts to pay **illegal gambling debts**
- contracts to create a **monopoly**
- **unconscionability** (almost impossible as a defense these days, but basically, that the contract shocks the conscience of the court)
- **accord and satisfaction** (basically, a settlement of a disputed amount, such as an agreement after a lawsuit).

Rescission (asking the court to declare the contract no longer exists) is a way of voiding a contract, but the person seeking rescission has to restore the other party to their original position. If, for instance, your character finds out after he buys his dream boat that a grisly murder happened on it, he might be able to rescind the sale, but he has to give the boat back in its original condition. Fraud, concealment, breach of warranty, and material misrepresentation may cause rescission to be allowed.

Damages

Remedies for breach of contract are specific performance (forcing someone to comply, which can't be done where a personal service is involved), damages, and attorney's fees only if the contract provides for them. Does the owner of the haunted boat try to force your character to buy it anyhow?

Damages allowed for a breach of contract are those only those that "naturally flow" from the breach. Damages that are speculative (you'd have to guess how much they are or how they were caused) won't be recovered. For instance, your character might assume he wouldn't have had to pay interest on his credit cards if he'd only been paid the money he was owed for repairing cars for a wealthy businessman. But it's unlikely that the court will allow the credit card interest as damages. There are too many other reasons why your character might not pay off his cards

Partnership Disputes

Unlike shareholders and officers in a corporation, partners are generally held personally liable for judgments against a partnership. There are multiple types of partnerships.

Limited partnerships: This is where limited partners have little say in the management, but their risk is only up to the amount of their investment. Limited partnerships have at least one general partner, which handles the day to day business decisions and bears personal liability for debts. The limited partners may be the primary investors, and the general partner the one investing mostly time and effort (sweat equity), or the general partner can be the primary investor. The best friend partners in your story could appoint one of them to be in charge. Do they agree with how she is running things?

General partnerships: Where partners share equal say in the management and decisions, and share equal liability for the debts. They are less common due to the advent of limited liability partnerships, but they are more informal to set up and are frequently used among friends or in new, less sophisticated businesses. For instance, your best friend characters could form a general partnership, then disagree on how to run it. Maybe one partner wants to buy a building and the others prefer to rent.

Limited liability partnerships: The limited liability partners aren't liable for the actions and debts of the other partners. They are structured the same as either a general partnership or limited partnership. Does one of the partners in your story get sued?

Partnership law varies from state to state. The partnerships are governed by both the partnership agreements and the laws of the particular state where they were formed. If one partner in your story is sued, the partner's interest could end up owned by someone new. Or the partners may disagree on day-to-day management and end up having to split up the partnership. How well the partners set up the partnership will determine what happens if the business dissolves or one partner needs to sell her interest.

Corporations

If you have a business in your story, its structure will determine how it operates, who makes the final decisions, and who will be liable if something goes wrong.

Corporations are business entities that have separate identities from their owners. They can sue and be sued, sign contracts, and basically do what individuals do. The shareholders are not personally liable for the debts of the corporation. For example, your character could get frustrated when he learns he can't sue the individual shareholders who made the decision to sell the product that killed his daughter. Only the company will be liable for the corporate wrongs.

Types of corporations

Corporations can be for-profit or not-for-profit. Each has its own rules. Does your character run his not-for-profit company as her personal bank account? He may lose his not-for-profit status and have to pay tax penalties.

A closely held corporation: Privately owned by stockholders, and is not traded on the stock market. Publicly held corporations are traded on the stock market. Closely held corporations have more control over the path the corporation is taking and can make decisions more quickly.

Publicly held companies: These have more capital and have more shareholders, so the risk is spread around more. Public companies are also more highly regulated than close corporations. Do your characters decide to go public with their company? They could make a killing by selling off stock in the stock market. But then there are huge numbers of shareholders making the decisions, and lots of government regulation. Do they regret losing the control they once had?

Limited liability companies: These are a sort of hybrid between partnerships and corporations, and provide advantages of both. They tend to be smaller companies that want more control, yet the insulation a corporate structure provides.. Does your character have to sue a limited liability company? If she knows the individual owners have lots of money but the company itself is small, she may want to sue the owners but be unable to. How does that affect her ability to recover money?

Private companies: Unlike public companies, these are subject to "piercing the corporate veil," that is, holding stockholders personally liable for corporate debts. If corporations neglect the formalities such as meetings, mix private and corporate expenses, or take other actions that negate the corporation as an entity, then the shareholders can be held liable for corporate wrongs. For instance, your shareholder character could get sued personally after the company decided to stop holding meetings. She could be on the hook for the corporate debts even though she thought she was safe by being a shareholder.

Officers and directors are also shielded from personal liability in all but a few instances. They can be personally liable for actions they took outside the scope of their duties, for personal motivation, and for some statutory claims like Fair Labor Standards Act. The company president in your story could, for instance, write a letter accusing his former secretary of being a thief because she turned him down for a date.

Shareholder Disputes

Shareholders may have claims against stockbrokers. These claims involve improperly manipulating the client's account or selling stocks that are inappropriate. Did your character lose money at the hands of his stockbroker?

Some of the claims your character could have are:

- Churning: buying and selling stocks too frequently to increase the broker's commissions to the detriment of the client.
- Unauthorized trading: trading without permission.
- Misrepresentations: guaranteeing results or misrepresenting a stock.
- Insider trading: using information from an inside source in the corporation.
- Risky investments: putting a client into stocks that are inappropriate for their level of risk. For instance, retirees need very safe investments, whereas younger investors may want higher risk for the chance of higher returns.
- Margin trading: margins are basically trading based on loaned money. The problem occurs when the customer didn't get a full explanation of the risks of margin trading.

Stockholder characters can also have claims against corporations, particularly public companies, for securities fraud. These claims could include overstating revenues or assets, or understating costs or liabilities. Failing to disclose potential losses such as major lawsuits in the works, or falsely inflating the value of shares, can result in major liability. Did your character buy a hot-sounding stock only to find out the CEO knew about a lawsuit he failed to mention? Did your character's company end up in bankruptcy because they didn't disclose potential losses? Or did the company go belly up when it finally had to produce real dollars? As we saw from Enron, securities fraud can put officers, directors, and even lawyers in jail, as well as result in massive judgments. Do any of your characters end up in jail over securities fraud?

While complaints about stockbrokers are almost always litigated in an arbitration, securities fraud claims against a corporation by stockholders are resolved in federal court. You can control the setting in your story by deciding what issues you raise. There are also state laws that protect shareholders, and require disclosure of records on request, compliance with certain corporate forms, and other shareholder protections.

Sarbanes-Oxley, the common name for the Public Company Accounting Reform and Investor Protection Act of 2002,[47] was enacted after the rash of scandals in companies such as Enron, WorldCom and Tyco. This law offers layer upon layer of protections, compliance mechanisms, and penalties, along with whistleblower protection. Does your story show how the new laws work to protect whistleblowers?With Enron and other corporate scandals, securities can be a great subject for your story. This isn't an easy subject, so you'll need to do some research to get it right.

---

[47] A great start for researching this is the Securities Exchange Commission website, which has a nice FAQ section about Sarbanes-Oxley. SEC is the entity that enforces this complex law.

Chapter 14 – Person to Business

Individuals in your story will likely have to deal with businesses. If their business transactions don't go smoothly (and if you're writing a story about it, odds are they didn't) you'll need to know some of the legal issues that come up when people go up against companies.

Landlord/Tenant

Landlord-tenant law deals with property rental. Each state has its own requirements regarding landlord-tenant law. Much of the relationship depends on the contract, that is, the lease. What principles might your lawyer character apply to residential landlord-tenant situations? I'll try to touch on a few.

Warranty of habitability

The "warranty of habitability" means that the landlord warrants the property is in good condition and will keep it in compliance with housing codes. It can be express (written) or implied. If the lease addresses who is responsible for repairs and how the tenant will notify the landlord of the need for repairs, the tenant needs to follow it. Most states have made it illegal for landlords to try to get tenants to waive the right to have the premises maintained. If your character has water coming from their ceiling, this may apply to them.

All tenants have the right to a certain level of safety and decent conditions. Broken plumbing, leaks, safety hazards, structural issues, common areas, and electricity issues all fall within this category. Where your character can run into difficulties is if they are poor and can't afford a lawyer to help, don't know their rights, or the parties dispute what is required.

As an example, your landlord character could encounter tenant-caused problems such as cleanliness, destruction, or failure to notify the landlord in time to stop damage from becoming major. Even if the landlord can pass the bill back to the tenant, it can be a problem if the tenant has no money to pay. If a tenant causes hazardous conditions in common areas or that leak over to other apartments, the landlord could have to foot the bill or be fined even though it wasn't his fault.

Lock-outs

I see this all the time in stories, and it really bugs me. The tenant shows up one day and is locked out. The landlord has kept their stuff or thrown it out on the sidewalk. That's illegal without a court order. So are threats, turning off heat, cutting off electricity or water, and other coercive measures.

Eviction notices

The landlord must first give written notice that the tenant is in breach of the lease. If that breach is failure to pay, then they may be able to post a notice on the door and give three to five days notice to pay up or get out. If it's something else like having pets or too much noise, there is usually either a lease provision or statute that tells how much notice has to be given and allows time to correct the problem. Some states allow "unconditional eviction notices" – that is, no opportunity to correct the problem. These are usually allowed in situations of illegal activity, repeated violations, or damage to the premises. Even if your landlord character has a drug dealer on the premises, the tenant can't be locked out.

Illegal activity on the premises can make for an interesting dilemma for your landlord character. For instance, the drug dealer can't be locked out, but just having them on the premises can subject the landlord to forfeiture of the property under the criminal "corrupt enterprises" laws (meaning the government can take property that was used in a criminal activity). If the tenants pay up after they owe rent, the landlord can get into trouble accepting money used in a criminal enterprise. If your landlord character calls police to get the dealer out, will they lose their building? The injustices of the criminal forfeiture laws could be the subject of a great story.

Tenant defenses to eviction

A tenant fighting eviction isn't helpless. He can bring up claims that the landlord didn't follow the lease, that the premises weren't kept up, or claim the landlord didn't follow the right legal procedures. The eviction case can last weeks or even months if the tenant fights it.

Taking possession

Even after the notice has been given, your landlord character still can't just throw the tenant out without some legal process. Generally, they have to file suit and get a "writ of possession" (the court order allowing them to evict). Even then, the landlord can't just toss the tenant's things out. A law enforcement officer will serve the writ of possession or court order, and even then the tenant may have time to vacate before they are forcibly removed.

Retaliation

If the tenant complains to a fair housing authority, a zoning entity, or other government agency about improper or illegal conditions, the landlord cannot retaliate by giving a notice to vacate or other coercive measures.

Fair housing

It is illegal to discriminate in housing due to race, age, sex, religion, national origin, color, having kids, being pregnant, or disability. There are specific requirements for senior-only housing (55 and older). It is also illegal to discriminate against someone for associating with a protected individual. For disabilities, the landlord will have to comply with laws requiring accessibility of the common areas and of the dwelling unit. The fair housing laws are enforced through the U.S. Department of Housing and Urban Development, the state agencies in states that have their own fair housing laws, and by civil lawsuits. Does the landlord refuse to rent to your characters because they're expecting a baby?

Does a wheelchair-bound character find herself unable to get into the apartment? Disability discrimination is the area most subject to litigation these days in the fair housing arena. Landlords can be hit with high bills regarding accessibility requirements, or may be ignorant of the requirements. If your landlord character doesn't know the law, their no-pets policy may illegally prohibit Seeing Eye dogs. Or, a tenant may be unaware of their rights and face hardships as a result.

Consumer Protection

While I addressed deceptive advertising and other deceptive practices in Chapter 13, there are many more consumer protection laws on the books. Many states have laws protecting consumers relating to specific practices. For instance, in Florida there are laws relating to price-gouging after hurricanes. It wouldn't make sense for Iowa to have that law. Regional differences require different types of consumer protection. Can you think of a problem in your story region that may have a law associated with it? Is there a law against price-gouging ethanol in Iowa after floods?

The big battleground right now is "federal preemption." Congress may pass a law on a topic that either accidentally or purposely overrides stricter state law. Sometimes the courts determine that a similar federal law preempts (trumps) state laws. Consumer protection isn't the only area where preemption is occurring. While this is also happening in employment law, big lobbying dollars are being spent to try to override strict state consumer protection laws. Your character's state could have a great consumer law. If there's a similar federal law, then your character could end up with the state's law thrown out.

Some examples of areas where consumer protection laws exist are:
Food: While the Food and Drug Administration has some safety requirements, most food safety is dealt with on the local level. Food production, wrapping, marking, restaurant safety and cleanliness[48], and specific items like meat and milk are subject to regulation to protect consumers.

Prescription drugs: The Food and Drug Administration regulates which drugs are allowed in the U.S. and how they are labeled and advertised. Yet drug labeling can still cause problems for your characters. If your Spanish-speaking character reads: "Take once daily," and thinks the word "*once*" is the same in English and Spanish (*once* is the Spanish word for the number eleven), he may have a serious overdose taking it eleven times a day.

Hospital safety: Most states don't require hospitals to disclose the numbers of patients that get infections inside the hospital. That is

---

[48] Think about characters with food poisoning or who find odd objects in food.

changing. Pennsylvania was the first state to pass such a law. Many states now have similar laws, or some in the works. Your character could get a worse problem inside the hospital than they had going in, like a staph infection. Hospital safety is mostly state-regulated in the form of building and sanitary codes.

Lemon laws: Most states have procedures where a car that has had multiple repairs can be returned as a lemon. If there have been three to four repair attempts on a vehicle under a year or two, or the vehicle has been out of service for 30 days, there is usually an arbitration procedure the buyer can go through to get a refund or replacement.

Fraud laws: If the seller misrepresented a car as new or sold a flood-damaged car, there are state anti-fraud laws that protect consumers. Does your character's car have suspicious water marks?

Airline travel: If you've ever traveled, you know your character has almost no rights in this arena. Airlines can overbook, bump, delay, hold your character prisoner without letting them go for hours on the runway, and they have to sit and take it. If they make a fuss in any way, they can be arrested when they get off, or while onboard if they're lucky enough to have a marshal aboard. Your character can go through a hellish flight full of frustration and be arrested for standing up to a flight attendant.

Banking: There are a slew of laws protecting consumers from bank fraud and bank discrimination. Consumers have privacy protections, keeping banks from disclosing their personal information. Interest rates must be properly disclosed in writing. Every aspect of banking is regulated. If your character has a banking dispute, you'll want to have an understanding of the laws and regulations that apply to their situation.

Cable TV: Cable companies are subject to the rules of each local government entity where they operate. They are generally monopolies in a particular geographic area and, as a result, don't have to care about the customer. Does your character's business lose internet service because the cable got cut? In order to force the cable company to fix it, they may have to go through their local government.

Consumer Product Safety

The Consumer Product Safety Commission (CPSC) issues recalls and regulations on unsafe consumer products. If your character is injured by a product, you might check the CPSC website on product safety standards for each product (http://www.cpsc.gov/cgi-bin/regs.aspx). Many products have voluntary standards that CPSC has issued, and are listed online (http://www.cpsc.gov/volstd/standards.html). This is a great source for personal injury attorney characters who are looking for well-known ways a product could have been made safer.[49]

Credit

The Fair Credit Reporting Act gives consumers access to their credit reports and the ability to dispute false or inaccurate reports. The Equal Credit Opportunity Act prohibits discrimination in granting credit. The Fair Debt Collection Practices Act prevents creditors from calling at night, at work, threatening, harassing, and requires them to stop calling if you tell them to do so. It also provides strict procedures for collecting debts. Your character could have a creditor hounding them at work, interfering with their ability to get their job done, even costing them their job.

There are consumer protection laws that apply to just about everything your character touches. A little research can add authenticity to your story of a character facing consumer woes.

Products Liability

Unlike traditional negligence claims in personal injury, products liability puts "strict liability" (meaning they're liable whether or not it was their fault) on the manufacturer if the product is defective. A product is defective if it varies from the intended design of the product. If the hair dryer blows up instead of drying your character's hair, it is defective. Other ways companies could be liable for injuries caused by their products are failure to warn of problems (thus all the

---

[49] If you ever doubt the value of personal injury attorneys, just remember lead paint on toys made in China and remember, there but for the grace of our plaintiff's bar would be the U.S. Do you think we would have had massive recalls without the personal injury bar? When your kid puts a toy in their mouth, thank a personal injury attorney that they don't have brain damage.

warnings you see on products)[50], breach of warranty, and standard negligence.

The warranty doesn't have to be a written warranty, like the ones you buy on your appliances. The "implied warranty of fitness for a particular purpose" would apply if, for instance, your buyer character purchases a microwave for the stated purpose of drying a dog. We know what happens then. The seller would be liable, because they knew the purpose, and they should have told the buyer to use a hair dryer instead.

Products liability is another entire course in law school, and there are many multimillionaire attorneys out there handling products liability. If your character was injured by a product, they may have use for an attorney who handles products liability. Or, you may write it so that Congress preempted the law in that area and your character can't sue the asbestos doll manufacturer. Or, you can make tort reform applicable so that the damages your character is limited to don't begin to cover the injury.

Products liability is a great area of law to use in a story.

Real Estate

Real estate law isn't that sexy, but everyone has to live somewhere and work somewhere. This area causes passionate disputes, and even murders. A little real estate law could be good for your plot.

What is real property? Essentially, land and buildings, and anything permanently affixed to or growing on them. Under this definition, the mold in your office air conditioning vent is real property. All other property - your character's car, clothes, bling, iguana, and CD of "Chipmunk Punk," - is called "personal property." You will give yourself away as a legal amateur if you refer to an oral contract to sell or dispose of real property. All contracts for the sale of real property must be in writing (the law that says this is called the "statute of frauds").

If you have a law student character, they may anguish about the "rule against perpetuities." This rule is that "no interest is good unless it vests not later than 21 years after the death of a person living at the time the interest is created." This is truly all you need to know. No lawyer not

---

[50] Warning: Do not use this book to whack your children or spouse on the head, slam on your genital area, or beat senseless the agent who rejected your manuscript. Oh, OK. Go ahead and smack the agent.

practicing real estate understands this. Few law students understand it. And most real estate lawyers will look at you funny if you bring it up. I have only met one lawyer in over 20 years of law practice who claimed it actually came up in a case. But it's a great term for law school stories.

Types of Ownership

Most property is held in "fee simple," meaning the owner and heirs can do what they want with it (zoning permitted, of course).

If more than one person owns the property, then the owners must decide what type of joint ownership they will have. Joint ownership can be of several types:

- **Joint tenancy** is the most common. Under this type of ownership, if one owner dies, the property goes to the remaining owner(s). This is good to know for murder mystery writers, since the person who inherits makes a great suspect.

- **Tenancy in common** means that the interest in each owner's share can be sold or inherited. Also great for murder mysteries. For instance, if your villain killed someone thinking they were going to get a piece of property, but it turns out that they held it as a tenancy in common, they will have a whole new co-owner to deal with.

- **Tenancy by the entireties** is reserved for spouses. While husband and wife are individuals, when they own as husband and wife by the entireties it is as if a third person, "husband-wife," owned the property. A judgment against only the husband won't attach to the property that husband and wife own by the entireties. If the wife dies, the husband who has the judgment against him is out of luck though, because the judgment will attach. Neither party holding property by the entireties can sell their share of the property without consent of the other.

- **Life estates** are useful in estate planning. Your character's parents can deed the property to the kids, with the parents having a "life estate." Then the property goes to the kids when the parents die. The kids have an ownership interest called a "fee tail"[51]. Do they fight over which one wags the tail?

---

[51] Also a great term to use in a humorous story. Way funnier than fee simple.

Some examples of where property issues go to court are where there are encroachments (buildings, fences, or other items crossing over the property line); title disputes (who owns it); easements (rights of way across property for things like utilities, roads, and beach access); specific performance (after signing a contract, the seller refuses to sell); and breach of contract (buyer refuses to buy).

Here are some of the types of lawsuits you might see in a real estate litigation practice:

- **Quiet title actions** – quiet title is a lawsuit filed where there is a problem with the property title. For instance, if your seller character finds, when the title search is done, that someone placed a lien on his property that doesn't belong, he could sue to quiet title, that is, to get rid of the dispute. Or your character, out for revenge, could file a bogus lien on an ex-boyfriend's house and sit back waiting for him to sue her. He won't be able to sell or get a loan on his property until he obtains a court order getting rid of the lien.

- **Adverse possession actions** – adverse possession is where someone has used all or part of a piece of property for a specified period of time, varying by state. For instance, if a fence is a foot over your character's property line, and has been there for 30 years, the owner of the fence can claim adverse possession and take away the one foot of land where the fence sits. Good fences make good neighbors, except when the fence is an encroachment.

- **Boundary or easement disputes** – if the owners disagree on where the boundary or an easement on property runs, they may sue to get a determination.

- **Disclosure disputes** - A big area of litigation is where the seller fails to disclose known defects. Your newlywed characters could buy a house that turns out to have had an infamous murder in it. Or, your character could be gravely ill if there was a leak painted over to disguise the toxic mold.

Admiralty

Admiralty law covers accidents and other liability of ship owners when in navigable waters. It is purely federal law, but many claims can be brought in either state or federal courts.

I dare you to make admiralty interesting in your story, but here's a little bit of how it works. Among other weird aspects of admiralty law:

Injuries

A ship owner's liability in an accident is limited to the value of the ship (this actually was invoked for the Titanic), under the Limitation Act. Are your attorney characters representing victims of a sea tragedy who have to compete with hundreds of victims for a small slice of the recovery pie?

Under the Jones Act, the law allowing injured seamen to sue their employer, the injured seaman can get a trial by jury for an injury or wrongful death. Your character's family could sue for his drowning at sea.

A "seaman" is anyone who works 30% of time or more on a vessel or fleet of vessels under the same ownership or control.

Injured seamen can use "maintenance and cure" to pay for their injuries. Under "maintenance and cure" the ship owner has to pay for medical treatment for an injured seaman and to provide basic living expenses while convalescing.

Under "unseaworthiness," the ship owner is liable to an injured seaman if the ship or part of the ship was defective in some way. For example, your sea captain character could get hurt when a railing collapsed due to faulty riveting.

Other injured workers are covered by the Longshore Act, a form of worker's compensation which has fewer remedies and may not allow them to recover much money. Your character could think she's a seaman but find that she's limited to recovery under the Longshore Act, and have to struggle to pay her expenses.

What if your character is a passenger, not an employee? Injuries to passengers have a one year statute of limitations set out on the ticket, which the courts enforce. Most personal injury lawsuits can be brought within four years. Did your character miss the deadline thinking the statute of limitations was like other personal injuries?

Liens for Wages

A seaman who isn't paid can actually get a lien on the ship and have it seized. This has to be done by a case in federal court. There was recently a case where a cruise ship that owed wages to workers tried to move to a different port. A federal judge ordered the ship seized and wouldn't let the owner move it until they paid the wages. Had the seamen not been paid, the ship could be sold to pay them. Does your character end up owning a cruise ship?

Treasure Hunting

Salvage is what you'll need to research if your character is a treasure hunter. It's probably the sexiest area of admiralty law. Treasure hunting is done either by contract or through pure or merit salvage. Whatever means they use, the treasure hunters don't get to keep it all. The owner will get a portion of the treasure, even if it has been sunken for hundreds of years. Salvage law may be useful in your pirate story. Aarrgh!

Small Claims

These are claims that are, well, small. The states cap them at, say, $5000 or $15,000. Ah, the *People's Court*. And that's what small claims court judges will tell you they are. The TV judge shows, like *Judge Alex*, are real small claims cases that were picked for their sheer entertainment value. Nothing is closer to a pure justice system or pure entertainment than small claims court. If you want to give your judge character quick, interesting cases, make him a small claims judge. Small claims judges listen to rank amateurs plead their cases and have to dispense justice based on the arguments. Can you think up a sitcom around this scenario?

People can sue landlords, contractors, vendors, employers, friends, and family members who owe them money. Corporations don't need counsel to defend themselves here. Many states have mediation programs for small claims that encourage people to try to settle out of court. Your character could settle a personal injury case in small claims court and realize later she had a bigger claim because her injuries were more serious than she thought. If she signed a release when she settled, she gave up those claims for the serious injuries.

Small claims court is full of real folks who come to the justice system because "someone done them wrong." They come, hat in hand, asking for justice. Your character may need to resolve a small matter quickly, so small claims court can be useful to your story. Many times, justice is dispensed in small packages. For entertainment, a quick resolution, drama, and wonderful dialogue, small claims court may be just what your story needs.

Chapter 15 – Person to Person

Family – can't live with them, can't kill them. Or can you? Divorce, child custody, will disputes, all provide opportunity for drama in your story. Whether you write mysteries, young adult fiction, romance novels, or newspaper articles, the family disputes are the messiest, most personal, and frequently the most dramatic fights. And a simple auto accident can thrust your character into a legal dispute with another driver. Here are just some of the ways you might use people suing other people in your stories.

Divorce

"Dissolution (divorce) movies are the absolute worst. They give a false impression of greedy and rapacious lawyers and their murderous...cheating...money-hungry husbands or wives...you name it. This makes for interesting entertainment, but is certainly not the norm. From what I've heard just in speaking with people is that the vast majority of the general population do not trust family lawyers, but view them as 'sharks' who glory in sensationalism and in making opposing counsel and the other spouse as miserable as possible. This is true, of course, with some lawyers in some cases, but is not the usual m.o. Most family lawyers are hard-working practitioners who represent individuals dealing with the stresses of separation, division of assets and debits, visitation and custody, sometimes, with debilitating physical problems (themselves or a child), depression, money problems (how will 2 people afford to live separately when they could barely make ends meet in one household?), and in the worst cases, domestic violence."

-Michelle Pivar, Florida Family Law Attorney

Whether you are covering a celebrity divorce, writing a murder mystery, doing a screenplay for a TV soap, or writing a children's coming-of-age story, few areas of the law are more emotionally charged and full of plot possibilities than divorce. A little understanding of how it works will go a long way toward making your story credible.

No-fault

Traditionally, divorce could be granted only upon specific reasons, called "grounds," which varied from state to state. States have drifted away from requiring grounds, and toward "no-fault" divorce. The idea behind no-fault divorce is that people shouldn't be forced to stay in a marriage for any reason. The only thing the petitioner needs to allege in a no-fault divorce is incompatibility, irretrievable breakdown, or irreconcilable differences. Sixteen states have purely no-fault laws. Most others have a hybrid, allowing the parties to divorce either upon no-fault criteria or upon grounds stated in their statutes. Only nine states have not adopted some form of no-fault law. So your character's divorce and how smoothly it can go may well depend on which state she's in.

States with only no-fault divorce		
Arizona	Iowa	Oregon
Colorado	Kansas	Washington
California	Kentucky	Wisconsin
Florida	Michigan	Wyoming
Hawaii	Montana	
Indiana	Nebraska	

Some states require a separation period before allowing a no-fault divorce. Evading the separation requirement is one of the reasons a party may choose to allege some fault. Do your characters have to go through a legal separation? Do they date while still technically married?

In the states that allow fault to be alleged (which may also affect property, alimony, and custody), there are several grounds considered to be "fault." The most usual are physical or mental cruelty (the most common), adultery, abandonment/desertion (the amount of time varies by state), imprisonment (again, the amount of time is set by the state), and inability to engage in sexual intercourse if it wasn't disclosed before marriage. You can have a character who's never hurt a flea suddenly accused of spouse abuse by a wife trying to get more alimony. Does he become so enraged he goes after her with his buzz saw?

The archaic concept that, if both parties were at fault, divorce could not be granted, no longer exists today. You could have older characters who tried to divorce in the fifties who were forced to stay together because both had affairs. Maybe that affects the way they react to their granddaughter who's about to tie the knot.

Common law marriage

If people hold themselves out to be husband and wife, intend to be married, and live together for a "substantial" period of time, some states will deem them married even if they did not go through a ceremony. This can be particularly fun for your story. That being said, it's hard to have an accidental common-law marriage. Just living together doesn't cut it. They have to both hold themselves out as spouses (refer to their live-in as "my husband" or "my wife"), and have an intent to be married (in other words, aren't just cohabiting). Do your con-artist characters who hold themselves out to be spouses in order to do a con end up married under the concept of common law marriage? They might have to go through a divorce proceeding when they have a falling out.

States with Common Law Marriage		
Alabama	Iowa	Oklahoma
Colorado	Kansas	Pennsylvania
District of	Montana	Rhode Island
Columbia	New Hampshire	South Carolina
Georgia (if before	(inheritance	Texas
1/1/97)	purposes only)	Utah
Idaho (if before	Ohio (if before	
1/1/96)	10/10/91)	

On the other hand, common law marriage provides a great chance to have a bigamist character, or a mystery spouse to make a claim in a will contest. There is absolutely no way to track this down in a court record, yet a common law spouse could surface if your character lived in the right state for even a short time.

Alimony

Unlike child support, alimony payments are tax-deductible. While alimony used to presume that the spouse would not work outside the home, that presumption has changed. Young spouses able to work for a living are generally expected to do so. Factors that go into alimony are age of the parties, length of the marriage, health, relative income, future financial prospects, and fault. Does your spoiled rich husband character used to being the boy-toy find, to his surprise, that he can't get alimony from the ex-wife when she dumps him for a younger model?

Rehabilitative alimony

Rehabilitative alimony is given in order to allow a spouse to get training, education, or sometimes to allow them to stay home with a child not in school full-time. It's usually for a set period of time, and can be reviewed if circumstances change. Does your spouse character who's never worked a day in her life have to go to school to learn something useful? She could find her life changing for the better when she realizes she's actually good at something.

Permanent alimony

Permanent alimony is increasingly rare in these days of equal rights and opportunities. Once granted, it can cease only upon death of one of the parties, remarriage, permanent co-habitation, or change of circumstances. Fun fact: a sex-change operation does not cease the obligation of permanent alimony, at least as of this writing. Could your character be paying alimony to his ex-wife who had a sex-change operation and is now a man? How does he react to having to write his alimony check to another guy?

Lump sum alimony

Lump sum alimony can be granted in lieu of property division, or can be done for tax purposes. It can be awarded regardless of the remarriage of the recipient. If your character gets a windfall, they could use it to do something life-changing.

Temporary alimony

This is alimony granted before the divorce is final. If your character has the better-paying job, she could have to pay her husband's expenses before they get divorced.

Reimbursement alimony

Reimbursement alimony is granted to reimburse for expenses, such as medical school or law school, paid by one spouse for the other. Your character might have put his wife through law school and been dumped. The lawyer-spouse may have to reimburse him for the expense of law school tuition on top of her student loans. Serves her right.

Child support

Child support is not tax deductible, other than the standard dependent deduction. It is granted to the custodial parent or, in the case of joint custody, the parent who has primary custody, to provide for the needs of the child. Sometimes the non-custodial parent can be awarded support to pay for expenses during the child's visitations. While the parent can seek enforcement, the right of support actually belongs to the child. Does your character go to court to seek child support only to have his teen daughter testify that she doesn't want it? Is he a sleazebag who's telling her that he'll go to jail for contempt of court if she testifies? You could have the mother character overhear what he's telling her. Does she whack him in the head with a shovel or go to the judge and ask for help?

If the person caring for the child finds out they are not the parent, yet served as the parent for a period of time, due to fraud or misrepresentation of parenthood, they can still seek child support from the real parent. The converse is also true. If the person served as the parent, the principle of "estoppel" (meaning you can't deny something you've said that someone else relied on – in this case, the kid) may require them to pay child support even if paternity proves false. You could have your character find out he wasn't the father, deal with all the emotional issues involved, and still have to pay child support.

Federal law now requires each state to set out child support guidelines, so you can easily calculate how child support would be factored in your story. The two general criteria the courts use to determine support are the needs of the child, and the ability to pay. How does the court in your story balance those factors?

States and the federal government will enforce child support, through both criminal and civil laws. A failure to pay will result in a judgment that is enforceable even if the courts later determine that there was a change in circumstances or other defense. If your character simply stops paying because she lost her job, she may be surprised to land in jail or have a judgment against her. Had she gone to court for a modification, she may easily have avoided this problem.

Custody

The movie *Losing Isaiah* is a heart wrenching story of child custody and the racial divide. What makes it more real is that it correctly reflects the standard used in all custody issues – the best interests of the child. Whether you are covering celebrity meltdowns or doing fiction, custody is dramatic and emotional. Under the Uniform Child Custody Jurisdiction And Enforcement Act, jurisdiction is with the court where the child resides. Does your character end up having to sue in Podunk, where the ex-husband moved?

Custody factors include many things, but they all boil down to "the best interests of the child." Most custody arrangements are done by agreement between the parties. Do your characters have to negotiate how custody will work?

If custody is disputed, then courts will consider:
- which parent is the primary caretaker,
- fitness of the parent,
- wishes of the child if the child is old enough,
- mental and physical health of parents,
- religion and cultural factors,
- discipline,
- excessive discipline/emotional abuse,
- domestic violence,
- contacts with the community,
- ability to interact with extended family,
- age and sex of child (the "tender years" doctrine provides a presumption in favor of the mother when the child is very young),
- drug and alcohol abuse.

Can your character get falsely accused of domestic violence or sexual abuse so the ex-wife can try to get sole custody?

Visitation

Just because a parent fails to pay child support doesn't mean the parent owed the money can deny visitation. Both visitation and child support can only be changed with a court order. One party doesn't just get to change it on their own. The parties can agree mutually to modify visitation arrangements. The problem with the parties agreeing to modify visitation without getting a court order is that they may have an argument that makes one of them change their minds. So say the father thinks he's okay to take the child to Montana for Christmas but the court order says the mother has the kid for the holidays. The mother gave a verbal okay, then saw his new girlfriend. What happens when she goes to court and complains he violated the court order?

Most court orders on visitation require "reasonable" visitation. If the parties can't agree, then the court may set a fixed visitation schedule. Frequently, courts will set a fixed schedule, and allow the parties to modify it by agreement or practice. What if your characters have a schedule they change all the time by agreement because they get along well? What happens to the flexible schedule if they have a fight?

Property division

How marital property is divided depends entirely on state law.

In "community property" states, assets acquired during the marriage, or with earnings from the marriage, are split evenly. Debts acquired during the marriage belong to both spouses. Other property belongs to the separate spouses. Does your character strike it rich right after getting married? Half of what they own may go to the spouse who cheated on her.

Community Property States		
Alaska	Louisiana	Washington
Arizona	Nevada	Wisconsin
California	New Mexico	Puerto Rico
Idaho	Texas	

Most states use equitable distribution. In those states, judges have discretion to be fair, considering the assets, earnings, potential earnings, and needs of both spouses. Does your character try to hide his earning potential? Did he sign a big book deal and put off the advance?

Generally, the parent with primary custody is the one who stays in the house. Although it does happen, spouses who change the locks and prevent the other spouse from entering are breaking the law.[52] They need a court order to do so. A spouse can ask the other to leave, but can't force the issue without an order. What if your character gets locked out? She shows up one night from school and can't get in. Does she get the police to open the door? Get a hatchet from the shed? Or just slink meekly away and get a hotel room?

Inheritances during the marriage and property owned before marriage are non-marital property as long as they are kept separate. Once commingling occurs, they are probably marital property. Did your character inherit billions from the uncle only to have the spouse take half the joint bank account in the divorce?

Collaborative law

Imagine, lawyers getting along, putting aside filthy lucre to work to resolve a matter in a way that works out well for both sides. That's the world of collaborative law, pioneered and still primarily used in the world of divorce law. I saw my first screenwriting reference to collaborative law in the movie *Juno*. The lawyers for both sides agree that they will try to settle the matter. If they can't, then they won't represent either party in the divorce. This is so that neither attorney is motivated by the potential of earning more fees. They work toward settlement only.

Of course, this has ticked off some traditional silk stocking Bar Associations to no end. Colorado has gone as far as to ban it as violating ethical rules against limiting an attorney's ability to represent a client. Do your characters want a collaborative divorce and find it's not allowed in their state?

The parties agree to disclose every single asset, to not play games in hiding information, and to work to resolve the matter amicably. If they get caught, the lawyer representing them has to withdraw, and the collaborative process is over.

I believe that this will be the trend in law. More and more, the justice system is moving at a glacial pace to forms of alternative dispute resolution. This is cutting edge stuff, a great topic for a story.

---

[52] On the one hand, seeing stories that have the spouse doing a lockout bother me because I know it's illegal. But I also know people it's happened to, so be careful if you use this in your story. Go for realistic, not trite. Have the lockout victim go for a court order or call the police. The police can help get them back in.

Annulments and "Gets"

Although not overly common, annulments and gets are frequently sought for religious purposes. If your character or subject is Catholic or Jewish, for instance, you may need to know about these devices.

Annulment

The difference between annulment and divorce is that annulment means the marriage never occurred. Grounds for annulment can be any "legal impediment." Examples are that the spouse was too young and failed to obtain parental consent; intoxication or drug use; a spouse was already married; consent to the marriage was under duress (shotgun wedding being a good example); consent to the marriage was obtained by fraud(a nice modern example is transgendered surgery); a spouse was a prisoner sentenced to life when the ceremony took place; concealment of a factor such as addiction, venereal disease, or criminal record; physical incapacity (inability to engage in intercourse); consanguinity (too closely related – in most states, second cousins and closer). Did your characters get married as teens? After 20 years, one character might try to claim they didn't get parental consent and the marriage is illegal.

The party responsible is not allowed to seek annulment, only the innocent spouse. Does your character claim it was the other spouse who brought the venereal disease into the marriage?

Religious annulments, on the other hand, are not necessarily granted on the same grounds as civil annulments, and you'll need to research the particular religion to find out each of the requirements. However, sometimes the civil divorce decrees might order the parties to participate in a religious annulment. This is usually ordered when the parties agree to it in the settlement. Do your Catholic characters argue over whether they will agree to an annulment?

Get

A Get is a bill of divorce which the husband gives to his wife to free her to marry again. A Get is a document that exists in Orthodox Judaism which says, simply, "You are hereby permitted to all men." Gittin law provides that only men can initiate the process. But the woman can refuse to accept it. A Get is the only way an orthodox Jew can remarry. This is an increasingly debated area of the law. More states are developing laws that allow courts to order the refusing spouse to grant the Get. If you have a story about orthodox Jews, you'll need to know about Gittin laws as well as civil laws.

Auto Accidents

One certain way to land in a legal dispute with another individual is to hit their car with yours. Movies, TV and books frequently show fender benders and serious accidents. This is one of the most common uses for the court system you might have in a story. Most people are probably in auto accidents or have family members in auto accidents at some point in their lives.

While much of auto accident litigation is covered in the Personal Injury and Products Liability sections[53], there are some areas unique to auto accidents you might need to know.

The most confusing is the difference between "fault" and "no-fault" laws. It's really just like it sounds. In fault-based states, before recovering for an accident from the insurance company, the person claiming must show the other person was at fault. In no-fault states, the parties each claim through their insurance companies, don't have to wait to get the repairs and injuries taken care of, and the insurance companies battle it out later.

No-Fault States:		
Arkansas	Maryland	Pennsylvania
Delaware	Massachusetts	South Dakota
District of Columbia	Michigan	Texas
Florida	Minnesota	Utah
Hawaii	New Jersey	Virginia
Kansas	New York	Washington
Kentucky	North Dakota	Wisconsin
	Oregon	

In no-fault states, your character can't sue anyone for injuries unless they are over a certain monetary amount or a certain level of severity. This varies widely by state.

---

[53] Chapter 10 page 98 and Chapter 14 page 166.

Many of the other oddities of auto accident law fall in the realm of criminal penalties, such as hit and run, failing to stop and exchange information, driving without insurance or a license. But these criminal violations may affect your character's ability to recover for the accident.

A fender bender can be an annoyance your character has to deal with, or can be a major story event.

Probate

Probate is what happens to a will after a person dies. The will doesn't just magically get honored. A probate court will have to determine who gets what.

> "'This is my testament,' I announce, taking a pen. 'A holographic will, every word written by me, just a few hours ago. Dated today, and now signed today.' I scrawl my name again. Stafford is too stunned to react.
> 'It revokes all former wills, including the one I signed less than five minutes ago.' I refold the papers and place them in the envelope."
> - **John Grisham**, *The Testament*

In inestimable Grisham fashion, *The Testament* captures the drama of a capacity hearing, a high stakes will contest, and the emotions of all involved. By getting the legal aspects of will signing and revocation right, Grisham adds to the authenticity of the story and demonstrates his mastery of the legal drama.

Death and taxes are certainties in your character's life. Probate is an area that many people will have to deal with at some point or other. Much property passes automatically and doesn't need to go through probate. Property owned with a spouse, or with a designated beneficiary, will not need to be probated. I hate seeing stories where the will is read and, next thing, the house is being sold by the person who inherited it. Nothing in the legal system is that quick. That house has to go through probate.

First, the will has to be shown in court. The court determines whether everything is present that is required to make a legally binding will. The will usually must have to be a certain number of witnesses, and the witnesses can't be the people inheriting. What happens to your character's will if he tried to cut the kids out by hand-writing a new will in the hospital? If he called the nurses in to be witnesses, will the will leaving everything to the hospital be upheld?

If the will cuts a spouse out, the spouse will usually still be able to claim a "spousal share," a percentage of the estate. In community property states, that is half. However, the spouses can sign an agreement waiving their share. Some states provide that a head of family cannot leave the residence to anyone other than a spouse or minor child, if either is alive. If your character tries to cut her husband out of the will, does he end up suing his own kids to get his cut?

Many states have provisions to prevent an accidental disinheritance. If a child is born after the will is made and it doesn't say, for instance, "equally among my children," then a child may be able to claim a percentage. If the intent is to disinherit a child, the will usually must say so. What happens in your story if the louse of a husband left his pregnant wife for the aerobics instructor? When he has a heart attack in bed, does the ex-wife have to fight the louse's new wife for her child's share of the money?

The probate court will designate a "personal representative" of the estate to gather all the property, pay the debts, and ultimately distribute the property. The court will determine the validity of any disputes to the will. The personal representative's and attorney's fees will be paid out of the estate, along with court costs. What if your story has a dishonest personal representative? If the personal representative character claims most of the estate as his fees and expenses, your feuding family might have to settle their differences to fight him together.

Estate taxes change with the political winds, so double check these. Right now, each year the exempt amount will go up, until 2010, when there will be zero estate tax. How much of your character's inheritance is lost to estate tax?

Will contests can be great story fodder, but they are rare in reality. Bases for challenging a will can be:

- **Mental incapacity:** person making will was mentally incapable of making will, such as Alzheimer's, drunkenness, drug abuse, or mental disorder. Your character could make a drunken will leaving everything to the bartender, then die in a DUI accident on the way home.

- **Duress:** the person was forced to make a will. Did the villain hold a gun to your character's head and say, "sign?"
- **Undue influence:** so the older invalid character leaves everything to the stripper young wife, the hot cabana boy, the caregiver. What the kids who want to challenge the will have to show is that that the person was so controlling that the geezer no longer had the ability to make the decisions. Did your Mrs. Robinson character marry the pool boy and leave him everything?
- **Fraud:** that the will was procured by some misrepresentation of facts. Did Grandpa change his will to favor your character's sister after sis told him she was pregnant?
- **Forgery:** the will itself was not signed by the person claimed.
- **New will:** a new will cancels out the old.

Only people with standing may challenge a will. These include spouses, children, and anyone included in a prior will that was left out.

You could use a will contest in your story that will be emotionally draining on your characters. An inheritance in a will could cause a surprise windfall leaving your character free to pursue her dreams. Or your character expecting a big inheritance could have to change his extravagant lifestyle when he gets nothing in the will.

Probate issues can be wonderful plot devices. A little understanding of the probate rules in your story's state will help add authenticity and spice to the story.

Chapter 16 – Person to Government

Tangling with government can be confusing and frustrating, but in the real world we all have to encounter government at some point in our lives. Whether arrested, tangling with the IRS, or exercising free speech, here are just some of the ways your characters may end up having to deal with government.

Civil Rights

Civil rights are laws protecting each person from governmental abuses.[54]. Some are protected under the constitution, some by statute. Discrimination is the one everyone thinks of, and it is certainly a big civil rights issue. However, there are many other civil rights that can be enforced through civil rights lawsuits. These include:

Color of law: a government official uses their authority in some way that is harmful or abusive. This can include excessive use of force; sexual assault, wrongful arrest, fabricated evidence, and failure to keep from harm. For instance, your sheriff character could use his badge to commit a rape.

Due process: this means that legal proceedings and anything that deprives a person of liberty or property are done with fairness. This includes hearings, trials, and other proceedings. Issues like requiring prisoners to wear prison garb at trial, location of trials, and other procedural issues are considered "procedural due process." The other area of due process law is called "substantive due process" and consists of issues like privacy, the right to marry persons of another race, the right to control education of children, and other limits government can or cannot place on individual liberties.

Due process doesn't just apply to arrest. It applies every time government takes away any kind of property (land or stuff), such as

---

[54] Not meant to be ironic.

expulsion from a public school, termination from a classified government job, taxation, and licenses. Procedures that may be required include being allowed to have counsel, to present evidence, to cross examine witnesses, to have somebody hear the case who isn't biased, and to have a written decision. There may also be appeal rights. You could have your teen character sue for due process when he's expelled from school for throwing bottles from the roof of the school.

Equal protection: that every category of person is to be treated the same as every other category. Typical categories can be race, sex, citizenship, national origin, disability, and can also apply to types of restrictions such a speech, travel, privacy, or association. The government will have to show some sort of "legitimate and compelling interest" (basically, a really good reason) if a classification falls within a protected category. For instance, if a minimum height requirement for police officers existed, the city having the requirement would have to show a compelling interest, such as safety, to counteract the fact that it mostly excludes women. How much the government has to prove depends on the classification. Race and national origin are subject to the highest level, "strict scrutiny," where government has to show the restriction is "narrowly tailored to serve a compelling government interest."

For example, if your character is applying for a job that is available to U.S. citizens only, the government would have to show some reason such as national security for the restriction. Odds are, the government wouldn't be allowed to keep this requirement. Gender is less protected. Is your character going up against men-only or women-only requirements? The cutting edge is going to be whether or not sexual orientation will ultimately be considered a "suspect class." Right now, it is not. Does your gay character make a federal case out of being excluded from a job or the right to get a marriage license?

Free speech: this is the protection that says government cannot interfere with the content of speech. It does not mean that businesses and individuals who aren't government can't restrict free speech. I can't tell you how many employees tell off their boss, get fired, then come to me saying, "But what about free speech?" This fundamental misunderstanding is shared by many citizens. Stores don't have to let your character scream abusive epithets at clerks, and businesses can tell your character to get out if they are creating a scene. Government can't restrict speech, other than within very narrow limits. These include defamation, perjury, treason, obscenity, creating a public danger (crying "fire" in a crowded theater), and trade secrets. My journalist readers will know all about this protection. If you are using free speech issues in your story, make sure you don't have a character claim a free speech issue against a private entity.

Free press: the companion to free speech. This is the concept that government cannot interfere with journalists. This protection also means that it is extra difficult to claim defamation against the press. Let's say a reporter prints a story saying your character killed her husband. If she wants to sue the reporter for defaming her, she'll have to show that the information was published with knowledge it was false, or with reckless disregard as to its truth or falsity. So the reporter had to know she didn't do it, or didn't care whether or not it was true when he wrote the story. Public figures have very little protection. Opinion can never be libelous. Is your elected official character upset at an article calling her a stripper when she is really a belly dancer? She'll still probably lose unless she can show malice.

Privacy: the right to privacy is not in the constitution. However, over the years the Supreme Court has found an implied right of privacy in the 9th Amendment. This right protects personal freedoms such as family, marriage, procreation, contraception, interracial marriage, private possession of obscene materials in the home, and abortion. Ten states also provide for privacy protections in their constitutions, above and beyond the implied right of privacy. Does your character sue over a law requiring a waiting period for abortion?

States with Constitutional Privacy Protections		
Alaska	Hawaii	South Carolina
Arizona	Illinois	Washington
California	Louisiana	
Florida	Montana	

Association: this is the right to be with whomever a citizen pleases. It can include friends, intimate association, or common factors such as beliefs. Government can require permits for demonstrations as long as they aren't unduly restrictive, can require buffer zones for protests, can keep felons from associating, but can't require government employees to hold certain political loyalties or punish employees for their beliefs. Is your character a member of a Muslim book club accused of harboring terrorists? Government also cannot impose restrictions on purely private individuals' and groups' rights not to associate with others. Does the town council try to force your character's women-only spa to allow men? Discrimination is allowed among private individuals, but is prohibited for public accommodations (anyplace the public is invited) and entities that receive government funding.

Condemnation

Under the concept of condemnation, government has the right to take away property for public use within certain limits. While "eminent domain" (the power to take private property for public use) has traditionally been used for purely public uses such as highways, railroads, public utilities, and government offices, the power has more recently been used to take private property for private use, on the grounds that "economic development" is a public use. This is a great area for a story. Does your character's mini golf course stand in the way of a proposed high rise?

The other area of condemnation allows government to prohibit property from being used until certain health or other hazardous conditions are corrected. This does not usually result in loss of the property unless the owner fails to correct the situation. Did your landlord character allow the roof to leak, causing the tenant character to be thrown out due to condemnation?

Where condemnation has been most controversial is where certain properties or areas are deemed "blighted." These properties can then be taken for fairly minimal dollars (the Constitution requires just compensation, but "just" is a matter of opinion and can cause disagreement). Is your character's property targeted to be sold to developers for shopping centers, offices, condominiums or other development? So far the Supreme Court is allowing it. The Supremes are saying it is up to the states to say whether or not they will allow cities and counties to take private property like this.

If your character lives in a state that allows government to take property for private use, they could have their dream home on the beach snatched from under them by a condominium developer; lose the family farm to a country club; or have their mom and pop store taken by a shopping center. Or, an entire neighborhood could be seized to build a luxury development.

Is your character doomed? Well, there are some defenses to this kind of taking.

Just compensation is supposed to be the fair market value of the property plus any "consequential damages." An example would be lost profits. Your character could hire appraisers or economists to demonstrate the real amount that would be fair.

The owner gets a hearing, and the government must prove that it engaged in negotiations for a fair price but were unable to agree. And the government must prove its public purpose, some use the taxpayers are getting out of taking the property.

More states are amending the law to prohibit what is essentially a handout to developers, but if your character is in one of those places that have not banned giving private property to developers, this kind of story can be full of tension, drama, and emotion.

Zoning

These laws, almost always done at the local level, protect existing property owners from having property near them used in a manner that will devalue their property. Not every city or local government has zoning laws. If an area is zoned residential, agricultural, commercial, or industrial, then the property zoned for that purpose can't be used for another purpose.

Zoning may prohibit mobile homes or multifamily residences in certain areas. Zoning may also have very specific structures, parking, or other practical or appearance-based requirements. Landscaping, setbacks, height limits, and lot sizes can all be addressed in zoning laws. Does your character buy a building for a beauty salon only to find out she has to pay for a bigger parking lot and palm trees?

These kinds of cases can be fun for a story because the initial zoning issue is decided at a local government level. There can be public hearings, local hearing officers, or other local proceedings that will add interest to your story. The procedures can vary wildly from city to city, county to county, and state to state.

These purely local decisions are usually subject to appeal, based upon due process, unconstitutional taking, or other grounds. But most cases stay at the local level. You can have hearings with mobs of irate neighbors, public comments, and other antics that most areas of the law don't provide.

While the nuts and bolts of zoning law are pretty dry and very area-specific, the emotions and opportunity for showing local government at its best and worst make zoning cases ripe for placement in your story.

Government Employment

Since I've already addressed employment law in another chapter, I'll just address here some specific quirks of the law relating to government employees.

Government employees are supposed to have free speech rights, unlike employees who work for private entities. The reality is that those rights have been severely limited over the past couple of years, making them virtually meaningless. There are few, if any, free speech protections left for government employees.

The constitution says government can't take property without due process of law. While most jobs aren't considered property protected under this law, government service jobs can't be taken without due process. That means government employees get a name clearing hearing if there is damaging information in their personnel files. Your character's hearing can be as meaningless as a meeting with the person who disciplined them, or a full-blown evidentiary hearing, depending on the entity. Your character will also get to have a hearing to dispute any discipline, such as a suspension without pay or a termination. This has to be before an impartial decision maker.

Many government employees have unions that give them additional rights in their collective bargaining agreements (union contracts). This can be a mixed blessing. I have seen recent cases where government employers argue that the employees must use the appeals process set out in the union contract before filing a suit. If the employee hasn't filed the grievance, they may lose their suit. But, if the employee filed a grievance, governments will argue that the case was already decided in the grievance and the employee can't sue. Catch-22? Yes. Illogical? Yes. Upheld? So far, mostly.

Tribal governments are immune from almost all state and federal laws. Those employees must go through the tribal councils to address issues, and many tribes have almost no laws against discrimination or other types of employment protections that most employees take for granted. Contracts with tribal governments sometimes contain a clause saying the tribe waives sovereign immunity if they breach the contract, so they agree to be sued in a U.S. court. You could have a tribal employee character who is fired in order to hire a tribe member. He could be rudely surprised to find out that U.S. laws against discrimination don't protect him.

Federal employees have much shorter deadlines for beginning discrimination claims[55], and have to jump through so many hoops to bring them that most get lost in the maze. One wrong step or missed deadline, and the claim is lost. These deadlines can be short – a matter of days or weeks.

Government whistleblower cases have similarly shortened deadlines. If you have an employee character who works for government, one way you can add tension is to have her confused about the procedures. She could even miss a crucial deadline and lose her right to sue.

Suing government is a pain in the neck. It's not their money, so they have no qualms about years of appeals, costs, and fees. These cases can drag on, exhausting the employee character and his funds. At the end, the employee's damages are capped (meaning that there are maximum amounts the employee can receive, no matter how much they are injured). The law has become such that fewer lawyers are willing to take on government entities.[56] Your character could go from lawyer to lawyer and end up getting turned down. If he ends up representing himself, does he win or get squashed under a mound of paperwork and expense?

---

[55] The first step is that the employee must initiate contact with a Counselor (someone the government entity designates internally) within 45 days of the date of the discriminatory action. That seems like a lot of time, but most employees who get fired or suspended are too stunned or too busy initiating grievances to think about the discrimination aspect until it's too late.

[56] This writer included. I chose sanity over suing government a couple years ago and doubled my income in the process. Less trouble, more income. A no-brainer.

Government employees are also great characters. In my experience, they tend to be more willing to tilt at windmills, go against their employers, sue and grieve over and over again, and litigate to the death. Is it because they work for governments that are willing to do the same? Does the mentality of the government entity rub off on the employee? I also find that, if government employees lose one case, they are willing to file another. This is exactly what government does.

Government lawyers and human resources people are also great characters. Bending the rules, intimidating witnesses, losing evidence, favoritism, and politics can be explored in your stories realistically if you have a case involving government. On the other hand, government employees and lawyers can also be written as true believers, defenders of the public good and the taxpayers' dollars. I find that many people go into government service because they have a personal crusade. Many never lose that idealism.

Any way you go, government employees can be written as more extreme than other characters, and your readers will believe. Nobody who has ever waited in a drivers' license or post office line will ever doubt any bizarre behavior you have a government employee engage in.

Government Unions

The right to "bargain collectively," that is, to negotiate a union contract, is protected by law, and most government employees have unions. The unions negotiate contracts with government employers containing all the rights and responsibilities of the government entity and the union members. The contracts usually are binding for 2 – 3 years.

The union contracts will have grievance procedures in them. Grievances are hearings where employees challenge employee disciplines and violations of the contract. They can have multiple steps, from informal meetings with supervisors, up to arbitrations with full evidentiary hearings. Frequently the chief executive of the entity, such as a city or county manager, will have the final say or can even override an arbitrator's decision.

Government union negotiations can be great fun for a story. They can be raucous proceedings and are usually open to the public. Both sides sit at a table and negotiate the terms of the agreement, or any amendments. Is your negotiation calm and businesslike or borderline violent? Are there protests if the negotiations impasse, or even strikes?

Government unions are full of their own politics. Employee characters on the outs may have the union refuse to take their grievances up the chain and may be forced to hire counsel to represent them, or can sometimes be cut out of the process. Their only redress would be to make an unfair labor practice claim against their own union, but the underlying claim (such as discrimination) may be lost forever.

The laws governing government unions vary from state to state, so you should make sure your story gets your state's law correct.

Elections

Anyone who was awake in 2000 knows something about election laws after the *Bush v. Gore* case. *Recount*, a television movie about that election contest, gave a birds-eye view into that election's legal battle. While most of us go to the polls, vote and leave, without thinking about what went into getting us there; there are laws about every single aspect of election law.

One law that applies to all federal and state elections since Watergate is that foreign nationals who are not citizens or permanent residents cannot contribute to political campaigns. Indeed, campaign contributions are highly regulated. Every dollar and its source have to be reported. Failure to report timely can result in catastrophic fines to a campaign. Does your character from Peru accidentally throw a campaign into an uproar by making a contribution that's exposed by the opposition?

Political candidates, political committees (commonly referred to as PACs, for Political Action Committee), and union committees (sometimes called committees of continuous existence), all must file reports of their contributions and expenditures regularly. These reports are on a strict schedule, usually quarterly in non-election years and more frequently as elections get closer. Does your well-meaning character start a PAC and get socked with ruinous fines for failing to file reports?

Contributions close to elections and during legislative sessions can be prohibited or regulated to avoid last minute surprises. Depending on the type of candidate, corporations may be prohibited from contributing to avoid the influence of special interests. You could have a mega-company in your story figure out a way to get around these limits so they can buy an election for a candidate they control.

Campaign advertising and activities are also regulated down to the minutest detail. Laws require specific disclaimers and disclosures in these advertisements, from buttons and bumper stickers to TV ads. A minor mistake can cost a candidate the election or result in fines. Did your character win only to lose an election challenge because she forgot to use a disclaimer in her TV ad?

Election Day activities such as campaigning at polls, vote counting, opening and closing of polling places, and polling machines are the subject of laws and ordinances.

Vote fraud, absentee ballot fraud, and other election wrongdoing that result in altering election results can be the subject of election contests that end up in court. These court cases are usually quick due to the need to fill offices. Does your character uncover forged absentee ballots?

Election law issues are timely and fun to deal with in stories. Because candidates are more likely to have legal teams in place, election litigation is becoming the rule, not the exception. These cases happen on a shorter timeline than many court cases, so can be easier to plot out realistically (as opposed to showing an auto accident case happening in less than a year) than other civil law story lines.

The most shocking thing I found out when I became involved in political campaigns is just how mean people are to candidates. Instead of congratulating them and thanking them for putting themselves on the line and participating, our citizenry feels free to abuse them at events, jeer, refuse to allow them to speak or attend events, and just be downright nasty to candidates. This can also be fodder for a story. It ticks me off when I see shows and stories about candidates being treated like gold wherever they go. The reality is much different and darker.

If your story is about elections, you need to know that every aspect of the process is subject to a law or ordinance. Whether your candidate or PAC follows the law, on the other hand, is up to you.

Administrative Law

If your character is dealing with a government agency that makes rules and regulations, they may have to deal with administrative law. Administrative law is how individuals and companies can dispute decisions government agencies make. Administrative law occurs outside the courts, usually with a person called a hearing officer, magistrate, or administrative law judge presiding. The person presiding might not even be a lawyer or have legal training. Whether your character is appealing a zoning decision, a termination of employment, unemployment, a fine, or another government decision, they may run into some sort of administrative law process.

There can also be boards or panels that conduct the hearings, giving you an opportunity to show the panelists arguing among themselves.. This can make for great fun and confusion in your story. Even better, many board members are political appointees. You could show an elected official putting political pressure on the panel.

Abortions

No matter your story's take on the morality or implications of abortions, you should have an understanding of the law. I'll try to give a brief overview. Until 1973, the legality of abortions was up to each state. Then the Supreme Court ruled in *Roe v. Wade* that the right to have an abortion was protected under the Constitution under the fundamental right to privacy. They cited the earlier contraceptive cases as precedent.

Since then, the Court has been expanding the states' rights to regulate abortions. For instance, after viability of the fetus, the states have much more latitude to regulate abortions. Does your teen character's state require parental consent? If so, there will be a judicial bypass so the minor character can prove to the court some compelling reason not to obtain consent. Does she prove she's been abused? States have been allowed to impose 24 – 28 hour waiting periods (longer would, of course, affect whether the fetus is viable or not and can be deemed unduly restrictive). This waiting period could be agonizing for your character, and add great tension. States can require the person seeking an abortion to have counseling. Some states require specific medical information or information about alternatives to abortion to be presented to the patient prior to the procedure. Many states have recordkeeping requirements (specific information about the patient and procedures that must be kept) for clinics. Is your character scared to give her name because her husband is a pro-life senator?

The latest battleground has been regarding partial birth abortions. The majority of states have banned or restricted these procedures. Most states allow exceptions to save the mother's life. However, some states do not allow the procedure to be used even to protect the mother's health. Does your character's doctor say the only thing that will save her life is a partial birth abortion?

A big area of contention, and more circumspect, is the regulation of abortion clinics themselves. Some states have passed regulations on everything from door sizes, hallway lengths, landscaping, and furnishings. Pro-choice groups argue that these regulations are an attempt to force clinics out of business, and indeed, they are having that effect. Anti-abortion groups argue that the regulations are necessary to protect the health of the mother. This could make for a twist to your story where you character's abortion clinic gets a surprise inspection of their furniture and front lawn.

The other area that is constantly in litigation is the regulation of anti-abortion protesters. The interests of free speech and association versus the right to privacy and the right to access the clinics are usually weighed and balanced. Buffer zones have been used to create a safe area where the patients and doctors can enter without threat of violence. The issues of bombings, murders, and threats of violence perpetrated by those who are against abortions are the subject of criminal law, which isn't a part of this book. Is your abortion protester sued for violating a buffer zone?

There is no doubt that abortion is an emotionally charged issue and makes a great subject for a story, fiction or non-fiction. Whether your character is a woman facing the choice, a doctor being threatened, a clinic owner whose clinic has been bombed, or a protester with sincere beliefs, you will be able to tug the heartstrings and write passionately about this subject. Some understanding of the state of the law and the areas of legal controversy will help your story ring true.

Civil Unions and other Gay Rights Issues

Like the civil rights movement before it, the issues involving gay rights and civil unions/gay marriages are the final frontier of the civil justice system. Whether for or against these types of rights, an understanding of the state of the law will help your story's authenticity.

You could have characters who tell their kids to love their neighbors and who want government to leave them alone argue passionately for the right to exclude homosexuals from jobs, housing, marriage, insurance, or even life itself. Your story could show the same arguments used to exclude blacks from the same rights in the 1950s being used against homosexuals. Oddly, groups that otherwise support civil rights sometimes oppose laws protecting homosexuals from the same type of discrimination. This area is a matter of extreme passion on both sides of the issue, and is thus a fabulous topic for a story.

State laws on whether same-sex marriages will be allowed are not settled. Under the Defense of Marriage Act, other states do not have to honor the Full Faith and Credit Clause of the U.S. Constitution by honoring or recognizing those marriages sanctified in states allowing them. Ultimately, there may be a constitutional amendment addressing the issue.

Some states recognize civil unions or domestic partnerships, giving some rights to homosexual partners such as property, custody, insurance, and medical decision making. Oddly, some of these same states have specifically banned gay marriages.

Some states have decided to recognize gay marriages from the states that allow them. There are some other anti-discrimination laws in a few states that protect homosexuals. Some states prohibit sexual orientation discrimination in employment or housing.

A story featuring a homosexual being denied housing or a job, a homosexual couple splitting up with no laws addressing property division or child custody, a person passionately involved in the anti-gay rights movement, or a legislature torn by this divisive issue can be exciting and timely. These laws change constantly, and probably won't settle down for 20 years, so do your homework and make sure your story has the legal aspects right. The rest is up to you and your sincerely held beliefs.

Chapter 17 – Discovery

Discovery is the way parties exchange information in a civil lawsuit. There are numerous means of discovery - I will address the most common. It is important to get the terminology right. Calling an affidavit a deposition or other misuse demonstrates an amateur's perspective on the legal system. If your character gets the terminology wrong, make sure it is on purpose to show they are a neophyte to the system.

Requests for Production

These are written requests made to the other side asking for documents, emails, electronic media, videotapes, or other physical evidence.

They will have the "style," (parties, case number, court) and then say something like:

"Plaintiffs request that Defendant produce the following documents at the offices of the undersigned within 30 days after service:"

There will be a list of the requested documents or evidence sought to be produced, followed by a set of seemingly ridiculous definitions of terms (defining what terms like "document," "record," "he" and "or" mean) that are sometimes longer than the request itself. Few people pay attention to the definitions until a dispute arises as to whether everything was produced. Is an electronic copy a "document"? The definitions may well decide this issue.

The response to the request for production is due within 30 days from the date it is sent. Any objections to what is requested can be asserted in the response. If the response is not sent within 30 days, the objections are waived. However, objections to privilege, such as attorney-client privilege, aren't waived by failing to object.

Frequently, the response will say something like:

"The documents responsive to request number 2 are available for inspection and copying in the offices of the undersigned."

For small quantities of documents, your attorney character may copy and send the documents as a matter of courtesy to the other side. Some attorneys of the jerk variety will require opposing counsel to review the documents at their office, designate which ones are to be copied, then will send them to a copy service. This takes two or three times as long as just sending the documents, and since delay is a defense attorney's friend, this can be an effective stall tactic in your story. Is an inspection at the opposing attorney's office necessary or even requested because huge amounts of documents are produced? If the attorneys in your story want to narrow down the documents to reduce costs and keep from being overwhelmed, they can do so in this way.

Big firms can use over-production to bury a small practitioner in paper and increase the costs of litigation. Destruction, called "spoliation," of evidence is both illegal and barred by ethical rules, but still occurs on occasion. Does the big firm dump a truckload of documents on your character? Does your client character know of a document the other side says never existed? Does the person who did the shredding hide when their life is threatened?

If an item is not produced, the party who fails to produce it may be sanctioned. Your character could have pleadings or defenses stricken, meaning that all or part of their case is lost. They could be prohibited from using evidence they failed to produce in discovery at the trial. They could be required to produce a document that's humiliating, like a love letter to someone other than their spouse.

If there are objections raised that have no merit or documents are not produced, your attorney character will file a "motion to compel," asking the court to require the other side to produce, which the court hears and decides what still needs to be produced and which objections will be upheld. The court will then give a deadline, usually 10 – 20 days, to provide the missing items.

Newbie lawyers frequently make the mistake of requesting too many documents. They aren't sure what to ask for and thus ask for so much they can spend lots of time going through nonsense. Does your newbie character request a warehouse full of paper? Does your character request documents solely to harass an opposing side by requiring them to spend massive amounts of time or expense sorting, or to produce items that are irrelevant or confidential and embarrassing? Discovery abuses can be dealt with by filing a motion for protective order, asking the court to limit discovery. Or they can make an objection to the request telling the judge why the documents should not be produced, so the judge can decide what gets produced.

Interrogatories

Interrogatories are lists of questions, usually limited to 20 or 30 including subparts, sent to the other side to be answered under oath. Interrogatories will have the style and a cover page that will say something like:

"Plaintiffs hereby give notice that they have propounded the attached interrogatories upon Defendant."

There will then be an attached set of the questions themselves, prefaced with language such as:

"The Plaintiff, by and through the undersigned counsel hereby propound the following interrogatories upon Defendant, and request that they be answered separately, fully and under oath within (30) days of service pursuant to Rule 1.340 of the Florida Rules of Civil Procedure."

The list of questions, with spaces for the answers, will follow, then a space for the signature and notarization. These will also be accompanied by an extensive definitions section.

Similar to requests for production, your character can object. Otherwise, they must be answered. These answers are admissible in court and are binding on the parties. If your character testifies differently under oath later, their answers may be used to impeach them.

Subpoenas

Subpoenas are the way non-parties can be forced to produce documents or attend a deposition. They are also used to compel attendance at a trial. Subpoenas for documents can be done with or without depositions. If they are for documents only, then they are called a "Subpoena Duces Tecum" or "Subpoena Duces Tecum without Deposition." The issuing party generally has to notify the other side in advance and give them an opportunity to object before a document subpoena can be issued.

If the documents are to be produced at a deposition, the character will get a "Subpoena Duces Tecum With Deposition." This will say something like: "YOU ARE HEREBY COMMANDED to appear before the following authority authorized to administer oaths and take testimony on the following date and time, and to have with you the documents on the attached list."

It will give the time and date of deposition, the court reporter, and the name of the issuing attorney. Some subpoenas will advise the witness how to file objections, while some leave the witness to figure it out on their own.

The other type of subpoena is a "Subpoena for Deposition." This one simply commands the person to appear to give testimony.

Affidavits/Witness Statements

An affidavit is a statement issued under oath in writing. There is no opportunity to cross examine the witness, no need for the other side to be present, and it's not admissible in court except for purposes of impeaching the witness if they testify contrary to the affidavit. It can be used in support of motions such as a motion for summary judgment.

I can't tell you how many people come into my office and say "I gave a deposition" when they mean they signed an affidavit. Use the term correctly.

A witness statement is sometimes under oath, but mostly not. It can be a recorded statement, can be in front of a court reporter, or can simply be something they wrote down and signed. These are informal means of preserving testimony, not admissible for any purpose in court other than impeachment. Does your character write down what happened? They just gave a written statement.

Depositions

A deposition is a formal question and answer session in front of a court reporter under oath. The parties can set them by sending a "Notice of Taking Deposition." The parties to a lawsuit must appear if reasonably noticed. Most attorneys will contact the other side to arrange scheduling as a matter of courtesy. The jerk lawyer character will not. The notice will simply show up, and then if it's not on a date the attorney or witness characters are available, they have to file a motion for protective order, asking the judge to stop the deposition, and go before the court to stop it.

Non-parties (people who aren't the plaintiff or defendant or their officers) are compelled to attend depositions by subpoena. They can file a motion for protective order to stop or limit the deposition, and they may have their own counsel present.

Normally only the parties, their attorneys, the witness, and the court reporter can be present at a deposition. Some depositions can be conducted in front of a court appointed Special Master or Magistrate if there are antics anticipated. If there has been prior misbehavior in depositions, or threats, a party may ask for a master or magistrate. Does your character have to depose a mobster and fear for her life? She may request a Special Master.

Witnesses must answer all questions, whether or not objected to, other than privileged matters. What will usually happen is, periodically, the attorney for the other side will say, "Object to the form." An inexperienced witness character will stop and wait to be told what to do. Then the attorneys will usually have to tell them to go ahead and answer. An experienced witness character will know to just keep going.

Does your attorney character make improper "speaking objections" that will give the witness a hint as to what they are doing wrong? "Lawyer: Objection. The witness can't possibly answer that because you're asking them to speculate. Witness: I wouldn't want to guess." "Lawyer: Objection. You know darned well that the car was going left. You are misleading the witness. Witness: The car was going left." Attorneys can get away with some of this some of the time, but it's considered to be sanctionable if they are really feeding a witness the answers or obstructing the deposition.

Attorneys can only instruct a witness not to answer if the matter is privileged. "Objection. Attorney client privilege. I instruct the witness not to answer." It sometimes throws off the witness to ask, "Are you going to follow your attorney's instruction?" I've had witnesses go ahead and answer after that.

Depositions are usually dull affairs, but my most dramatic stories of my own law practice came from depositions. There was the battery, where an opposing counsel grabbed a document out of my client's hands and we had to threaten to leave in order to get it back. That same deposition was the one where opposing counsel leaned over the table and shook her fist in my face. There was the one where opposing counsel stood up and blocked the door to keep my client and me from leaving the room, which is a false imprisonment. I also figured I was going to get punched. We managed to escape unscathed. There was the one where someone called my court reporter and told them the deposition was cancelled, and the deposition was delayed, resulting in the witness going berserk and the police having to be called. The court ordered the deposition to occur in the judge's office after that one.

I know one attorney who prided himself on how many times he was able to get opposing counsel to make death threats to him during depositions so he could call the police and have them arrested. This guy was so obnoxious that he had the police in his office several times a year.

Because no judge is present, a deposition may be the best opportunity for you to have a truly dramatic episode in your story. Shootings, fights, threats, arguments, all can occur in depositions with no risk of being stopped by a bailiff or judge. If this behavior occurs in court, it will be ended quickly, usually with an arrest or contempt jailing.

Requests for Admissions

Requests for admissions are a list of statements that the other side wants to be admitted are true, or a list of documents sought to be admitted to be authentic. For instance, the plaintiff may know that her dates of employment aren't disputed. Rather than have to prove the dates up at trial, a request for admission will allow her to present the dates as already proven. Requests for admissions are technically not considered "discovery," but most lawyers and judges treat them as discovery for purposes of deadlines. Failure to answer timely means everything in the request is considered admitted.

Requests for admissions will say something like: "Plaintiffs hereby request that Defendant within 30 days after service of this request to make the following admissions for the purpose of this action only and subject to all pertinent objections to admissibility which may be interposed at the trial:

A.   That the following statements are true:
    List of statements

B. That the following documents, attached hereto, are authentic and are true and correct copies of the originals:
List of documents."

Why wouldn't everyone just deny everything? Because if they deny and the statement is deemed true or the document deemed authentic at trial, they have to pay the attorney's fees and costs of proving the denied statement or document.

Does your character throw a request for admissions in the garbage because he doesn't want to be bothered with answering? He will find out he just admitted everything on the list and lose his case, because anything not denied by the deadline is considered admitted.

The reality of requests for admissions is that usually courts frown on admissions by default. Courts tend to like to let people prove their cases with evidence and testimony. Even if a party fails to answer for months or years, the courts usually allow them to cure this failure.

Discovery Disputes

How do your characters deal with discovery issues? There are three types of motions they can file if they think there is a discovery problem:

- **"Motions to compel"** seek to have the court order discovery that hasn't occurred. They are filed when objections are raised; documents are not produced; a party or witness fails to appear; or interrogatories are not answered.
- **"Motions for protective order"** ask the judge to stop or limit discovery. They are filed to stop or limit abusive discovery practices.
- **"Motions for sanctions"** ask the judge to sanction the other side for discovery abuse. They are filed for repeated discovery abuses. A judge can impose a sanction anywhere from a small fine or requiring costs or fees to be paid, up to ending all or part of the case.

Chapter 18 – Alternate Dispute Resolution

Alternative dispute resolution is a means of resolving disputes outside the court system. Courts love alternative dispute resolution. When I started law practice it was unheard of, controversial, communist even. Now courts mandate mediation in almost every court case. Arbitration is the darling of the defense bar. Courts can order non-binding arbitrations where parties either accept the rulings or go to court anyhow. Collaborative law is the newest, least accepted form of alternative dispute resolution. As an arbitrator and a mediator, I am a big fan of alternative dispute resolution.

Mediation

Mediation is where a neutral third party tries to help the parties reach a settlement. Mediators aren't able to make decisions in the case, and won't be the person deciding the case if it goes to trial or arbitration. Their job is to get the parties to reach an agreement so that everyone walks away and says, "I can live with that."

You may remember *The Wedding Crashers* as a funny movie about two guys who crash weddings. But do you remember how it started? The crashers are family mediators, and the mediation scene is fabulous. It's funny but realistic. These mediators are creatively trying to get the parties to move off entrenched positions, which is exactly what real mediators do:

Lawyer: "I knew this was a bad idea."

Mediator 1: "You know what Ken, the bad idea would be to let your client walk out of here today and drag this thing out another year, wasting more time and wasting more money. The only good idea is to let me and John do our job and mediate this thing right here."

Mediator 2: "You wanna hear the crazy thing? I know it doesn't feel like it, but we're making progress. We settled the deal with the cars. Let's see, that takes us to frequent flyer miles. We're flying."

The mediators took an argument and made it turn around. They got the couple to remember some of the good days of their marriage and the case settled. This is a great example of using a realistic scene, adding some humor, and giving the story authenticity.

Mediations can be a fun or serious aspect of your story. They can be a brief interlude or the climax of the story where everything resolves.

Mediator characters will tell the parties that, if everyone is a little unhappy with the settlement, it is probably about right. They are trained in tactics to help the parties reach a consensus. Mediation will usually start with a session where everyone is present. The attorneys, a party representative if it's a corporation, the party if it's an individual, and the insurance adjuster (if there's insurance), will be present, or sometimes on the phone. The mediator will explain the process and give each side time to explain their side of the dispute and what efforts have been made to settle the matter.

Most mediations then break into "caucuses," where the mediator will meet with each side and discuss the upsides and downsides of the case, and settlement offers to be relayed to the other side. What is discussed in caucus is confidential unless the party relaying the information gives the mediator permission to relay it to the other side.

The mediator will then go back and forth between the parties, relaying information and offers, asking questions, making sure both sides understand the risks of going to trial, and try to reach a settlement. They can't give legal advice or put pressure on any side, and they can't prefer one side over the other. Does your mediator character try to bully the parties into a settlement?

Mediators have to disclose any conflicts, prior dealings with either side or the attorney, or other potential matters that could affect their impartiality. Does your mediator character fail to disclose that he is a shareholder in the defendant company? The parties can object to any mediator, and will usually be asked to agree on one. Sometimes the court or mediation group will appoint one, subject to objection.

The mediator is paid by the hour, and is paid whether or not the case is settled. Most cases that are mediated settle at mediation. Mediation with a trained, competent mediator may be the best thing that has happened to the justice system in the past century. It has done much to unclog the court systems and move the parties toward amicable resolutions. Can your story's case end with a mediation instead of a trial?

If a mediation is successful, the parties walk out with a signed settlement agreement. If unsuccessful, impasse is declared and the case goes on to the next step.

Arbitration

Arbitration is where a neutral third party or panel of neutrals acts in place of a judge. Arbitration is a private proceeding where evidence is presented, witnesses heard, and a final decision made. It is like a trial, but quicker and sometimes less expensive.

Arbitrators don't need to be lawyers. They have expertise in a particular area, which means that the case will be decided by someone familiar with the issues. In court, judges know some about lots of areas of law, but few are experts in, say, complex construction law. Having someone who knows the area of law cuts through some of the need to brief on basic issues and educate the decision maker. It is another big reason why parties like arbitrations.

Arbitration is done mostly when the parties agree to resolve their disputes through arbitration rather than court. Sometimes, the parties disagree on whether or not they consented to arbitrate (whether the dispute is "arbitrable."). As an arbitrator, I can tell you that courts are mostly striking down arbitration clauses found in places like receipts, small print, backs of tickets and other places where consumers might not realize they are agreeing to arbitrate.

On the other extreme, courts are tending to uphold arbitration clauses in employment cases, even where the clauses are in small print on job applications, employee handbooks, and pre-employment agreements. Did your character's employment application say she would have to arbitrate any employment issues?

In the middle are commercial (meaning business-related) arbitration clauses, which tend to be more evenly negotiated, and thus are being upheld in most cases.

The advantages of arbitration are that discovery (depositions, document requests, written questions) is usually much more limited, the process is quicker, and the hearing process is more informal. Affidavits and hearsay evidence can be admitted. Other than in employment cases, depositions and formal discovery requests are rare.

Courts in some states use a process of court-appointed arbitrators who issue opinions under seal (in a sealed envelope in the court file that the judge doesn't look at unless the parties accept the opinion). The parties can accept the opinion, in which the case is over. Or the parties can request a "trial de novo," which means the case goes forward in front of the judge. This sounds meaningless, but could your characters settle after hearing the view of an impartial third person about the case? Sometimes a party is shocked that an impartial arbitrator ruled in favor of the other side. Realizing they might lose may be what your characters need to move them toward a settlement.

Another means of arbitration that is extremely cost-effective and speedy is the "paper arbitration." This means that there is no hearing with testimony. The arbitration is done just on paper. The parties submit their briefs and evidence, along with affidavits or deposition transcripts, and the arbitrator decides solely on the parties' written submissions. If you are looking for a way to get around showing witnesses testify in your story, you may want to use a paper arbitration.

There are some downsides to arbitration. One disadvantage can be the cost. Arbitrators' fees and filing fees can sometimes be much more than the cost of going to court. Whether arbitration is cheaper or more expensive depends on the case. If the court proceeding would result in a huge number of depositions, an arbitration may be a way to keep those costs down, since court reporter fees can be huge. If the court case is relatively simple, then an expedited (shorter, speedier) arbitration with smaller, non-hourly arbitrator fees may still be worthwhile. Where arbitrator fees (normally arbitrators are paid by the hour) will be more expensive than what a court case would have been, then the only advantage to selecting arbitration is that it's faster.

The other downside of arbitrations is the bias of the arbitrator. Many arbitrators are paid by a particular employer or company to conduct a series of arbitrations. Sometimes, the parties not paying may believe the arbitrator to be afraid to rule against the party who pays the bill. Defense side firms tend to have more of their attorneys become arbitrators in their particular area of practice. Does your character sue her stockbroker only to end up with an arbitrator who spent 20 years representing stockbrokers? She may fear she won't get a fair hearing because of bias.

Arbitration is a marvelous process when both parties are in it willingly. They will cooperate in exchanging information and speeding up the process because they understand arbitration's advantages. When one party is dragged in kicking and screaming, the cooperation that is the backbone of arbitration can break down. Your arbitrator character may need to get involved in more discovery disputes and exercise control over the process if the parties are forced into arbitration.

The end of the arbitration process is an award. The arbitrator resolves all issues and decides who wins and who loses.[57] The award is either voluntarily paid, or the winner takes the award to court to enforce the award. This will usually end up in the issuance of a judgment confirming the award. Does your character win and then still have to go to court to enforce the award?

The only grounds for vacating an arbitrator's award are failure to disclose a conflict, fraud, corruption, or exceeding authority. Failure to follow the law or legal errors are not reversible, unlike court. Does your character discover the other side bribed the arbitrator with cruise tickets?

Arbitration awards and proceedings are confidential and are not made public, which is another incentive for parties to agree to arbitrate. Does your character push for arbitration to keep some damaging information from going public?

While arbitration is not perfect, it can be a great way to resolve a case quickly, privately, and relatively inexpensively. It is another means of unclogging the courts and getting disputes resolved. Can it unclog your story by giving you a quick resolution?

Private judging

A seldom used but available means of alternative dispute resolution is private judging. The parties hire a judge to decide the dispute, similar to an arbitration. The difference is that the private judge doesn't necessarily have expertise in a particular area of law, and is more likely to be a retired judge. These procedures are done more formally and with the use of formal discovery procedures and evidentiary rules. The idea is that, in a complex case, a judge who focuses on fewer matters and who is

---

[57] The issue of prevailing party attorney's fees has to be resolved in court unless the parties specifically agree to let the arbitrator decide that as well.

available on short notice to resolve hearings can speed things up and save the parties time and expense.

Collaborative Law

Collaborative law is where the attorneys are hired solely to settle the case and agree to withdraw if the case doesn't settle. I discussed it extensively in the family law section in Chapter 15. Collaborative law can be used in other areas of legal practice, but the vast majority is still done in the context of divorces. Collaborative law will ultimately expand to areas such as employment, commercial, construction and consumer law.

Online dispute resolution

The internet has forced arbitration and mediation to evolve. Online arbitrations and mediations are starting to develop, where the dispute resolution is done entirely online. Online mediations can be done by live chat, and can be from a few minutes to an hour. Online arbitrations allow parties to submit brief written statements and some evidence, and the decision can be made quickly without a hearing. Because they are just developing, the online processes are in flux. Eventually online dispute resolution will become more common, and the procedures will be standardized. For right now, you can use them in your story, limited only by your imagination. You could have a Twitter mediation in your story, where the parties resolve their case one sentence at a time.

Conclusion

Other forms of alternative dispute resolution will evolve and emerge. The practice of law is increasingly becoming about resolving disputes rather than about simply going to court and getting a judgment.

If your story has a dispute, you can utilize alternative dispute resolution as a minor plot point or as the story's climax. There are plenty of opportunities for emotions, conflict, character development, and plot twists in these proceedings. The best part for writers is that they aren't as controlled as court proceedings, so there's more opportunity for extreme behavior. They can also be shown as shorter than court proceedings without bending reality too much.

Chapter 19 – Trial Preparation

Preparing for and conducting a trial is the single most time-intensive, stressful thing civil lawyers do. Cases don't go from intake to trial without hundreds of hours of effort. Discovery is long and drawn out. Trial preparation is intense, done in the weeks or months right before trial, and will make or break the case. An unprepared lawyer can win, but will have a much harder time and will be doing the client a disservice.

A trial done by well prepared lawyers will run more smoothly and is more pleasurable for the judge and jury. If your lawyer character is unprepared, it's important to know what they should have done and show the other side doing it as a contrast. And you will need to show things going wrong as a result. This provides great tension for your writing. If both sides have prepared, you need to know what they have done to get ready.

Jury instructions

This is what is read to the jury out of the judge's own mouth right before they go to deliberate. In my view, the jury instructions are the single most important part of the trial. Jurors take them extremely seriously. If instructions are confusing or have an incorrect statement of the law, the jury will punish the plaintiff, not the defense. When in doubt, I believe juries rule against the party seeking relief.

Most jury instructions are standardized. Negligence, medical malpractice, defamation, the more common tort and statutory claims, are standard and the parties have to argue and prove to the judge the need for any changes or modifications. Because standard jury instructions are pre-approved (panels of judges and lawyers write and publish them) judges can't be reversed on appeal for selecting a standard instruction. Judges in your story will err on the side of using the standard instructions.

In developing areas of the law like employment, the jury instructions are constantly in flux, and lawyers need to carefully use model instructions and update or modify them to reflect the facts and law of the case. You could write a funny jury instruction on, say, when an employer is liable for the janitor leaving a bag of ball-bearings spilled in the hallway, causing an injury. Or your jury instruction could show that your character can't prove a key part of her case.

Jury instructions will be drafted by one or both attorneys. The parties have a conference to see which ones they agree on.

The disputed ones are then presented in a "charge conference," usually the day before or the day of jury deliberations. The lawyers argue over which version of the proposed instructions should be read to the jury. Then the judge picks. She may decide to give the defense instruction on one issue and the plaintiff's instruction on a different issue. This is tough on the lawyers, who don't know until the last minute what the judge is going to say to the jury. Your character's case strategy could get thrown off by an unexpected jury instruction. The lawyer may have to change his closing because the jury is getting an instruction that damages his case.

Most judges get the proposed instructions on DVD from both attorneys. After the charge conference, they make any changes to the instructions and create the final set, using the versions they selected from each side. Instructions will then be presented to both sides for final review for errors (typographical, or the judge copied the wrong side's instruction). The instructions are printed right before the jury comes in, then the judge reads them straight through to the jury.

I just saw a TV show where the judge read an instruction that both attorneys were hearing for the first time. The attorneys' jaws dropped in shock when they heard the instruction. There had been no charge conference. This galls me. It would never happen. They might not find out until ten minutes before closing arguments, but the attorneys always know what instructions the judge will give before they are read to the jury.

The instructions should be organized so they make sense. There will be initial instructions to the jury about what they are supposed to do when they go into the jury room. Select a foreperson, discuss the case, etc. Then the judge will summarize for each count what both parties are alleging. Here is where careful crafting on the attorneys' part is important. Does an awkward statement or, worse, a statement that makes clear the judge doesn't buy one party's position, damage your character's case? For instance, your judge could say, pointedly, "I instruct that you may disregard any or all of a witness' testimony. You may disbelieve a witness's testimony based upon lack of credibility." Then he could look at or point to your character. The jury gets the message that the judge doesn't believe her.

The judge will then describe what specific issues the jury must decide in order to find in favor of the plaintiff. He will describe what the defenses are to the claims, and what issues the jury must consider in order to decide to find in favor of a defense. He will describe what they need to do if they find a particular way on certain points. If there is more than one count, the judge will go through each count. The jury will then be told about how to compute damages if the plaintiff has won. Finally, they will be told how to fill out the verdict form.

Some judges let jurors take a copy of the jury instructions in the deliberation room with them, some do not. If your characters don't spend the time working on the jury instructions, they can have a great trial and still lose because the judge gives a confusing or erroneous instruction. And if they don't object to the instruction, they will not be able to get an erroneous instruction reversed on appeal.

Exhibit/Witness Lists

These are the lists of each document or other piece of evidence that each side plans to introduce, and each witness the party plans to call. Expert exhibit lists will require the specifics about what the expert is expected to testify on and the opinions that will be rendered. Regular witness lists will have the name and address of each witness so they can be subpoenaed for deposition and trial.

The purpose of these lists is so the other side can get copies or inspect any exhibits they haven't seen yet, and depose any remaining witnesses.

Any exhibits or witnesses not put on the list will normally not be allowed to be used in the case. Many judges will allow a disclaimer at the end of the lists:

15. All exhibits on Defendant's exhibit list. (Meaning if the other side lists something, the Plaintiff can use it at trial)
16. Impeachment and rebuttal exhibits. (Meaning if a witness testifies, any documents can be used to counter what they've just said, whether or not they are listed)
17. All exhibits produced in discovery in this matter. (This can be everything that either side provided in the case, whether or not it is listed)

These catch-all categories still allow for surprises to happen. But the purpose of discovery and disclosures is to avoid surprise. Does your judge character allow parties a continuance or postponement of a trial if they are surprised? I've seen judges allow a party to issue a trial subpoena where a witness shows up with documents neither disclosed nor previously seen, and still allow them to be introduced. Your plaintiff character could be shown his bank statements from five years ago and be asked to explain certain entries on the spot. If he guesses wrong under oath, it's the same as lying. If your judge wants to throw out the case, allowing surprise exhibits may confuse a witness enough to damage or destroy the case.

Subpoenas

Trial subpoenas, like deposition subpoenas, can be with or without a request for documents. A subpoena duces tecum (subpoena asking a witness to come with documents) at trial is more rare than at deposition, but may be used, for instance, if a doctor was called and they need to bring the patient file so they can use it during testimony.

Since trials are scheduled for a long period, usually 2 weeks to three months, the subpoena will say, "For the three week trial period commencing June 5, 2010" as an example. My own subpoenas state that witnesses should contact me to schedule their specific date and time of appearance. That way I know they've received it, they intend to show up, and I can work around their schedule as best I can to make it more convenient for them. A witness cooling their heels for a week sitting outside the courtroom in your story will be very, very unhappy. An unhappy witness will not be a good one.

Subpoenas will usually be served by a process server or the sheriff. Some states allow attorneys, or any person over 18 who isn't a party (the plaintiff or defendant in the case), to serve a subpoena. The subpoena will come with a small witness fee, from under $10 to around $40. This is theoretically to pay the witness for gas mileage and parking. It is illegal to pay a witness money to testify[58] other than the witness fee, unless the witness is an expert.

Sometimes witnesses fail to show up. They can be held in contempt for doing so. The sticky issue comes up if they fail to show during a trial. Judges don't like mistrials or continuances for no-show witnesses. Some will send the sheriff to haul them into court that day. Some will make the attorneys proceed without. Does a witness fail to show up for your character's trial? If the key witness doesn't show up, your character could lose their case because they couldn't prove it at trial.

If the witness fails to show, sure, your character can have them jailed later. But what good is that if the case has already been lost? Your characters could lose a case or have it damaged by a no-show witness.

Verdict forms

A verdict form is what the jury uses to write their verdict. A confusing verdict form (one that uses words the jury doesn't understand, legalese, or incorrect statements of law) can tank a case as easily as a confusing jury instruction. These forms are, again, prepared in advance. The parties try to agree on them, and any disputed issues get decided right before the forms go to the jury. Defense attorneys like to make them unduly complex because this works to their advantage. Plaintiff's attorneys will try to keep them simple. Each side will try to put in language that favors their position. These distinctions can be minute but important. Here's a great example that comes up all the time.

Was the harassment so severe and pervasive that it altered the terms and conditions of Plaintiff's employment?

Was the harassment either so severe or so pervasive that it altered the terms and conditions of Plaintiff's employment?

Was the harassment either so severe or so frequent that it altered the terms and conditions of Plaintiff's employment?

---

[58] I once had a witness tell me that the Plaintiff (I represented the Defendant) had a lot of nerve listing her as a witness because she had turned down the offer of a trip to Hawaii if she'd testify for the Plaintiff. When I got that witness to put that in an affidavit, the case settled amazingly fast.

The first version is an incorrect statement of the law, but it also appears on some pattern verdict forms issued out of the federal courts. The standard is severe OR pervasive, not severe AND pervasive. This is discussed in **Chapter 11**. If the incident was severe, such as a rape, it might not also be pervasive. I like the third version because jurors don't know what the heck pervasive means.

Errors in verdict forms are reversible, but only if the error was raised at trial when the attorneys were arguing which form was correct in front of the judge.

Motions In Limine

These are motions that try to limit or exclude evidence or testimony. The idea is to simplify the trial itself, limit the number of arguments that need to be made in front of the jury, and to exclude evidence or testimony that is duplicative, inadmissible, or prejudicial. Some of your character's key evidence could be thrown out, such as an email they got by hacking into the former employer's computer, excluded on the grounds that it was a trade secret or a privacy violation.

The motions are usually brought up in the weeks before trial. Most judges give deadlines for them. But they can also be used sometimes in mid-trial if some piece of evidence is a surprise or a new theory of the case arises that was unexpected.

One argument lawyers use to exclude evidence is that it is "more prejudicial than probative." This objection covers many issues – prior drug use, sexual history, prior bad acts, convictions, and other pieces of evidence. The idea is that the evidence may be slightly relevant, but it will also be so damaging that the harm it will cause outweighs any proper purpose. For instance, in a sexual harassment case, the defense might want to introduce promiscuity. However, her private sexual history has nothing to do with whether or not her supervisor made repeated sexual comments to her. So it wouldn't be allowed in.

Motions in limine can also be used to exclude items that weren't raised in the pleadings, that have already been decided, that weren't previously disclosed, that contradict an admission already made, or that aren't admissible under a rule of evidence. For instance, the defense in your story wants to claim that the plaintiff failed to send a demand letter required under a statute requiring notice before bringing a negligence claim. However, if they never put in their answer that she failed to comply with a condition precedent (legalese for she didn't do something she was supposed to do before filing suit), the court might not allow them to raise that issue in the trial.

These can be used for so many purposes, they are going to be helpful (or devastating) to any lawyer character you have. The parties rarely understand them, so your party character can be confused or distressed that they can't testify on a topic, or think their attorney is brilliant for getting a damaging piece of evidence thrown out. You could have the defense try to bring in your character's casual drug use, show the panic your character has that he'll lose the case, then provide relief by getting the evidence excluded.

Pretrial Dispositive Motions

Dispositive motions are ones that end all or part of the case. One kind of motion that could end the case is one I already talked about: motions to dismiss in **Chapter 8**. These can be brought right up through the end of the trial. There are two other commonly used dispositive motions that can throw a wrench in the story.

Motion for Judgment on the Pleadings

The purpose of the motion is to say that, based on the pleadings, one side or the other should win the case. This is a motion done, usually shortly after pleadings close, but which can be brought up before trial.

For example if, in response to a complaint, the defendant admits he was negligent and doesn't raise any defenses, the plaintiff could move for judgment on the pleadings. A mortgage foreclosure, other debt, breach of contract, or other case that involves relatively undisputed facts could warrant this type of motion. In a mortgage foreclosure story, the homeowner might admit they hadn't paid for six months and try to say it's because they lost their job. Losing their job isn't a defense, so the judge could enter judgment on the pleadings.

Motions for judgment on the pleadings are relatively rare in civil practice. The greater risk to your plaintiff character's case is a motion for summary judgment.

Summary Judgment

Summary judgment is used where the important facts in the case are undisputed. Once the facts are agreed, one side might think the law is on their side and judgment is required on all or part of the case. So they would file a Motion for Summary Judgment. If they are only entitled to judgment on part of the case, such as on a defense or on liability (meaning the money owed still has to be proven), then it's called a Motion for Partial Summary Judgment.

Motions for summary judgment used to be rarely granted, and judges used to disfavor them. However, they are becoming more common, particularly in cases judges dislike such as discrimination and defamation cases. Federal courts use them more frequently than state courts[59] to clear their calendars.

The person making the motion attaches affidavits (sworn statements) and certified copies of any documents that support their claim that the facts are undisputed. For instance, your sexual harassment plaintiff character could testify that the only sexual harassment she's claiming was the supervisor sending her an email asking her for a date. The defense would attach the plaintiff's deposition transcript and a copy of the email. The defense would argue that the single instance isn't enough to be sexual harassment. Based upon that, the judge would probably enter summary judgment in favor of the defense and the case would be over.

If partial summary judgment is entered, then the court will state which issues remain to be decided. The trial will proceed only on the undecided issues. For instance, if partial judgment was entered on liability in favor of the plaintiff, saying the defendant is liable for the claims, then the case would proceed only on the issue of the amount of money the plaintiff will get.

---

[59] I am happy to report that I just had a defense lawyer announce bitterly in a mediation that, had the case been brought in federal court, summary judgment would have been granted by now. The case then settled in the mid-six-figures. See, when opposing counsel make statements like that to me, my clients always tell me later that they're glad I advised them correctly to stay in state court. So I always appreciate it when opposing counsel makes me look smart.

Chapter 20 – Court Practice Before Trial

Calendar Call

Calendar call or docket call is where lawyers literally are called to the court to bring their calendars to set the trial. There will be a trial notice well in advance setting deadlines for discovery (discovery cutoff), motions, witness and exhibit lists, mediation, expert discovery, pretrial stipulations, and the trial period.

The trial period will be anywhere from two weeks to the longest I've ever seen, three months. The order will set the calendar call day, usually the week or two before the first day of the trial period. The lawyers all show up and the cases are called, emergency cases first, then according to age of the case, oldest first. Picture tens if not hundreds of lawyers milling about, socializing, arguing, settling cases. Calendar calls can be lots of fun.

The judge always asks if the lawyers are ready for trial. Many times, one or the other will give a reason why the case should be continued, or rolled over to the next trial period. Sometimes the parties agree, sometimes not. The judge will then decide if there is good cause shown to move the trial, or if it will go forward.

If the case is going forward, the judge will ask how many days the trial will last and which week the lawyers want. If they agree, then the judge will give them a number for that week. "You're case number 1 on week 1." If one has a conflict a particular week, the judge will accommodate the conflict. "Your honor, I'm set number one for a trial the first week, so I'd prefer week 3." "OK, you're number 2 on week 3."

The other lawyers will be waiting carefully keeping track of the numbers assigned to each case. That's because, when they get their trial number, they have to keep in touch with the lawyers for the cases in front of them. They will want to find if the case ahead of them has settled, or if it will get resolved.

For instance, the lawyer whose case is number 3 on week 1 knows that the two trials ahead of them (number 1 on week 1 and number 2 on week 1) have to settle before they get to go. If theirs is a four or five day trial, then the cases ahead must settle because their case will take the whole week. If theirs is a one or two day trial, then they also want to track any trials in progress. If number 1 on week 1 settles and number 2 on week 1 is the trial that is starting Monday, the lawyers for number 3 on week one are "on deck." They will have to see if the trial in front of them ends by Tuesday or Wednesday that week so they get a chance to go.

As another example, if case number 1 is a three day trial and it goes; case number 2 is a five day trial, so it gets rolled over to another trial period (once the first day is used up, they won't be able to finish that week); case number 3 is two days, so if all goes as planned, case number 3 should be ready to go on Thursday because they can finish in two days. Theoretically. The lawyers frequently underestimate how long their trial will take. If they run out of time, they may end up with a mistrial and have to start over.

Sounds confusing? It's pandemonium. Let's say you're number 1 on week 2. Theoretically, you're definitely going to trial, right? Wrong. If case number 1 goes long, you get rolled over. Does the judge forget to tell your character that she has a day off during a particular week? They can be ready to go only to find out the judge has a short week, theirs is a 5 day trial, so they're rolled over.

Only number 1 week 1 has a pretty much guaranteed chance of going to trial. Even then, I have had judges bump our trial for one reason or another.

This is particularly distressing to clients and witnesses who are left hanging, unsure of when the trial will go. Lawyers are used to the "hurry up and wait" of trial scheduling. Usually the first time a trial is set is sort of a dry run. The office gears up, witnesses are subpoenaed, evidence organized, and then you realize everything that was forgotten, overlooked, depos that need to be taken, exhibits the other side never got you, an instruction that needs cleaning up, etc. When the trial doesn't go, the parties get to stand down and fix everything they realized was wrong or incomplete.

Of course, your characters can't count on the trial not going. They have to prepare and be ready, because anything can happen in a trial period. I've actually had judges call the parties from week 2 during week

1 and say, "All my trials settled. Can you be here in 2 hours?" And your characters had better say yes if they want to get the case tried.

Sometimes judges will say, "I have a judge who is doing overflow work for me. Will you try the case in front of Judge Smith in order to get your trial done this period?" Your character's upside is speed. The downside is having a judge who knows absolutely nothing about the case. The lawyers have to make a snap decision, with the clients, as to which way to go.

Clients have to take off work, witnesses also have to miss work, and the uncertainty causes much anxiety. Delays are frustrating when your character wants it over. The defense is usually relieved when the trial is delayed, and the plaintiff wants the whole thing over.

Calendar call and the frustrating uncertainty of whether the trial is actually going can add to the drama and tension of your story. A trial that goes the first time it is set is rare. Showing how it really works may be just what you need to make your story realistic.

Motion Calendar

"Motion calendar" or "motion docket" is how short motions get set for hearing in front of the judge. If there's anything crazier in the civil justice system than motion calendar, I don't know what it is. Clients hardly ever see it, so they think I'm exaggerating when I try to describe it. Here's motion calendar in a nutshell.

Hearings that can take a short time, usually limited to 5 – 15 minutes, depending on the judge, can be set on a "motion calendar," usually occurring 2 – 3 days per week for the judge at a particular time, mostly at some ungodly hour of the morning. Why? Are all judges morning people? Do they like getting up at 5 or 6 a.m.? I have no idea. Motion calendars can go as early as 7 or 7:30, but are usually somewhere between 8 and 9 a.m.

Here's where it gets fun. The attorney setting the motion sends a notice, say a week or two in advance, setting the motion on a designated motion day. Some judges' offices won't confirm whether or not the motion made the calendar or got bumped. Usually the first, say 20 or 50 cases, make the calendar. The rest aren't set, and the lawyer has to try again.

Sometimes the only way to find out your character's case didn't make it onto the judge's calendar is to have them show up. Some clerk's offices or judge's offices have a method of confirming whether the hearing made the calendar or not. Bad enough yet?

It gets better. If 20 or 30 or 50 cases are on the calendar, who goes first? Usually the first case to "have a pair," that is, both lawyers show up. The bailiff or judicial assistant will sign each lawyer in, and when both are present they assign a number. They then call the cases into chambers or the courtroom in numerical order[60]. If your character's opposing counsel wants to be a jerk, they can show up late and make your character sit all morning for the case to be heard. Lawyers can sit or stand in a crowded hallway for hours waiting to be called. This is great for defense lawyers who are billing by the hour, and lousy for plaintiff's lawyers who aren't paid until the case is over.

And when the judge runs out of time, the judicial assistant will tell everyone left that they have to reset the hearing.

Is there any wonder why legal bills get so high?

Your client character can be frustrated by the repeated delays in getting hearings on basic motions. Your attorney character can spend so much time cooling heels with opposing counsel in a hall that they become friends or resolve the matter that is the subject of the motion. More action occurs in the hallway than in chambers during motion calendar. Attorneys can sit far apart and ignore each other, talk to each other, socialize with other attorneys, get to know hapless clients who try to attend these hearings, or befriend the judicial assistant. Attorneys are incapable of sitting and doing nothing, so they will either talk to someone or bring work if they plan to ignore the other side.

If the judge is in a bad mood, the lawyers who don't go first get a heads up and could decide to submit an agreed order (the parties agree on how the issue is going to be resolved, so they prepare an order for the judge to sign reflecting the agreement) on the issue or reschedule. Lawyers arguing will usually have other lawyers listening to their arguments, so a judicial slapdown can be doubly humiliating in front of colleagues for your character.

If the hearing is in a courtroom for motion calendar, the attorneys will usually have to argue in front of the bench, with no place to put down papers and files.

---

[60] I know one courthouse that posts the lists the night before, just to mess with out of town lawyers. The locals run in and sign up first.

Motion calendar arguments are very seat-of-the-pants. The argument has to be condensed into a minute or two, and many attorneys come with little or no preparation. These hearings are usually discovery disputes or other quick beefs with opposing counsel.

Motion calendar can be a place to put your plot twists or to develop your villains and other characters. Have fun with it.

Specially Set Hearings

Motions that aren't on motion calendar are specially set in order to get a date to appear before the judge. The hearing is where the parties make their arguments to the judge about how the motion should be decided. These settings can take weeks or months to get. And sometimes they get bumped at the last minute, only to take weeks or months more to reschedule. Litigation is all about living with delay.

The hearings themselves are usually in chambers. The lawyers will sit around a table, with the judge at a desk at the head of the table. The party making the motion generally gets to go first. How the hearings are conducted can vary wildly from judge to judge. Some allow a free for all, with lawyers interrupting each other. Most will let one side be heard without interruption for slightly less than half the allotted time, then the other side. Then the moving party gets the last word.

Sometimes the judge will ask questions. Some judges will take up most of the hearing time themselves with comments, questions, and asides. I have one judge who will get up, pace, and make the arguments to himself. It seems to help him sort through the arguments in his head so he can make the decision. Which kind of judge do you have in your story?

If the hearing is in a courtroom, the attorneys and clients, if they attend, will sit at counsel table and will either argue by standing at counsel table or will stand at the podium.

Common Pretrial Motions

Motion to Compel	Pleadings
Motion for Protective Order	Motion for Summary Judgment
Motion to Dismiss	Motion for Leave to Plead
Motion to Strike	Punitive Damages
Motion for Judgment on the	Motion for Sanctions

Motion for Attorney's Fees	Motion to Remove
Motion for	Motion to Transfer Venue
Rehearing/Reconsideration	Motion to Intervene
Motion for Stay	Motion to Recuse or Disqualify
Motion for Temporary	Judge
Injunction	Motion to Disqualify Counsel
Emergency Motion for Ex Parte	Motion to Withdraw
Injunction	Motion in Limine
Motion to Quash Subpoena	

Specially set hearings are usually more scripted, with the lawyers having prepared memoranda of law for the judge in advance. Some hearings require testimony, so witnesses will be called and evidence presented. Injunctions, attorney's fees, and sanctions hearings are just a few that may need live testimony.

Because these hearings aren't in front of a jury, the judge in your story could show more of their real personality to the attorneys. Judges behave drastically differently in front of a jury than they do with just the lawyers.

The presence of a court reporter can also make a big difference in a judge's behavior. When I was pregnant, I once had a judge order me to get co-counsel because he said he wasn't going to continue the trial if I gave birth. Fortunately, I had a court reporter. I asked him, just to be clear, if he was ordering me to hire co-counsel because I was pregnant. He wisely thought again, and backed off.

Judges in your story who are abusive, inattentive, biased, or unprofessional can behave quite well when their words are being transcribed. On the other hand, sometimes the lawyers may want the judge to feel freer to speak his or her mind, in which case they can go off the record or just not have a court reporter at the hearing.

Most hearings will result in a ruling and a written order on the spot. These orders are either pre-prepared by one of the attorneys, or are handwritten in the hallway and sent to the judge for signature. Sometimes the order is complicated and the attorneys go back to their offices to do the order, which usually results in a disagreement about what the judge actually said. Does your character think he's won only to have to go back for another ruling because both sides can't agree what the judge said? For instance, the defense could believe the judge said a motion to dismiss was granted with prejudice, meaning the case is over. The plaintiff could claim they didn't hear the words "with prejudice," which means they could file an amended complaint. If they didn't have a court reporter, and the judge doesn't remember, they could have to argue the case all over.

Some judges will take a complicated matter under advisement and issue an order later. The problem with this is motions are sometimes forgotten, and the judge fails to rule for long periods. The issue can become moot (not mute), meaning the issue no longer matters because something already happened (for instance, a motion to delay a deposition becomes moot once the deposition has occurred), or the case can be delayed, if the ruling is not made timely.

The order on a hearing will have the style (case name, number, court identification), and then say something like:

THIS CAUSE, having come before the Court on Plaintiff's Motion for Protective Order regarding the deposition scheduled for October 31, 2010, and the Court having heard the argument of counsel and being otherwise advised in the premises, it is hereby

ORDERED AND ADJUDGED:

1. The deposition scheduled for October 31, 2010 shall not proceed on the date scheduled.

2. Plaintiff's deposition shall be rescheduled by cooperating with Plaintiff's counsel to find a date convenient for both sides in which Plaintiff will not be undergoing a heart transplant.

DONE AND ORDERED this 19th day of September, 2010 in chambers in Broward County, Florida.

Hon. Jane Smith
Circuit Court Judge

Copies furnished:

James Patoot, Esq.
Jane Newbie, Esq.

Motion practice can be tedious, but it is the backbone of civil trial practice. Your most entertaining or pivotal moments can be in motion hearings rather than at trials, and you can have greater authenticity because of the flexibility and freedom the judges have when they aren't in front of a jury.

Chapter 21 – The Trial

Admit it. Ninety percent of you skipped chapters 1 – 20 and went right here. Despite all my pleas that you write about some of the pretrial stuff that is 99% of civil law practice, you are going to go right to the trial. Trials are exciting, no doubt. Anything can happen. If you haven't looked at some of the sections on other places to put some action, such as depositions, mediations, and pretrial hearings, please, go back. Trials have a pretty strict structure, and some of your zanier moments can't happen here realistically.

Your character's trial day is going to start with either jury selection or motions. In a busy courthouse with lots of judges competing for a jury pool, the jury selection goes first so the judge can get a shot at the top jury picks.

Jury Selection

Unless the trial is exceptionally complex and high profile, jury selection goes pretty quickly. Most judges will do some initial voir dire, which means asking the jury questions. The judge will ask the basics. Do they know any of the attorneys or parties? Do they know anything about the case? Most jurors will have filled out a form giving some basic information about job, criminal history, and prior lawsuit involvement.

The lawyers will not know anything about the jurors until they walk in the door. Jurors are selected randomly from a pool, and are assigned to the particular trial at the last minute. Or, does one side have the jury pool list in advance in your story?

Lawyers, jury consultants if the lawyers or parties have the money, and the parties will participate in the jury selection, discussing the decision in a huddle at counsel table.

The lawyers are given the questionnaires shortly in advance, and have a chance to note any questions that arise regarding particular jurors. After the judge asks the initial questions, the lawyers will have a chance to voir dire the jury. This is usually very, very short. The lawyers can have as short as 15 minutes, as long as an hour, depending on the judge and the trial, to ask everything they could possibly want to know of the jury. You can have some fun with your writing by thinking up strange/goofy questions for your lawyer character to ask.

Some judges require the questions to be submitted in advance. Sometimes they will place parameters on the questions. I had a judge state that she hated bumper sticker questions (As in, "Do you have any bumper stickers on your car? What do they say?") and would not allow them.

Usually there isn't enough time to ask all questions of each potential juror. So the questions will be directed to the whole panel. "Did anyone here ever _____? Raise your hand if you _____?"

The plaintiff goes first with questions, which actually gives the defense a small advantage in that they don't have to ask some of the more basic questions because they'll already be covered. They get to have more information and can focus on follow up.

Jury voir dire is the first time a jury in your story will hear about the case, and the first contact they will have with the lawyers. A likeable lawyer can make big points during voir dire. And the lawyers can subtly give hints about the case and get a feel for any biases the jurors might have.

Here's an example of a few of questions a jury might be asked (there are usually dozens of questions):

JURY VOIR DIRE

- Have you or has any member of your family ever been a plaintiff or defendant in any lawsuit? If yes, what kind of lawsuit and what was the result?
- Have you ever been a witness in a lawsuit? If so, was there anything about being a witness in a lawsuit that would cause you to favor one side over the other in this lawsuit? Was there anything about being a witness in a lawsuit that gave you any particular feelings, either negative or positive, about our judicial system?

- Do you have a member of your family or a close friend who was either a party or a witness in a lawsuit? If yes, what kind of lawsuit and what was the result?
- Do you have certain thoughts or concepts or feelings regarding the judicial system in this country? If you do, would you please tell me about them?
- Have you ever served on a jury before? If so, when and how many times? In what court? Were the cases civil or criminal? If the cases were civil, what did they concern? In those civil cases, what were the verdicts? In those criminal cases, what were the charges? Was the verdict guilty or not guilty?
- I would like to ask if you have any reason at all, however private, that would make you feel you would not like to serve on this case? If so, please raise your hand.

The questions would be tailored to the particular type of case. If anyone answers yes to the questions, they will raise their hands and the lawyer will ask follow up questions. Many times the lawyer won't have time to ask everything on the list, so they will have to pick the most important questions and decide which to ask.

The defense will follow up with their questions. Then the lawyers will huddle with the clients and/or consultants. Sometimes this is done in front of the jury, but mostly done away from them. The jury will be sent back into the hall or some other waiting area.

Challenging the jurors

The defense and plaintiff can challenge jurors, meaning they don't want that particular juror to serve. The judge will go in order, starting with juror number 1.

There will be peremptory challenges (challenges that each side gets to make without a stated reason) allowed to each side, that is, each lawyer can strike that number of jurors for no stated reason. The most common number I see is three peremptory challenges per side. Peremptory challenges can also be the subject of appeal in your story if they are used in an improper fashion, such as to strike all black jurors.

Challenges for cause (for a stated reason) will be argued, and the judge will decide whether cause exists. Challenges for cause will be for specific biases or conflicts. For instance, the Plaintiff's attorney in your discrimination story might challenge a juror who was an HR person for 24 years and who admitted she never encountered a situation where she believed there was merit to an employee's discrimination claim. Defense will vigorously defend the honor of the challenged juror. The judge will decide. If the juror is allowed to stay on, then it may be a matter for appeal later if the Plaintiff loses. Most judges err on the side of not striking the juror. Counsel gets unlimited challenges for cause.

The selection will go something like this.

> **Judge:** Juror number 1. Plaintiff?
> **Plaintiff's attorney:** No objection.
> **Judge:** Defense?
> **Defense attorney:** We'll strike.
> **Judge:** Juror number 1 is stricken. Juror number 2. Plaintiff?
> **Plaintiff's attorney:** No objection.
> **Judge:** Defense?
> **Defense attorney:** No objection.

This goes on until there are 6 jurors (yes, I know you think juries have 12 members, but this is rarely the case in civil matters, although some courts still have 12 member juries) and up to two alternates seated.

Then the judge may allow what are called back strikes (going back to jurors that were already discussed) if the lawyers have any peremptory challenges left.

> **Judge:** Any back strikes? Plaintiff?
> **Plaintiff's attorney:** We strike number 5.

If a juror is back-stricken, then the judge asks about challenges to the next one on the list.

Once the jury is seated, the remaining jurors are either sent home or back to the jury pool to start over.

The judge will give the jurors initial instructions. A little bit about the case, whether or not they can take notes, when lunch will be, whatever the judge thinks the jury needs to know about how things will work. Elected judges like to take this time to show the jury just how great they are and why they should vote to re-elect Hizonor. Then the judge turns it over to the lawyers.

Order of Presentation

Just to give you a summary of how the case will go, here's the order:

Opening by plaintiff

Opening by defendant

Witnesses called by plaintiff, followed by cross examination of each by defendant, then re-direct by plaintiff.

Plaintiff rests

If defendant is going to move for directed verdict, it's done here.

Witnesses called by defendant, followed by cross examination of each by plaintiff, then re-direct by defendant.

Defendant rests.

Post-trial motions by both sides are done here – motions for directed verdict.

Plaintiff's closing argument.

Defendant's closing argument.

Plaintiff's rebuttal argument.

Jury instructions are read.

Jury deliberates.

Jury verdict read.

More post-trial motions, although many are done days or weeks later because everyone wants to go home.

Protocol

"Most TV is not about reality; it's about entertainment. If you can't keep an audience captivated, you won't be on for long. So when I watch a show like *Boston Legal*, where the judge is openly mocked in the courtroom and the closing argument is extremely powerful and completely improper, I smile and enjoy the heck out of it. I get enough reality at work."

-Alex Ferrer, TV's *Judge Alex*.

Judges are properly referred to as "Your Honor." Some attorneys just say, "Judge." As in, "Judge, I object." I have a preference for "Your Honor," but both are commonly used, so your characters can use either. Absolutely not, "Mr. Smith" or "hey you" or "dumba--."

Here's the thing about judges. They are human. Some have biases, some are just dumb, and all can be infuriating when they rule against you. But when they are acting in their official role, they are the office, not the individual. And when they are the office, they are what stands between each one of us and tyranny. A judge is the cornerstone of a democratic justice system. As such, they don't have to earn respect. They must be respected.

If your character fails to bite her tongue, your story should carry consequences. A trip to the jail for a few hours, only to be released upon calming down and being ready to apologize profusely, sanctions, even disbarment or being disallowed from practicing in that particular court again, are all sanctions that can and should be levied against a lawyer who can't hold in the snarky comment. Sometimes the judge will go even further, dismissing the case. That's a total disaster, because it's malpractice city. Say the judge dismisses the case because the lawyer called her a witch. The client, who had a good case, could come back and sue the lawyer because the loss was the lawyer's fault.

Your judge character may not deserve respect. But your characters have to give it anyhow. In private, they can moan and complain, and say all the things they wished they could say to the judge. But mocking judges to their face is very, very dangerous. And it should be. If the office of judge does not command respect, and we don't fear the consequences of disobedience, people will stop obeying. There lies despotism or anarchy.

Bench Trials

The differences between bench and jury trials are pretty striking. Openings are shorter or non-existent in bench trials. Objections are fewer because the judge won't be prejudiced by improper evidence, mistrials are almost impossible, and almost all the theatrics are spared. Judges don't want to see dramatics, hear poetry, or suffer the nonsense lawyers put on for the uninitiated. They want to see the evidence and hear the witnesses. Then they focus on the legal arguments. Closings may be short, or may be in writing in the form of briefs.

Bench trials take half the time of jury trials, or less than half. They are no-nonsense. Some claims can only be decided through a bench trial, such as a lawsuit seeking an injunction to stop someone from using a trade secret, or a small claim (under $5000 or so). If your story has one of those, you can make the judge quirky or biased, or do something besides attorney antics to entertain your reader. The other thing that happens more in bench trials is the attorneys carping and sniping at each other. If this happens in front of jurors the judge stops them, and they realize it makes them look bad. It ticks the judge off too, but most attorneys can't help themselves. Attorney sniping is another way to increase your story's tension.

Opening Statement

The plaintiff's attorney will give an opening statement first. This is not, I repeat, not, called "opening argument" (there's no such thing as opening argument and I see this all the time on TV). The opening statement is a non-argumentative statement of what the lawyer believes the evidence will show in the case. The smart lawyer will, like a writer, tell a story about the case, with enough drama and plot twists to keep the jury listening and enough information to tell the jury why they absolutely will want to rule in favor of the plaintiff.

From the writer's perspective, your opening will be much shorter than a real one. Openings can be 15 minutes to many hours, depending on the complexity of the case. Most are 15 – 30 minutes. A screenwriter with a 15 minute opening has just used 1/8 of their screen time. A writer's opening is more like 2 – 5 minutes.

The defense will be allowed to do their opening at the end of the plaintiff's opening, or they can reserve and do their opening at the beginning of their portion of the case. It's a matter of personal taste and strategy, but most defense attorneys do opening at the start of the case so the jury gets a balanced perspective at the beginning.

If motions weren't heard before the jury was selected, they may be heard either right before or right after opening, out of the jury's presence.

There is no rebuttal in opening, because it's not an argument. It's just the facts, and how they will play out. At the end of openings, the judge will say, "Plaintiff, call your first witness."

Witness Examinations

The order of witnesses is a matter of personal style and the attorney's judgment. They need to be called in a way that makes sense so that the story gets told in a logical fashion. Sometimes, witnesses who are available only a short time need to be called out of order. The plaintiff's witnesses go first, then defense, then plaintiff gets to present rebuttal witnesses. If the defendant has a counterclaim, they also get rebuttal witnesses. If the witness needs to be called out of turn, sometimes attorneys will allow the courtesy of having the witness called on their portion of the case. Even if the courtesy isn't granted voluntarily, the judge will usually allow it.

There are different types of witnesses that may be called in the case. Here are the basic types.

Fact witnesses

Fact witnesses are those who are going to testify about, well, the facts. They are not allowed to give opinions or testify about anything they didn't actually see, hear, taste, smell or touch. They cannot be paid, other than a statutorily determined witness fee to compensate them for travel expenses and very little of their time. $6.00 to $40.00 is not an unusual range. The fee doesn't compensate them for the day they missed of work. Many employers will pay, and some are required by law to pay, an employee who is subpoenaed to testify in court their regular wage.

It is unlawful to terminate an employee for their testimony under subpoena or for missing work to testify under subpoena. Does your character have to testify against her employer? Or have her boss resent the work she missed under subpoena?

The witness will be called and asked questions first by the side calling them, and then will be subjected to cross examination. Other than adverse witnesses, the side calling the witness cannot ask leading questions, that is, questions suggesting the answer. These are usually yes or no questions. On cross, the witness can be led. On redirect, they cannot.

Sometimes a witness will be called on both sides. This can be dealt with one of two ways. On cross, the examining attorney can only ask questions on the same subjects as direct examination. The attorneys can agree to dispense with that rule to allow the witness to finish and go home. Or the cross examining attorney can reserve the right to recall the witness on their portion of the case. Sometimes the examining attorney reserves the right to recall the witness on rebuttal. Does your witness character think it's over only to hear the judge say, "The witness will remain available until further notice"?

The real joke on newbies to the justice system is how many witnesses will lie, especially to save their jobs. I've seen witnesses turn on their best friends to save their livelihoods. In *North Country*, a story based upon a real sexual harassment case, Michael Seitzman used this kind of development to good effect:

> **Witness/friend:** After that, she started ranting all the time about how we shouldn't take it anymore. The company wasn't protecting us. The union wasn't protecting us.
> **Female defense lawyer:** What did she think you needed protection from?
> **Witness/friend:** Don't know.
> **Lawyer:** Did you have any problems getting along with the men in the mine?
> **Witness/friend:** I didn't bother them, they didn't bother me.

The scene then switches to men making graphic sexual comments and graphic sexual graffiti on the job. The stark contrast between the testimony and the visual showed she was lying through her teeth. It was powerful.

Lying witnesses are frustrating, and most laypeople don't expect it, no matter how much their lawyer warns them. I hear all the time my trial-virgin clients saying, "If they're subpoenaed, they'll tell the truth." They're supposed to. But the one who does at any kind of personal or professional risk is rare. You can use a lying witness to traumatize a party in your story who naively believes in justice and the power of putting someone under oath.

Adverse witnesses

Adverse or hostile witnesses are those who work for, are friends or family with, or otherwise have an affiliation with the other side. They may be led by asking questions that suggest the answer. They may need to be called to prove an element of the case; for instance, that the employer failed to take corrective action.

"You didn't do anything to discipline or terminate Mr. Jones after he beat up that customer for returning an item, did you?"

"That wasn't the first time Mr. Jones was violent in the workplace, was it?"

Expert witnesses

Expert witnesses are ones who offer opinions on something technical or scientific. They didn't observe any of the events, but are brought in for their training and expertise. I try to avoid them like the plague because bad ones can harm your case beyond repair. In *The Verdict*, the expert witness testimony didn't go so well:

> "Mr. Galvin, sometimes people can surprise you. Sometimes they have a great capacity to hear the truth."

That's what Paul Newman's expert said after blowing it with the judge's questions. *The Verdict* is a good example of how an expert, that is, the hired gun who gives an opinion about some aspect of the case, is just as likely to tank a case as help. Of course, in *The Verdict*, the jury didn't cut through the nonsense and hear the truth. A surprise witness surfaced. They heard the testimony, then the judge told them to disregard it. That's what they cut through. Telling a jury to disregard something they've heard is like telling someone, no matter what, not to think of the theme song to *Gilligan's Island*. It can't be done.

Expert witnesses can be necessary, even beneficial to the case. In medical malpractice, other professional malpractice, products liability, and other complex cases, they may be required to prove an element of the case, such as that the medical treatment failed to meet the standards of practice in the community. There are some experts who make their living being experts, and some who come to court kicking and screaming. Either way, they make lots of money for their testimony.

Cross examination

The purpose of cross examination is to poke holes in the testimony just given. Mostly it's done by the opposing side, but judges can chime right in. Here's the exchange when the judge in *The Verdict* proceeded to slice and dice Paul Newman's (his character was an attorney named Galvin) expert.

> **Expert:** "In my opinion it took much longer. Nine, ten minutes. There's too much brain damage."
> **Judge:** "Are you saying the failure to restore the heartbeat within nine minutes in itself constitutes their medical malpractice?"
> **Galvin:** "Your Honor."
> **Judge:** "Yes, Mr. Galvin."
> **Galvin:** "If I may be permitted to question my own witness in my own way."
> **Judge:** "I'd just like to get to the point, Mr. Galvin."
> **Galvin:** "I am getting to . . ."
> **Judge:** "Mr. Galvin, I believe I have the right to ask the witness a direct question. Now let's not waste these people's time."

The judge proceeded to ask a series of damaging questions. And don't think it doesn't happen. I once had this happen to me, in a case where the judge did everything he could to tank my case after I failed to give a campaign contribution to his wife that she requested three days before the trial was to start. Fortunately, I managed to turn the judge's questions back on him and he ended up making points for my side.[61]

Paul Newman's snap back at the judge is something every lawyer subjected to the same behavior wishes they could say. "Your Honor, if you're going to try my case for me, I wish you wouldn't lose it." That kind of comment would land the real lawyer in jail for contempt or at least with some sanctions and a dressing down in front of the jury.

Other than judicial questioning, the cross examination is a chance for the opposing side to rehabilitate a favorable witness or tear down a damaging one.

The trick to cross is to have your characters ask only questions they know the answer to. If your character doesn't know an answer, the results of a cross examination can do more harm than good. You can use cross examination to humiliate a character, redeem them, develop a plot

---

[61] Of course, he threw out my verdict anyhow. Judges have almost infinite power to harm one side if they set out to do so, and there is little the victim attorney can do to save the case.

twist, or to increase tension. This is a good opportunity to have some fun in the story.

Objections

Throughout the trial your character will hear or make objections. Here are some:

Improper argument: During opening, objections are extremely rare. It's considered discourteous to interrupt. But if the lawyer in your story crosses the line between statement and argument during opening, this is the objection. Openings that go beyond what the evidence is going to show cross that line. Argument in an opening would be opinion, and appeals to emotions, comments on credibility of witnesses, or attacks on opposing counsel.

Other types of erroneous comments in trials would be telling the jury something they aren't supposed to hear – prior bad acts that aren't admissible, settlement discussions, insurance coverage, or poverty or wealth of an opponent, for instance.

The ruling can be simply, "sustained." If there is something more serious, the judge can give either a "curative instruction" (something to fix it such as telling the jury they have to disregard the statement) or grant a mistrial. That means the jury is dismissed and the parties have to start over.

Hearsay: An out of court statement offered to prove its own truth is hearsay. That's the standard definition. And that's about the best I can do to help you with the concept of hearsay. I didn't understand it in law school, and it took me years of law practice to get a handle on it. Some judges don't understand it at all.

Most documents are hearsay because they were made out of court. "Mr. Jones told me that Shirley told him that . . ." is hearsay. "Mr. Jones told me that . . ." is hearsay. The truth is that there are so many exceptions to the hearsay rule that most hearsay is admissible. Use it sparingly in your story.

Beyond the scope of direct: Cross examination questions can only cover topics addressed on direct examination. If the direct examination only asked a witness about the color of the traffic light, the cross can't then go into what other traffic was around during the accident. The other side would have to call the witness as part of their own case. Or, the parties can agree or seek leave of court to go beyond the scope of direct.

Irrelevant: Unrelated to anything at issue in the case.

More prejudicial than probative: While it may be related to something in the case, it will so inflame the jury that the resulting prejudice will outweigh anything of value it might add. Usually drug use, sexual activity, criminal activity, or something else considered very damaging.

Prior bad acts: Something the witness did that was bad, whether criminal or otherwise, that fails to be so similar that it establishes a pattern. Say you come in the house and see the beagle, looking sheepish. Next to her is a chewed up $20. She's bitten you three times in the past. Her lawyer would say the chewed bill was not similar to the bitten hand. It isn't similar enough to show a pattern. It's not admissible. Now, if she chewed up a $1 and a $5 in the past two weeks, the judge will let the similar chewings into evidence.

No predicate: The attorney skipped a step and jumped to a conclusion or asked the witness to jump to a conclusion without establishing the underlying facts.

Assumes facts not in evidence: The question contains a presumption, an unproven fact, such as, "When did you stop beating your wife?"

Best evidence: There is a document out there that is more probative of the issue than testimony, usually when a witness is testifying about the content of a document. "And what did the letter say?" "Objection. The letter is the best evidence of the content of the letter." So the letter has to come into evidence, not the testimony about the letter.

Not on the witness/exhibit list: An exhibit or witness not listed usually won't be allowed in.

Arguing with the witness: Self-explanatory, and a no-no.

Asked and answered: Lawyers don't get to keep asking the same question over and over again.

Compound question: Two or more questions together. Juries and the witness get confused, so it's not allowed.

What your attorney characters will likely say is simply, "Objection, Your Honor." Or, just plain, "Objection." If the judge is paying attention, he or she will probably know what it's about. (I once had a judge read comics and do crossword puzzles for the whole trial. She would rule alternately in favor of plaintiff and defendant. And I had a judge who kept falling asleep. My opposing counsel and I would take turns making loud noises near him when we needed a ruling.) The judge's response will be either "Sustained," "Overruled," or "Counsel, please approach." If the judge needs more information about the objection, they may ask for a "sidebar."

What the Jury Doesn't See/Hear

The jury will sit and cool their heels in the jury room for long periods of time during the trial. That is because they will be sent back to the jury room during lengthy motion arguments.

Sidebar

Shorter arguments can be done at sidebar, so the jury will see the attorneys approach the bench, but won't know what happened.

Sidebar will start with, "Your Honor, may I approach?" That's the clue to the judge that counsel wants to say something the jury shouldn't hear. It may be a speaking objection, needing an explanation. It may be something the lawyer wants to say or ask that could get them slapped down or get a mistrial if the judge doesn't like it. It could be a motion for a mistrial or a delay. The judge, lawyers and court reporter will huddle together and speak quietly so the jury can't hear. There will be a ruling, and the lawyers go back to their places. The court reporter moves the equipment back to the front of the bench, and the lawyers proceed based on whatever the ruling was.

Motions during trial

Motions during trial (as opposed to pretrial, which we addressed in Ch. 19 and Ch. 20) can relate to evidence or the case and whether or not it should proceed. Here are some of the more common motions during trial:

Motions in limine: to exclude or allow a particular piece of evidence or testimony.

Motions to strike: to strike a piece of testimony or evidence that came in.

Motions for mistrial: to end the trial because the jury heard something so damaging and improper that no curative instruction (just what it sounds like – an instruction to correct the error, such as telling a jury not to consider the testimony they just heard) can be made. The lawyers may compare it to hearing a bell ring. "You can't unring the bell, Your Honor. The jury's heard it, and they won't be able to ignore it, no matter how much they try."

Motions to amend the pleadings to conform to the evidence: the lawyer forgot to add a claim, or thought of a claim or defense during the trial. If the parties have tried the case allowing the elements of the claim or defense to be proven, and if no prejudice will result, the motion will be granted. For instance, a requirement before filing the case is the plaintiff had to send a demand letter. The plaintiff testified about the demand letter. Then the defense moves to dismiss because plaintiff failed to plead she complied with a "condition precedent" (something she had to do before filing suit). The plaintiff's lawyer may say, "I move to amend my complaint to conform with the evidence, and to say that Plaintiff complied with all conditions precedent." Since the testimony already came in, the motion will probably be granted.

Motions for continuance: something came in that the lawyer needs either a brief or more lengthy delay in order to prepare to deal with.

Motions for contempt: opposing counsel, the other side, or a witness failed to obey a court order, including a subpoena or order on a motion in limine.

Motions to dismiss: these are unusual in the middle of the trial, but if it becomes clear that the plaintiff doesn't have a legal claim, they can be made at any time.

Motions during trial can cause your biggest surprises. All kinds of "gotchas" can come up. A motion may be just what you need to cause suspense or tension in your story.

Closing Argument

The closing argument is the end of the case. It can be extremely dramatic in the story. This is where the lawyers wrap all the threads together and argue to the jury why they should find in favor of the lawyer's client, and how much damages they should award. By the time of closing, everything that can happen has happened. The lawyers know what the witnesses have said, what evidence is in, who did well and who didn't, what the jury instructions will be, and what the verdict forms will look like.

Regarding Henry starts with a great example of the unemotional, factual, defense side closing argument. It's an effective illustration of an argument typically used by a big corporate defendant, condensed into about two minutes. Henry, the lawyer played by Harrison Ford, starts with telling how sorry he is about what happened, what a tragedy it was.

> "It would seem poetic that someone else was to blame. It would feel right. But it wouldn't be fair. Let's think for a second. Who's being blamed here? It's not some big bad hospital corporation. We're talking about human beings. Four doctors, five nurses and the hospital chief of staff present at the time, all of them there for no other reason than to try and save Jonathan Matthews' life."

This is the corporate defendant putting the human face on the company. Then he proceeds to attack the plaintiff, his character, and how the whole thing is really the plaintiff's fault.

> "Here's my point. We all understand why Mr. Matthews is blaming the hospital. But nobody could have prevented Mr. Matthews' suffering except Mr. Matthews."

The writers did a terrific job of showing a closing argument without boring the audience with the specific details of the facts and the law.

Contrast that one with *The Verdict*. Paul Newman starts the argument with, "Today you are the law." One of the great lines for a jury of all time. The emotional closing of *The Verdict* doesn't deal with the facts at all, but is an appeal to truth and justice. That's because Paul Newman's case had totally, utterly tanked. All he had was the jury's emotions to play with. In reality, the other side would have objected like crazy. But it was effective for the story (just not very realistic).

A closing is the writer's chance to get creative, because this is where lawyers get creative. Lawyers quote poetry or movies, appeal to emotions, tell stories, and do everything they can within the rules of the game and the way the evidence played out to persuade the jury to find for their client.

Jury Deliberation

Once the instructions are read, the jury retires to the jury room. That is the first time during the trial they are allowed to discuss the case with anyone. Any discussions among each other or with family and friends can get them thrown off the jury or cause a mistrial. They first select a foreperson who chairs the deliberations.

Then they talk about the case. And there's no right or wrong way to deliberate. They discuss anything and everything about the case. Showing the jury deliberations can be the center of your story or just add tension. The parties and attorneys are waiting. The wait can be minutes, hours, or days. And there are few things worse than waiting for a jury. The lawyers and parties rehash what went right and wrong. Sometimes the attorneys talk settlement with each other. Sometimes everyone sits and chats with the judge for awhile. Some pace, some throw up, some rest.

Most people don't realize that attorneys don't get to eat, rest or sleep during most of the trial. Breaks are used to argue motions and do charge conferences (where the lawyers and the judge decide what the jury instructions and verdict forms will say). Lunches are short because they were eaten up with motions, and are used to prepare for the second half of the day. Evenings are used to prepare for the next day. A few hours sleep a night is pretty normal during trial.

If jury deliberation is expected to last a while, your characters may go to lunch or dinner, go to their offices if they are close, or just sit and drink coffee in a local coffee shop. I once lay down on a bench outside the courtroom and took a nap, having had no sleep for five days. This is a wonderful spot to develop your characters, reveal why they have their quirks, and humanize them further.

If a jury has a question, they give a note to the bailiff. The judge calls the attorneys back to the courtroom, and the jurors are led back into the jury box. The question is read. The attorneys and judge usually have a sidebar as to whether or how to answer the question. Many questions are ones that can't be answered. Points of law that aren't part of the case, evidence that never came in, witnesses who weren't called, can't be addressed. The judge will say something like, "I'm sorry, but I can't answer that question. You'll just have to go back and do your best."

Sometimes the question can be dramatic, a hint about which way the jury has decided. "Can we award more than what the plaintiff asked for?" is a plaintiff's dream question. Questions about defenses can indicate that they found for the plaintiff on the plaintiff's portion of the case, but they can also be a red herring. I once had a jury ask about a defense, and everyone thought the plaintiff had won. Then they jury came back with a verdict form that only found for the defendant on one defense, and that was enough. Because the defendant only needed to win on one defense to win the trial, the case was over. This can be fun for you to play with, to create a dramatic climax, ramp up tension, or give relief.

If the attorneys leave, they will give the bailiff or judicial assistant the party's and their cell phone numbers so they can be reached if they have to be called in for questions or a verdict. Does your character leave and forget to turn on her cell phone?

Verdicts

If your story has the case going to verdict, know that the lawyers may already view it as a failure, because lawyers mostly want to settle their cases. They know there is no justice, only money.

> **Lawyer:** "Look Josey, the illusion is that all your problems are solved in the courtroom. The reality is that even when you win, you don't win."
> **Josey:** "I know I'm right."
> **Lawyer:** "Yeah, I'm sure you are. But right has nothing to do with the real world."

North Country was based upon *Class Action: The Landmark Case that Changed Sexual Harassment Law*. It was written by lawyers, Clara Bingham and Laura Leedy Gansler, who obviously had the same experiences with the justice system I've had.

Your most dramatic moment may well be when the lawyers get that fateful call. The jury has a verdict. They rush back to the courtroom. When everyone is there, the jury is called back. The lawyers anxiously look for signs. If the jury comes in smiling and looking at the plaintiff, the verdict may well be for the plaintiff. If they won't meet the plaintiff's eyes, it may be a defense verdict. Or could it be another red herring with a quirky jury?

The judge asks, "Do you have a verdict?"

The foreperson says, "Yes, we do."

The bailiff takes the completed verdict form. The judge looks to make sure it is filled out correctly. If something is incomplete that keeps it from being a full verdict, the judge may well call the attorneys up to discuss whether or not to send them back. And an incomplete form does happen. If they failed to decide on all the defenses, for instance, then the judge in your story sends them back with instructions on what was missing. If it is complete, as it usually is, the judge hands it back to the foreperson and asks them to read it. The reading of the verdict is tense, full of anticipation, drama, and then relief and rejoicing for one side, disappointment and disgust for the other.

The attorney who lost may ask the judge to poll the jury. The judge will then say, to each member, "Juror number __, was that your verdict?" And I've actually had a juror answer, "No, that was not my verdict." What a plot twist. The judge will then send the jury back with instructions to reach a unanimous verdict. In my case, the juror came back again and answered, "No, that was not my verdict." It turned out she didn't understand what she was hearing when the judge read the verdict form. The judge finally asked her what the problem was, and then the juror figured out the verdict she was hearing was indeed her verdict.

If each juror answers, "Yes," then the judge thanks them for their service. The judge will tell them whether or not they are allowed to speak with the attorneys afterward. Some judges allow it, some prohibit it.

If the jurors are allowed to speak to the attorneys, they will usually go up to the winning side and do a post mortem. Do your characters get some surprising information about why they won? Jurors don't like speaking to the loser immediately after trial. Some jurors will reach out to the losing attorney or party well after the trial. I once got a letter from a juror telling me why they made a ruling, and how bad they felt about it. Not that it did my client any good. Unless some jury misconduct is disclosed, the only thing that talking to the jury accomplishes is to help the attorney understand what they did right, what went wrong, and just how a jury thinks. Every time I've spoken with a juror post-trial, it was educational.

A post-trial juror communication can be a celebration or another plot twist. It's just one more thing you can use in your arsenal of tools for your story.

Immediately Post Trial:

Motion for Judgment Notwithstanding the Verdict, Remittitur, Additur, Fraud on the Court

The verdict doesn't end the case. Once the jury is dismissed, post-trial motions (to resolve issues about the conduct of the trial) will be either heard, or more often, postponed. The attorneys want to celebrate or go home and curl into a fetal. They want to rest. The judge wants to get dinner. The bailiff and judicial assistant want to go home. Whether they happen the same day or later, here are the most frequent post-trial motions.

Judgment Notwithstanding the Verdict

This is a motion based on the same grounds as directed verdict, that is, that the winning side failed to prove their case. This motion can only be made if a motion for directed verdict was made at the close of the opposing side's case. The motion could say a key piece of evidence or testimony wasn't introduced, or an element of the case or a defense wasn't proven.

Remittitur

When you see those crazy jury verdicts for gazillions, know that the judge will probably cut them. That's called "remittitur." If the amount of the verdict isn't supported by the evidence, or shows that the jury's passions were inflamed, then the judge will reduce the amount of the verdict to something more sensible.

Additur

"Additur" means that, if the jury's verdict is too low, the judge can also increase it. For instance, if there is a clear monetary loss on a contract and the jury omits an element of damages that was proven, or if they got the number wrong, the judge can fix it.

Fraud on the Court

Fraud on the court is where the judge or jury was misled. If a party discovers post-trial that the other side lied, withheld evidence, or committed something else so severe that it would be a fraud on the court, they have up to a year to set aside the judgment based on fraud. The reality is that I've seen lots of cases throwing out a plaintiff's verdict if the court decided the plaintiff lied, but defendants who lie usually get a pass. If I knew why, I could sell it and retire.

A post-trial motion can yank victory from the jaws of defeat in your story. Your character can win, only to suffer crushing defeat, or win despite having lost the trial. The other way to lose the trial after the win is on appeal.

Chapter 22 – Post Judgment

The decision at trial has to be put on a piece of paper called a "judgment." This says who won, what they won, and whether there are any issues left such as attorney's fees and costs.

Motions

After the post trial motions, the judge will enter a judgment reflecting the final decision. Is the case over yet? No. It can still settle. But more important, for a bench trial the attorney who lost can ask for a rehearing or new trial. And for any kind of trial there can also be a motion for relief from a judgment.

Motion for rehearing or new trial: The losing party argues that the judge in a bench trial misunderstood the evidence or the law, and should have entered judgment for them instead. In both jury and non-jury trials, it can also be based upon newly discovered evidence that could not have been discovered in time for trial.

Motion for relief from judgment: This is a motion to overturn the judgment, and it can be based upon a number of grounds:

- **Mistake:** if the judge made a clerical error, say, an extra zero, or some other mistake that is correctable, then the judgment can be set aside and a corrected judgment issued.
- **Fraud, misrepresentation or misconduct of opposing party:** if there was fraud, misrepresentation, or misconduct of the other side (such as hiding evidence) that could not have been discovered prior to or during the trial, the judgment can be set aside. Sometimes judgment will be entered for the person making the motion, sometimes a new trial granted.
- **Newly discovered evidence:** this is where the evidence was discovered too late to move for a new trial.

- **Judgment is void:** one of the parties was under a guardianship (meaning they were incompetent or senile and couldn't be sued) or in bankruptcy (meaning they can only be sued in the bankruptcy court), or some other issue regarding a party's capacity to sue or be sued is discovered. Maybe the case was against someone serving overseas in the military. Or the person sued was a minor.
- **Judgment has been satisfied, discharged, or released:** the case has been settled or the judgment paid.

The moving party has up to a year to move to set aside a judgment for fraud, newly discovered evidence, or mistake. If the judgment is void or has been satisfied, discharged or released, there is no time limit. The motion must be made within a reasonable time.

Appeals

"I dislike shows where the lawyers yell at the judges, particularly appellate judges. Not that I didn't fantasize about doing that on occasion. But lawyers would be held in contempt if they did this in real life. Moreover, lawyers don't win all the time. I wish! Programs that show lawyers winning all of their cases lead the average Joe to think that is how it is in real life so they won't listen when you try to explain the potential downside to litigating instead of settling. "

-Cynthia Greenfield, Colorado Appellate Attorney.

Appeals are yet another of the many downsides to litigating. The appellate court can yank the judgment away from your character, or force them into a new trial.

If the verdict was against the weight of the evidence, then the appellate court can reverse the decision. Does your character's case get overturned because the appeals court thinks she failed to tip the scales in her favor? Maybe the appellate panel doesn't think her testimony was strong enough to outweigh the 20 people who testified on the other side.

The most common grounds for appeal are some error of the judge. If the error was harmless, that is, would not have caused a different result (like using the wrong word in the standard instructions, but the word that was used had the same meaning), the appellate court won't reverse. Most appeals can only consider the record of the trial court (the transcripts of trial, pleadings, and evidence), and if the issue was not preserved on the record, by an objection made at the time of the error, the appellate court will not reverse.

Appellate lawyers prepare written briefs that go to the appellate court. Sometimes they also get an "oral argument" meaning they have a hearing where they can make their arguments and answer any questions the judges have.

Some common judicial errors that can justify reversal are:

Erroneous instruction on the law: the jury instructions were incorrect, misleading, or confusing.

Excluding or allowing evidence: either disallowing something that should have come in or allowing something prejudicial that should have stayed out.

Allowing improper behavior of counsel: the attorneys said or did something that was damaging and improper, and the judge either failed to give a curative instruction or grant a mistrial.

Bias: the judge had a demonstrable conflict of interest or was improperly biased (not just that they ruled against one side).

Juror misconduct: the jurors did something wrong, like watch a TV program about the case or discuss the case before deliberations.

Unconstitutionality: the underlying statute or some conduct of an official violated the constitution.

Preemption: a statute or claim is preempted by an act of Congress or some higher authority. For instance, a state case on whistleblowing could be preempted by a federal whistleblower statute, meaning the plaintiff can only bring her case under the federal statute.

Some things that can be used to overturn criminal judgments can't be used in civil matters. For instance, ineffective assistance of counsel is grounds for appeal in criminal cases. Yet, no matter how badly the lawyer in your story messes up, the client doesn't get to use that as an excuse. Having a bad lawyer doesn't get a civil judgment overturned.

Because appeals are so formal, with most of it on paper, only the oral argument in the appellate courtroom may be exciting enough for your story. The oral argument will usually begin with, "May it please the Court." Justices are referred to as "Mister Justice" or "Madam Justice." Chief Justices are referred to as "Mister Chief Justice" or "Madam Chief Justice." Appellate judges are still called, "Your Honor."

Appellate judges keep lawyers on a strict clock, usually only 15 minutes for oral argument per side, including questions. There is absolutely no nonsense or posturing here. This is dry recitation of the law. Any theatrics will show that the lawyer is inexperienced in appellate court. And unlike trial court, the client does not get to sit at counsel's table. They have to sit behind the bar, that is, the railing that separates the viewing gallery from counsel table.

Your story could show the tension of a new lawyer arguing before a staid appellate panel the first time, or having counsel getting peppered with questions. There is no ruling on the spot. The opinion may be issued days, weeks, or even months after oral argument. How your characters react during the wait is the stuff of good drama.

Appellate lawyers and judges don't think like you or I. They have their own language and way of thinking. Dabbling in appellate law is dangerous. There are so many procedures and protocols, that minor violations can cost the client their appeal.

Writs

A writ is an order commanding somebody to do something specific. The other thing appellate courts do is hear writs. These can be either during the course of lower court proceedings or after. Here are some of the writs appellate courts hear.

Writ of certiorari: A writ of certiorari claims there was an error and asks the appellate court to review it. This is a purely discretionary writ (meaning the court can hear the case if they think an error is bad enough, or choose not to hear it). The Supreme Court hears most of its cases on certiorari. Lower appellate courts hear "cert petitions" when there is no appeal as of right (meaning the party is entitled to appeal and be heard). If the petition is accepted, the appellate court issues the writ to the lower court notifying it that it intends to review the decision. That doesn't mean the appeal is granted, only that the appeal will be heard.

Writ of prohibition: A writ of prohibition claims the lower court doesn't have jurisdiction (meaning the authority to preside over the case). Your character's case can be speeding toward trial only to have the appellate court stop the proceedings from going forward.

Writ of mandamus: Lower courts can issue these too. A writ of mandamus is a writ directed to some public official. The writ directs the official to do something they are required to do. For instance, if your county manager character refuses to provide public records, a writ of mandamus could order him to do so.

Writs are a weird little remnant of English law that can be useful to you in the right circumstance in your story.

Collection

So, your main character won their case, won their appeal, and is holding a million dollar judgment. The loser is just going to write a check now, right?

Sometimes. But unless it's a suit covered by insurance, it is more likely that your character still has a big problem – collection. A million dollar judgment against an individual is usually almost worthless. If they hold assets with their spouse, or most of their net worth in their main residence, they may be untouchable. Or they can declare bankruptcy to avoid or delay a judgment that isn't based on fraud.

Let's assume that your character thinks the judgment is collectable. How can they force the deadbeat judgment debtor to pay up? There are some weapons in the collection arsenal.

Discovery in aid of execution

These are just like pre-trial discovery requests, only the requests are for the purpose of discovering assets. The requests will demand the debtor disclose stocks, property, artwork, bank accounts, everything of value they hold. Once your character finds the assets, they can force payment. You can have fun with this. I once set the depositions of the mistress and wife back to back, and the judgment was suddenly paid.

- **Record the judgment:** recording the judgment with the correct authority, sometimes the clerk of court in the county of any real property, sometimes with a central agency of the state, will create a lien on real property so that, if the debtor sells, the debt has to be paid first (after mortgages).

- **Writ of execution:** a writ of execution directs the sheriff to collect on the judgment. All enforceable monetary judgments will have language to the effect of, "for which let execution issue." That is an instruction to the clerk of the court to issue a writ of execution that is delivered to the sheriff. The sheriff can then grab any designated property belonging to the debtor. You can have fun here. I once had a writ issued for a beloved family dog. The judgment was paid pretty quickly. If the assets are worthless or there are bank liens that have priority over the judgment lien, the expense of the execution may outweigh any amounts collected. The sheriff has to be paid for execution and storage of the asset, and then the asset has to be put up for public sale. The proceeds of the sale are used to pay expenses first, then liens in the order of priority. If there are other judgments, the first one with a recorded writ gets priority. Does your character win only to find out there are dozens of creditors that have to be paid first?

- **Writ of garnishment:** money owed to the debtor by a third party, such as wages or judgments, can be garnished. So can property held by a third party, such as bank accounts. The writ issues to direct the person holding the property or owing the debt to give it over to the judgment holder. The person named in the writ can have reasons they claim they should not have to turn anything over. They could claim they have a right to the property in the writ, or the debtor is not the owner of the property. If the property or debt does belong to the debtor, then the judgment holder gets it. Your character could find a big bank account to garnish. They would issue a writ of garnishment to the bank holding the money. Unless the bank claimed the account belonged to someone else, the bank would turn over the money.

Your character could end up with a worthless piece of paper, or can collect and have a major lifestyle change. The end result is up to you. By now, you have an overview of just some of the basics of civil law in order to enrich and enhance your writing.

I hope you have found *The Writer's Guide to the Courtroom: Let's Quill All the Lawyers* useful to your story, and maybe you've gotten some inspiration for ways to twist your story or develop your characters. If you've used this book to help craft your story, shoot me an email or a letter to let me know, and I promise to buy your book or watch your movie when they are released.

Good luck, and may all your novels be bestsellers, all your screenplays win Oscars, and all your newspaper stories win Pulitzers!

Acknowledgements

I give my undying thanks and praise to some people who helped me along the way. My special thanks:

To my fellow Litopians: Carolyn, who "discovered" me and gave me lots of encouragement; and Lynn, the first editor to read my children's books and call me a "real writer." May all your books be bestsellers.

To Raquel, who keeps me together every day, runs my office with amazing efficiency, and who was the first to read the words here. Simply put, I would not be successful without you. I appreciate you more than you know.

To Pete, whose terrific work and dogged determination to be a good lawyer gave me the time to spend on my writing. You are on your way to being a great lawyer. You are already a great human being.

To Jordan, whose precision research kept me on the straight and narrow. Anything correct in this book deserves your thanks. Any errors are mine and mine alone.

Special thanks to Brad Meltzer and Alex Ferrer, who believe that success doesn't mean you can't lend a helping hand to someone else. You are both extremely classy and excessively handsome. Here's to your continued success.

And finally, to my family: Madeline and Amelia, who inspired me to be a children's writer, and who encouraged me to pursue writing more to follow my heart; and Ben, who put up with seeing me behind a computer way too much, and who kept things together in the family when I was gallivanting off to writer's conferences. To my mom and dad, without whom I wouldn't have my adoration of books. Dad, I'm glad you got to celebrate my first publishing contract, even though you didn't get to see my first book in print. I love you all, too, too much.

BIBLIOGRAPHY

CHAPTER 1

National Federation of Paralegal Associations, *ABA Commission on Non lawyer Practice*, http://www.paralegals.org/displaycommon.cfm?an=1&subarticlenbr=3 38. (accessed November 14, 2007).

Arthur G. Greene, Therese A. Cannon, *Paralegals, Profitability, and the Future of Your Law Practice* (American Bar Association 2003).

Sperry v. Florida Ex Rel. Florida Bar, 373 U.S. 379 (1963).

PBS.org, Justice for Sale, www.pbs.org/wgbh/pages/frontline/shows/justice/que/map.html

U.S. Department of Justice, Office of Justice Programs, Bureau of Justice Statistics, State Court Organization 2004

CHAPTER 10

Fla. R. Civ. P. Form 1.945

Fla. Stand. Jury Instr. Civ. § 4.1 (The Florida Bar 2007).

Beth Claire Eisenman, *Florida Forms of Jury Instruction* vol. 4, § 143 (Lexis 2007).

Liebeck v. McDonald's Restaurants, D-202 CV-93-02419, 1995 WL 360309 (Bernalillo County, N.M. Dist. Ct. Aug. 18, 1994)

Andrea Gerlin, *A Matter of Degree: How a Jury Decided a Coffee Spill Is Worth 2.9 Million Dollars*, The Wall Street Journal A1 (Sept. 1, 1994).

Restatement (Second) of Torts at:

§ 21, Assault
§ 13, Battery: Harmful Contact
§ 35, False Imprisonment
§ 558, Elements of a Cause of Action for Defamation
§§ 158-164, Intentional Entries on Land
§ 218(b), Liability to Person in Possession

§ 652E, Publicity Placing Person in False Light
§ 479, Last Clear Chance: Helpless Plaintiff
§ 496A-G, Assumption of Risk

CHAPTER 11

Statutes:

Age Discrimination in Employment Act, 29 U.S.C.S § 630(b)
Title VII of the Civil Rights Act of 1964, 42 U.S.C.S § 2000e
Age Discrimination in Employment Act, 29 U.S.C. §§ 621-634
Americans with Disabilities Act of 1990, 42 U.S.C. §§ 12101-12117
Equal Pay Act, 29 U.S.C. § 206(d)
Rehabilitation Act, 29 U.S.C. § 791
Older Workers Benefit Act, Pub. L. No. 101-433; 104 Stat. 1978
Pregnancy Discrimination Act, 42 U.S.C.S § 2000e (k)
Federal Sector Equal Employment Opportunity, 29 C.F.R. 1614
Electronic Communications Privacy Act, 18 U.S.C.S §§ 2701-2712
Family Medical and Leave Act, U.S.C. § 2601
Whistleblowers Protection Act, 5 U.S.C.S. § 2302
Military Whistleblower Protection Act, 10 U.S.C.S. § 1034
False Claims Act, 31 U.S.C.S. §§ 3729-3733

Cases

Faragher v. City of Boca Raton, 524 U.S. 775 (1998).
McDonnell Douglas Corp. v. Green, 411 U.S. 792 (1973)
Myers v. Central Florida Investments, Inc., 2006 U.S. Dist. Lexis 51504 (M.D. Fla. 2006).
Maldonado v. Publix Supermarkets, 939 So. 2d 290 (Fla. 4th DCA 2006).
Samedi v. Miami-Dade County, 134 F. Supp. 2d 1320 (S.D. Fla. 2001).
McPherson v. City of Waukegan, 379 F.3d 430 (7th Cir. 2004).

Web pages:

USA.gov, Government Employees,
www.usa.gov/Government/Government_Gateway.shtml
American Medical Association, *American Medical Association Annotated Model Physician Employment Agreement*, (2000), http://www.ama-assn.org/ama/upload/mm/46/model_physician_aug.pdf.

CHAPTER 12

Florida Standard Jury Instr. Civ. § 4.2(a)-(c) (Florida Bar 2007).

David Louisell & Harold Williams, *Medical Malpractice*, vol. 1, §§ 4.01-4.14 (Lexis 2007).

Kelly v. Riverside Medical Ctr., 499 So. 2d 1135 (La. Ct. App. 1986).
(In a medical malpractice action the surgeon and hospital were held liable for leaving a lap sponge in the plaintiff following surgery to remove the gall bladder and appendix).

Mack v. Lydia E. Hall Hosp., 121 A.D.2d 431, 503 N.Y.S.2d 131 (1986).
(The court held that the doctrine of *res ipsa loquitur* was available to a plaintiff who suffered burns from an electrocoagulator used in the course of a surgical procedure for treatment of rectal cancer).

Gravitt v. Newman, 114 A.D.2d 1000, 495 N.Y.S.2d 439 (1985).
(The tip of a vein stripper instrument was left in the plaintiff following surgery for varicose veins. The court held that the plaintiff had demonstrated a sufficient evidentiary basis for invoking *res ipsa loquitur*).

Fla. Stat. § 766.102 (2007)
(Medical negligence; standards of recovery; expert witness)

Findlaw.com, Proving Fault in Medical Malpractice Cases,
http://injury.findlaw.com/medical-malpractice/medical-malpractice-law-overview/medical

Model R. Prof. Conduct (ABA 2007).

Restatement (Third) of The Law Governing Lawyers §50 (2000).

CHAPTER 13

Lanham Act, 15 U.S.C.S. §§ 1051- 1127 (2007) (purpose of Act is to ensure integrity of registered trademarks).

National Nu Grape Co. v Guest, 164 F2d 874 (1947), cert denied 333 US 874 (1948).
(Gist or value of trademark is to signify origin or source of product, and to provide symbol for article to aid manufacturer in advertising and selling).

Retail Services Inc. v. Freebies Publishing, 364 F.3d 535 (4th Cir. 2004). (Whether trademark protection extends to a proposed mark is tied to the mark's distinctiveness. In determining the distinctiveness of a given mark, courts use a categorical approach, placing the mark in one of four classifications that increase in distinctiveness as follows: generic, descriptive, suggestive, and arbitrary or fanciful. On the opposite end of the spectrum from the generic category are marks that are fanciful or arbitrary - inherently distinctive marks. Fanciful marks are, for the most part, nonsense words expressly coined for serving as a trademark. Arbitrary marks consist of recognizable words used in connection with products for which they do not suggest or describe any quality, ingredient, or characteristic, as if the trademark was arbitrarily assigned).

Copyright Act of 1976, 17 U.S.C.S. § 107 (2007).

Harper & Row Publishers, Inc. v Nation Enterprises, 471 US 539 (1985). (Copyright does not prevent subsequent users from copying from prior author's work those constituent elements that are not original, such as quotations borrowed under rubric of fair use from other copyrighted works, facts, or materials in public domain, as long as such use does not unfairly appropriate author's original contributions).

Donald Chisum, *Chisum on Patents*, vol. §§ 1.01-1.06 (Lexis 2007).

Federal Trade Commission Act, 15 U.S.C. §§ 41-58 (2007).

Securities Exchange Act of 1934, 15 U.S.C.S. §§ 78a et seq. (2007).

Sarbanes-Oxley Act of 2002, 107 P.L. 204; 116 Stat. 745 (2006).

SEC.gov, Division of Corporation Finance: Sarbanes-Oxley Act of 2002 – Frequently Asked Questions, www.sec.gov/divisions/corpfin/faqs/soxact2002.htm

CHAPTER 14

Restatement (Second) of Property: Landlord and Tenant § 5.5 (1977); Obligation of Landlord to Keep Leased Property in Repair

Restatement (Second) of Property: Landlord and Tenant § 12.5 (1977); Use of Leased Property for an Illegal Purpose

Nolo.com, Chart: Deadline for Returning Security Deposits, State-By-State, www.nolo.com/article.cfm/ObjectID/491C49DA-D208-4876-BEA5092CCB39FE1

Nolo.com, Chart: Landlord-Tenant Statutes, State-By-State, www.nolo.com/article.cfm/ObjectID/1682EC3F-6144-4D2B-9F5C6971C36F2928/2

Nolo.com, Chart: Notice Requirements to Enter Rental Property, State-By-State, www.nolo.com/article.cfm/ObjectID/FE2A286B-BD9F-41A5-B6C332C6FCF8E4D

Thelpa.com, Landlord-Tenant Laws and Statutes that Affect Our Rentals and Landlord Legal Rights, www.thelpa.com/lpa/lllaw.html

65 Am. Jur. 2d Quieting Title and Determination of Adverse Claims § 34 (2007).

61 Am. Jur. 2d Perpetuities and Restraints on Alienation § 5 (2007).

Answers.com, Property Law, www.answers.com/topic/property-law?cat=biz-fin

67A Am. Jur. 2d Sales § 638 (2007).

Fair Housing Act, 42 U.S.C.S. §§ 3601-3619 (2007).

Fla. Stat. § 501.160 (2007). (Rental or sale of essential commodities during a declared state of emergency; prohibition against unconscionable prices)

Megalaw.com, Admiralty/Maritime Law, www.megalaw.com/top/admiralty.php

Federal Food, Drug, and Cosmetic Act, 21 U.S.C.S. §§ 301 et seq. (2007).

Magnuson-Moss Warranty Act, 15 U.S.C.S. §§ 2301-2312 (2007).

Board of Governors of the Federal Reserve System, *Major Consumer Protection Laws*, http://www.federalreserve.gov/pubs/complaints/laws.htm, (accessed November 28, 2007).

USA.gov, Consumer Guides and Protection, www.usa.gov/Citizen/Topics/Consumer_Safety.shtml

The Fair Credit Reporting Act, 15 U.S.C.S. § 1681(a)-(x) (2007).

Equal Credit Opportunity Act, 15 U.S.C.S. § 1691(a)-(f) (2007).

Fair Debt Collections Practices Act, 15 U.S.C.S. § 1692(a)-(p) (2007).

Restatement (Third) of Torts § 2 (1998); Categories of Product Defect

U.C.C. §§ 2-314, 2-315 (2004).

Restatement (Second) of Contracts § 125 (1981); Contract to Transfer, Buy, or Pay for an Interest in Land.

Lawbore.net, www.lawbore.net

Hookedonlaw.com, Contract Formation Basics, www.hooledonlaw.com/quizzes/contracts/contracts_basic_offer_acceptance_consideration

Chandris v. Latsis, 515 U.S. 347 (1995).

The Jones Act, 42 U.S.C.S. App. § 688 (codified under 42 U.S.C.S. § 30104 (2007)).

The Longshore and Harbor Worker's Compensation Act, 33 U.S.C.S. § 901 (2007).

CHAPTER 15

Uniform Child Custody Jurisdiction and Enforcement Act §§ 201-202 (1997).

Wikipedia.com, Alimony, www.wikipedia.org/wiki/Alimony

Nolo.com, Common Law Marriage FAQ, www.nolo.com/article.cfm/pg/2/objectID/709FAEE4-ABEA-4E17-BA3483638831
Findlaw.com, Focusing on the "Best Interests" of the Child, http://family.findlaw.com/child-Custody/custody-who/child-best-interest.html

Divorcelawinfo.com, Grounds for Divorce,
www.divorcelawinfo.com/Pages/grounds.html

Divorceinfo.com, Divorce State-by-State,
www.divorceinfo.com/statebystate.htm

Findlaw.com, Temporary and Rehabilitative Alimony,
http://family.findlaw.com/divorce/divorce-alimony/temporary-
alimony.html

American Bar Association, 40 Fam.L.Q. 591(2007), Charts,
Alimony/Spousal Support Factors

Findlaw.com, Lump-Sum Alimony,
http://findlaw.com/divorce/divorce-alimony/lump-sum-alimony.html

I.R.C. § 215 (2007). (Alimony, payments, etc.)

I.R.C. § 71 (2007). (Alimony and separate maintenance payments)

Fla. Stat. § 61.08 (2007).

42 U.S.C.S. § 667 (2007). (State guidelines for child support awards)

Wikipedia.org, Annulment, http://en.wikipedia.org/wiki/Annulment

ABAnet.org, A Warning to Collaborators,
www.abanet.org/journal/ereport/my4ncolab.html

Restatement (Statement) of Conflict of Laws §§ 283-285 (1971).

Aflalo v. Aflalo, 685 A. 2d 523 (N.J. Super. Ct. Ch. Div. 1996).

Mallard v. Mallard, 771 So. 2d 1138 (Fla. 2000) (criteria to be used in
determining "need" are the parties' earning ability, age, health,
education, the duration of the marriage and standard of living enjoyed,
and the value of the parties' estates)

Fla. Const. Art. X, § 4 (2007).

26 U.S.C.S § 2010 (2007). (Unified credit against estate tax)

Findlaw.com, Probate Overview,
http://estate.findlaw.com/probate/probate-overview/

No Fault Insurance States & Statutes:

Arkansas: Ark. Code Ann. § 23-89-202.
Delaware: Del. Code Ann. tit. 21, § 2118.
District of Columbia: D.C. Code Ann. § 31-2401-31-2413.
Florida: Fla. Stat. §§ 627.730-627.741 (repealed effective October 1, 2007).
Hawaii: Haw. Rev. Stat. §§ 431:10C-101-431:10C-103.
Kansas: Kan. Stat. Ann. §§ 40-3101-40-3121.
Kentucky: Ky. Rev. Stat. Ann. §§ 304.39-010-304.39-340.
Maryland: Md. Code Ann., Ins. § 19-505.
Massachusetts: Mass. Gen. Laws ch. 90, § 34M.
Michigan: Mich. Comp. Laws §§ 500.3101-500.3179.
Minnesota: Minn. Stat. §§ 65B.41-65B.71.
New Jersey: N.J. Stat. Ann. § 39:6A-4.
New York: N.Y. Ins. Law § 5102.
North Dakota: N.D. Cent. Code §§ 26.1-41-01-26.1-41-19.
Oregon: Or. Rev. Stat. § 742.520.
Pennsylvania: 75 Pa. Cons. Stat. §§ 1791-1798.
Puerto Rico: 9 P.R. Laws § 2054.
South Carolina: S.C. Code Ann. § 38-77-10.
South Dakota: S.D. Codified Laws §§ 58-23-6-58-23-8.
Texas: Tex. Ins. Code Ann. § 1952.151.
Utah: Utah Code Ann. § 31A-22-307.
Virginia: Va. Code Ann. § 38.2-2201.
Washington: Wash. Rev. Code § 48.22.085.
Wisconsin: Wis. Stat. § 632.32.

Freeadvice.com, Fault and No-Fault Car Accidents: Who Pays the Bills?,
http://accident-law.freeadvice.com/auto/fault-no-fault-car-accidents.htm

CHAPTER 16

18 U.S.C.S § 242.
(Deprivation of rights under color of law)

FBI.gov, Color of Law, www.fbi.gov/hq/cid/civilrights/color.htm

FBI.gov, Civil Rights, www.fbi.gov/hq/cid/civilrights/civilrts.htm

Cornell.edu, Wex, Due Process,
www.law.cornell.edu/wex/index/php/Due_process

Usinfo.state.gov, Libel Law in the United States,
http://usinfo.state.gov/products/pubs/press/press08/htm

USConstitution.net, Things That Are Not In the U.S. Constitution,
www.usconstitution.net/constnot.html

NCSL.org, Privacy Protections in State Constitutions,
www.ncsl.org/programs/lis/privacy/stateconstpriv03.htm

Supreme.justia.com, Privacy after Roe: Informational Privacy, Privacy of
the Home or Personal Autonomy?,
http://supreme.justia.com/constitution/amendment-14/32-privacy-
after-roe.html

Meyer v. State of Nebraska, 262 U.S. 390 (1923).

Fuentes v. Shevin, 407 U.S. 67 (1972).

Board of Regents of State Colleges v. Roth, 408 U.S. 564 (1972).

U.S. Const. amend. I.

U.S. Const. amend. V.

U.S. Const. amend. XIV.

United States v. Carmack, 329 U.S. 230 (1946).

The Boom Co. v. Patterson, 98 U.S. 403 (1879).

Gertz v. Robert Welch, Inc., 418 U.S. 323 (1974).

Constitutional Privacy Protection States:

Alaska Const. art. I, § 22.
Ariz. Const. art. II, § 8.
Cal. Const. art. I, § 1.
Fla. Const. art. I, §§ 12, 23.
Haw. Const. art. I, §§ 6, 7

Ill. Const. art. I, §§ 6, 12.
La. Const. art. I, § 5.
Mont. Const. art. II, § 10.
S.C. Const. art. I, § 10.
Wash. Const. art. I, § 7.
United States v. Winans, 198 U.S. 371 (1905).

Pub. L. No 83-280 (August 15, 1953).

Wikipedia.org, Eminent domain,
http://en.wikipedia.org/wiki/Eminent_domain

ABAnet.org, Law and Procedure of Eminent Domain in the 50 States,
www.abanet.org/litigaiton/committees/condemnation/compendium.ht
ml

Findlaw.com, What is Eminent Domain?,
http://libaray.findlaw.com/1999/May/25/130971.html

Wikipedia.org, Zoning, http://en.wikipedia.org/wiki/Zoning

Uniform Relocation Assistance Act, 42 U.S.C.S. §§ 4601- 4638.

Craigslist.org, Fair Housing is Everyone's Right,
http://www.craigslist.org/about/state.fair.housing.laws.html

Bush v. Gore, 531 U.S. 98 (2000).

Sandra M. Stevenson, *Antieau on Local Government Law* vol. 1, *§ 86.20* (2d
ed., Lexis 2007).

Roe v. Wade, 410 U.S. 959 (1973).

Planned Parenthood of Southeastern Pennsylvania v. Casey, 505 U.S. 833 (1992).

Partial-Birth Abortion Band Act, 18 U.S.C.S. § 1531.

The Abortion Law Homepage, http://hometown.aol.com/abtrbng/

Firstamendmentcenter.org, Assembly, Abortion protests and buffer zones,
http://www.firstamendmentcenter.org/assembly/topic.aspx?topic=buffer_zones
Defense of Marriage Act, 1 U.S.C.S. § 7, 28 U.S.C.S. § 1738C

Wikipedia.org, Same Sex Marriage Legislation by State,
http://en.wikipedia.org/wiki/Same-
sex_marriage_legislation_in_the_United_States_by_state
Wikipedia.org, LGBT Rights in the United States,
http://en.wikipedia.org/wiki/LGBT_rights_in_the_United_States

Goodridge v. Mass. Department of Public Health, 798 N.E. 2d 941 (2003).
(The Supreme Judicial Court of Massachusetts declared that barring an
individual from the protections, benefits, and obligations of civil
marriage solely because that person would marry a person of the same
sex violated the Massachusetts Constitution).

CHAPTER 22

Steven Alan Childress & Martha S. Davis, *Federal Standards of Review*
(Lexis 2004).

U.S. Const. art. IV, cl. 2. (Supremacy Clause)

Fed. R. Civ P. 50.
(Judgment as a Matter of Law in a Jury Trial; Related Motion for a New
Trial; Conditional Ruling)

Fed. R. Civ. P. 51.
(Instructions to Jury; Objections; Preserving a Claim of Error).

Fed. R. Civ. P. 64.
Seizing a person or property

All Writs Act, 28 U.S.C.S § 1651.

Fla. R. Civ. P 1.560.
(Discovery in Aid of Execution)

Fla. R. Civ 1.570.
(Enforcement of Final Judgments)

Federal Debt Procedures Collection Act of 1990, 28 U.S.C.S. §§ 3001-3308

APPENDIX – ADDITIONAL SOURCES YOU MAY WANT TO USE

CHAPTER 1

Roger LeRoy Miller, *West's Paralegal Today: The Legal Team At Work*, (3d ed., Thompson 2003).

CHAPTER 10

Joseph W. Glannon, *The Law of Torts: Examples and Explanations*, (Aspen 2005).

CHAPTER 11

U.S. Equal Employment Opportunity Commission, http://www.eeoc.gov. (accessed November 14, 2007).

Lambda Legal, http://www.lambdalegal.org/ (accessed November 27, 2007).

Bully Busters, http://bullybusters.org/ (accessed November 10, 2007).

National Right to Work Committee, http://www.nrtwc.org/rtws.php3 (accessed November 27, 2007).

The Reporters Committee for Freedom of the Press, http://www.rcfp.org/ taping/states.html (accessed on November 14, 2007).

U.S. Department of Labor, Occupational Safety and Health Administration, http://www.osha.gov/index.html (accessed November 27, 2007).

Mack Player, *Federal Law of Employment Discrimination in a Nutshell*, (5th ed., West 2004).

CHAPTER 12

American Board of Liability Attorneys, http://www.abpla.org/. (Last accessed November 19, 2007).

Medical Malpractice.com, http://www.medicalmalpractice.com/ (Last accessed November 21, 2007).
- great information website

Myrtle Flight, *Law, Liability, and Ethics: For Medical Office Professionals* (4th ed., Delmar Pub 2003).

Clifford Elias & Diane Bissonette Moes, *Medical Liability in a Nutshell* (2nd ed., Nutshell Series 2003).

CHAPTER 13

Trademark Law Glossary, http://www.marklaw.com/index.htm. (Last accessed November 19, 2007).

Charles R. McManis, *Intellectual Property and Unfair Competition in a Nutshell* (5th ed., Nutshell Series 2004).

Restatement (Third) of Unfair Competition § 21 (1995).

Cornell.edu, Wex, Unfair Competition, www.law.cornell.edu/wex/index.php/Unfair_competition

United States Patent and Trademarks Office.http://www.uspto.gov/index.html. (Last accessed November 19, 2007).

Bitlaw.com, Patent Law in the United States, www.bitlaw.com/patent

Cornell.edu, Wex, Patent, www.law.cornell.edu/wex/index.php/Patent

Cornell University Law School, *Law by Source: Uniform Laws*, http://www.law.cornell.edu/uniform/vol7.html#dectr (Last accessed November 21, 2007).

Federal Trade Commission, https://www.ftc.gov.(Last accessed November 20, 2007).

Anthony Skrocki & Claude Rohwer, *Contracts in a Nutshell* (6th ed., Nutshell Series 2006).

U.S. Securities and Exchange Commission, http://www.sec.gov/ (Last accessed November 20, 2007).

Securities Law.com, http://www.securitieslaw.com/index.html (Last accessed November 21, 2007).

Securities.com, Common Complaints Against Stockbrokers, www.securitieslaw.com/complaints.html

Louis Loss & Joel Seligman, *Securities Regulations*, vol. 3, § 9-C-4 (Lexis 2006).
(Churning)

Alan Palmiter, *Corporations: Examples and Explanations* (5th ed., Aspen 2006).

Jeffrey Ferriell, Joel Goldstein, & Michael Navin, *Understanding Contracts* (Lexis 2004).

CHAPTER 14

D. Barlow Burke and Joseph A. Snoe, *Property: Examples and Explanations*, (2nd ed., Aspen 2004).

U.S. Food and Drug Administration, http://www.fda.gov/, (accessed November 28, 2007).

Board of Governors of the Federal Reserve System, http://www.federalreserve.gov/, (accessed November 28, 2007).

U.S. Consumer Product Safety Commission, http://www.cpsc.gov/index.html, (accessed November 28, 2007).
Washingtonpost.com, Trial Lawyers on the Offensive in Fight Against Preemptive Rules, 9/11/07, Cindy Skrzycki

AARP.org, AARP Bulletin, Consumer Alert, State-By-State Guide to Do-Not Call Registration, www.aarp.org/bulletin/consumer/a2003-06-30-statenocall.html/page=2

Cornell.edu, Wex, Products Liability, www.law.cornell.edu/wex/index.php/Products_liability

Dealerselect.com, Lemon Law Information and Sites,
www.dealerselect.com/lemon/Lemon.html

Federal Trade Commission, http://www.ftc.gov/index.shtml, (accessed
November 28, 2007).

About Health Transparency, Summary of States requiring disclosure of
hospital infection rates,
http://www.abouthealthtransparency.org/node/125 (accessed
November 29, 2007).

CHAPTER 15

Roger Clark, *No-Fault and Uninsured Motorist Automobile Insurance* vol. 1,
§ 1.20 (Lexis 2007).

Lawrence H. Averill, *Uniform Probate Code in a Nutshell* (5th ed., Aspen
2000).

John Dewitt Gregory, Peter N. Swisher & Sheryl L. Wolf, *Understanding
Family Law*, 3d ed., Lexis 2005).

CHAPTER 16

American Civil Liberties Union, http://www.aclu.org/ (last accessed
December 4, 2007).

John DeLeo, *The Student's Guide to Understanding Constitutional Law*,
(West 2005).

National Conference of State Legislatures, *Privacy Protections in State
Constitutions*,
http://www.ncsl.org/programs/lis/privacy/stateconstpriv03.htm (last
accessed December 4, 2007).

Mack A. Player, *Federal Law of Employment Discrimination in a Nutshell*
(5th ed., West 2004).

Library of Congress, http://www.loc.gov/index.html (last accessed
December 6, 2007).

Tribal Court Clearing House, http://www.tribal-nstitute.org/index.htm

(last accessed December 6, 2007).

National Right to Work Committee, http://www.nrtwc.org/rtws.php3 (last accessed December 6, 2007).

Lambda Legal, http://www.lambdalegal.org/ (last accessed December 6, 2007).

CHAPTER 22

Joseph Glannon, *Civil Procedure: Examples and Explanations* (5th ed., Aspen 2006).

James. J. Brown, *Judgment Enforcement* (2nd ed., Aspen 1995).

U.S. Marshals, *Writ of Garnishment*, http://www.usmarshals.gov/ process/garnishment.htm (last accessed December 5, 2007).

63C Am. Jur. 2d Prohibition §§ 1-7

52 Am. Jur. 2d Mandamus §§ 1-17

~~~

Authors,
You may send any questions regarding your story and the law to Donna Ballman's blog at writereport.blogspot.com.

Index

Other fabulous Writer Tools from Behler Publications:

A personalized tour of the publishing industry; how the various people who comprise this business think, why they make the decisions they do, and how authors can avoid the pitfalls. The four sections cover every aspect of the industry:

- Interviews by industry professionals
- An inclusive "holy Maalox, Batman!" behind-the-scenes tour of the submission process
- Defining the various types of publishers currently populating the industry
- The writer's survival style guide – complete with a four-part manuscript autopsy and punctuation beerfest.

978-1-933016-34-4
Trade Paperback * $19.95 * 6 x 9 * 380 pages
www.behlerpublicatsions.com

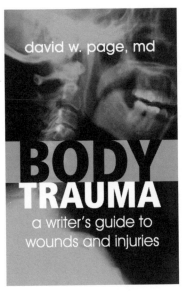

From murder/mystery to medical fiction, surgeon and trauma expert Dr. David W. Page is a writer's best friend.

Credible storytelling is the key to plausibility and Dr. Page offers the perfect prescription on deciding how severe a character's wounds should be and then writing the action that causes the pain. You'll put your characters in harm's way and mistreat them-believability-to within an inch of their fictional lives.

978-1-933016-41-2
Trade Paperback * $17.95 * 6 x 9 * 254 pages
www.behlerpublicatsions.com